Also by James D. Squires

Read All About It!:
The Corporate Takeover of America's Newspapers

The
Secrets of the
Hopewell
Box

The
Secrets of the
Hopewell
Box

STOLEN ELECTIONS, SOUTHERN POLITICS,
AND A CITY'S COMING OF AGE

James D. Squires

RANDOM HOUSE

Copyright © 1996 by James D. Squires

All rights reserved under International and Pan-American Copyright Conventions. Published in the United States by Times Books, a division of Random House, Inc., New York, and simultaneously in Canada by Random House of Canada Limited, Toronto.

Library of Congress Cataloging-in-Publication Data

Squires, James D.
The Secrets of the Hopewell box / James D. Squires.—1st ed.
p.   cm.
Includes bibliographical references and index.
ISBN 0-8129-2428-2 (alk. paper)
1. Nashville (Tenn.)—Politics and government.   2. Political corruption—Tennessee—Nashville—History—20th century.   I. Title.
F444.N257S68   1996
320.9768'55—dc20   95-22284

Manufactured in the United States of America on acid-free paper
24689753
First Edition

BOOK DESIGN BY DEBORAH KERNER

To the memory of my mother,
BILLYE WHITE SQUIRES,
and my grandfather
DAVID LEMUEL WHITE,
to whom this story belonged

Contents

Contents

◼

PART ONE

The Powder Puff Boys

Prologue

From my point of view, eye-level with the pistols on their belts, my granddaddy Dave and his friends were big and dangerous men. I learned to tell one from another by the guns they carried. Blue-steel automatics and nickel-plated revolvers, some stuck handle-up in belt holsters and others hung upside down under their arms in shoulder harnesses.

When I closed my eyes—which I did sometimes to hide my discomfort at being the only kid among them—I could still tell them apart by whether they smelled of sweat, cigarettes, spicy after-shave lotion, or a new haircut. And in my mind I ranked them all by their boots and shoes—whether they were scuffed and unkept, or polished like my granddaddy's until you could see yourself in them. I'd been told so many times how he'd kept his shoes that shiny even during something called the Depression, when he'd worn out the soles and had to put cardboard in them every morning when he went out to walk the streets looking for work. He said you could always tell a lot about people by the shoes they wore.

When I was a boy of four or five he took me with him to the sheriff's office uptown at the courthouse on Nashville's public square, which was the most exciting place I'd ever been. The sheriff was my granddaddy's best friend, Garner Robinson, who wore a friendly grin and a white cowboy hat cocked over his right eye. He was so big that my granddaddy called him "Fat Pappy" when nobody else was around. Garner's office was narrow as a bus. It was a tunnel of ringing telephones, laughs and curses, and roosters strutting with sharp-pointed badges on their chests and creases in their pants sharp enough to cut.

Handcuffs and clumps of keys hung from their belts. Billy clubs, blackjacks, or long-handled flashlights filled their fists, which always seemed to be clenched before my eyes. They brought in red-faced men with tattoos on their arms and their hands manacled behind them, white around the wrists. Everybody looked tough and like something was about to happen.

Their words were menacing, too, usually about "sonofabitching judges," "fucking corpses," and "goddamn niggers." They spoke of wrecks on the highways, blood on the walls, and shacking up. They grinned when they talked about "pussies," which I thought were cats, so I grinned, too, not knowing why until I was older.

I saw these same men over and over, not only at the sheriff's office, but at the Phillips-Robinson Funeral Home near where we lived, which the sheriff and his family owned. His men worked there, too, not in their patrol uniforms but in neckties with suit coats over their pistols.

Hands in their pockets or clasped behind their backs, they stood in circles in the vestibule, on the porch, farther down on the sidewalk, or out back in the ambulance shed, usually with the sheriff in the center.

At the crackle of a shortwave radio, one or two of them would break off and speed away in a red Cadillac ambulance, lights flashing and siren screaming. They'd come back with details of heart attacks and descriptions of an old lady who had choked on her food or a kid who had fallen through a glass window. Sometimes they brought back more than fodder for talk. There were naked bodies in bloody sheets or swollen blue ones that had been fished out of the Cumberland and delivered in rubber bags. Those from the morgue had tags on their toes and all were laid out on the tables to be "prepared"—for what I was not exactly sure. How tough grown-up men have to be, I marveled, to drive the big cars so fast, to argue with and curse one another while carrying loaded guns, to grab hold of whatever task confronted them, unafraid even of touching the disfigured and putrid dead.

The coroner, sloppy old Dr. Core, would show up in the back room and peer down over his glasses at the new arrival. Inevitably, one of the funeral-home guys would inquire as to his medical opinion. "Well, what happened to him, Doc?" they'd want to know.

"He died," Core would deadpan.

"No shit," they'd all say, laughing as if it were the first time he'd ever said it.

Each of "those who have passed" had his or her own room and was laid out for viewing in a casket at one end with undertaker chairs lined up in rows in front, and flowers around the sides. Sometimes my grandfather would sneak away from the group, and then I would spot him hiding among the flowers. He would make a loud noise with his mouth to make it sound like the corpse was breaking wind.

Everyone would laugh but Garner, who told them not to because "it will only encourage the silly sonofabitch." Then he would put his hand on my head and say, "I hope you grow up to have more sense than your granddaddy. I don't know what I'm going to do with him."

"Why don't you arrest him? You're the sheriff," I always asked.

"I think I'd rather shoot him," Garner would say, patting the pistol at his waist and giving me a wink. Then, with his huge hand clamped on the top of my head, he would march around me like I was a maypole. "For a kid you make a good walking stick," he'd say.

Garner made a point of introducing me to everybody, which was the only thing I didn't like about being around him. He would say, "This is Dave's grandson—Billye's oldest boy, James." No matter how hard I tried not to, I always looked down at my feet, which always caused my granddaddy to speak sharply to me.

"Look 'em in the eye, boy. When somebody talks to you, always look 'em in the eye." Then I wanted to crawl under the rug. Having flattened me with words, he would right me again with them. "Except when you're in the barnyard, of course. Your granddaddy has stepped in some mighty nasty stuff when he was looking people in the eye instead of watching where he was walking."

Even Jake joined in the laughter. Of all the men around my grandfather, I was most afraid of Jake Sheridan. He was not gruff, but he had a sharp, serious face that showed little time for other people's children. He was not big but when he said something all the other men listened, and everybody did what he said, even my grandfather, who never talked back or made jokes like he did with Garner. Jake spoke mostly of money and precincts, voting machines and election days, which meant little to me at the time.

Long after Garner wasn't sheriff anymore, we would stop in the parking lot of Jake's motel and my grandfather would go in "to see the man a minute." Sometimes, a Cadillac that I knew to be Garner's would be parked there, too. And I would wait in the car outside imagining that the meeting going on in the motel was like those I had witnessed in the sheriff's office, the three of them gathered around an old desk with Jake whispering to someone on the telephone while Garner and my granddaddy eyed each other knowingly. Secrets, I supposed, about money and guns, fast cars, election days, and dead people, the kind of talk that demanded someone stay outside to act as lookout.

It was not until I became a rookie reporter for Nashville's morning newspaper, *The Tennessean*, that I learned what they had been up to all those years. The pages of my own newspaper carried the startling disclosures: Garner Robinson and Jake Sheridan and the other dangerous men of my boyhood were the heart of a dastardly ring, a group of devious and corrupt politicians, a machine like the infamous Tammany Hall crowd in New York and "da" organization of "da mare" of Chicago, Richard Daley.

Now it finally made sense. No wonder Jake had seemed so ominous. He had been the big boss, a shadowy, behind-the-scenes manipulator who for two decades pulled the levers that made the city work. He had been the Svengali to Garner, who had gotten himself elected to more offices for more years than almost anybody else in Tennessee. And both had gotten rich in the process.

And as for my own granddaddy, no wonder he and I spent so much time waiting in restaurant parking lots or outside motels for quick meetings with strangers. No wonder he had disconnected the dome light inside his Pontiac, so it would not illuminate his face when other people climbed in and out of the car at night. No wonder he sometimes drove without license plates and had a garage full of cases of Coke and whiskey and new automobile tires. He had indeed been a leader of the machine's gestapo, quick to violence, not only capable but guilty of killing in the interest of racism, corruption, and political power.

The implications of all this were slow to dawn on me, but eventually they did. Whatever these men had been, I knew firsthand. As a boy and as a man I had known them and all their friends—the cops, the gamblers, the bootleggers, the saloonkeepers, the preachers, and the ward heelers. I saw them with their wives, with other people's wives, with the waitresses and barmaids. And I had grown up with their children. Their secrets were mine. I had been inside the machine without ever seeing it as such. Whatever else I was or would become, I had been part of it—one of them. Whatever I knew, they had taught me. For I had spent my childhood at the knees of the bosses, in the laps of the front men, and in the hands of the enforcers.

As an adult, I observed and wrote about them as if they were strangers and not the family of which I had been a part, as if becoming a reporter had somehow severed me from my roots and blessed me with a detachment from which I could view and judge them objectively.

I was not objective then, though I tried to be. Nor can I be now, some thirty years later. But I can tell what I saw and heard all that time, how it looked through eyes that saw it all up close. To the Robinsons I would always be "Billye's oldest boy"—nothing else. All of my life Garner and my granddaddy had talked politics in front of me as if I were another cop or an ambulance driver, and they never stopped when I became a reporter. Likewise, I never once reported a word I heard, although I was tempted constantly. It was one of those conflicts that couldn't be resolved so therefore was better left unacknowledged.

However subjective the prism of my hindsight, the story of my grandfather's friends is a remarkable tale of American politics. It is more than the story of a classic machine that demanded tribute, stole elections, and engaged in practices that by today's definitions would be considered corrupt to an extent beyond even a newspaper's imagination.

It is an epic saga of the urban revolution in America and the birth of a two-party South. It is a crucial chapter in the life of a city that became the breeding ground for the civil rights movement and the launching pad for what is perhaps the most significant political development of the century—the equalization of voting rights that shattered tradition and remade the country's political map.

Moreover, it is a case study in the power of the three most irrepressible forces in politics—class struggle, racism, and personal friendship—and a forty-year journey down the potholed road of change in American life with one of the damnedest crowds that ever traveled it.

Dave

The car was like the man at the wheel—shiny and fast. It was part of the Tennessee Highway Patrol's prewar fleet of black-and-cream Fords, a 1942 that had been stored unused for two years. By the time it was finally rolled out of mothballs and assigned to Patrolman Dave White, the new tires that had come with it had been taken off and used on another car. His new car was wearing old tires, which irked him. He promptly found a set of new tires on an old patrol car and pulled an unauthorized swap. This earned him a three-day suspension without pay, which might have stalled somebody else's career. But not Dave's.

His car had the old worn tires back, but there on his sleeve, just above the elbow casually extended through the open car window for anyone to see, was a set of brand-new gold sergeant's stripes, as much a testament to his political stroke as to his law enforcement prowess. The war had not been too bad to him after all.

Actually, when he thought about it, each of the two great wars had brought him prosperity. What his family gained after the first had been wiped out by the Great Depression. But now, after the second, with Hiroshima and Nagasaki still echoing around the world, life was better than ever. Drafted at age thirty-seven, he had returned to a job better than the one he'd left. All about him were the trappings of a dream come true. Around his waist and over his shoulder was a shiny black Sam Browne belt with a swivel holster and in it the polished blue-steel walnut-handled .38-caliber revolver that was standard issue from his employer, Governor Jim Nance McCord. On his chest and above the glistening black bill of his olive green gabardine hat were twin gold shields that authorized him to enforce the laws of Tennessee.

Sgt. Dave White shined the badges religiously, along with each copper-nosed bullet in his gunbelt. And in the spit-polished, round-toed black boots on his feet he could see his own reflection, the face of the person his wife Sallie regarded as "the best-looking man I ever saw." Dave was tall and lean, with black hair, prominent cheekbones, and deep-set, unreadable eyes. He always dressed to kill, favoring three-piece suits of gray gabardine in winter and cream-colored linen in summer, with two-tone shoes or boots of fine leather. His one clearly unflattering physical feature—a set of prominent pee-pot ears—he worked hard to disguise with snappy felt fedoras or sailor straws. One winter he chose a suit in a deep maroon, which he topped off with a white felt hat. And just before Christmas, the village newspaper warned children that "Santa Claus might not be coming because Dave White has his suit." But one thing the women all agreed on was that Dave looked his best in a uniform.

Sergeant White thought so, too, and leaned out the window to catch a glimpse of his own reflection in his side mirror as he eased the Ford along Donelson Pike, a narrow lane ten miles northeast of Nashville, not far from the airport and the bluffs of the Cumberland, toward the intersection with Highway 41, the Murfreesboro Road. The August sun was climbing into the late-morning sky. With it the humidity rose inside the patrol car. The only air stirring was the warm wind whipping through the open windows and the dashboard vents. He knew from experience that the minute the car stopped moving his sharply creased olive gabardine uniform pants would begin sticking to his thighs and the starched freshness of his shirt would start to melt. But as he approached the bus stop in front of Central State Hospital, the end of the line and turnaround point for city buses, he realized that stop he must.

Central State was Nashville's only mental institution, a state-run asylum. Crouched a scant one hundred feet off the Murfreesboro Road behind barred windows and barbed-wire fences, Central State resembled a small prison. Sergeant White could not remember a week passing since the day he became a policeman in 1937 when he had not been there on some business having to do with the criminally insane. During the thirties, he had helped get a whiskey-crazed cousin admitted there, and he never passed the place without visions of old Will Henry, straitjacketed, sitting atop a chest of drawers, pretending to be driving a car, imploring visitors to "give me five gallons of gas and check my oil." By the time they had wrung all the alcohol from Will Henry and sent him off on the straight and narrow to become a famous preacher, Dave White knew the doctors and inmates by their faces, if not their names. He knew hospital rules and procedures, too, and as he passed the bus stop that hot August day he thought it unusual for a patient in white inmate's fatigues to be out on the curb with a shovel on his shoulder.

Sergeant White made a U-turn in the middle of the Murfreesboro Road and went back. The patient he had seen was a lifelong hospital resident, a mildly retarded man trusted to work in the yard, with whom he had frequently exchanged the time of day. The man had a tooth missing at approximately the same spot in the front of his mouth where the sergeant had capped one of his own completely in gold, a little jewelry for his smile. The contrast had since become a grinning joke between them.

"What are you doing out here with that shovel?" Sergeant White asked the patient.

"Cleaning up shit," the patient grinned. He pointed his shovel at the green-and-white bus stop bench. On the ground beside it was a substantial pile of human feces. The flies had begun to buzz it.

"Goddamn," said the sergeant. "Who did that?"

"A nigger boy."

"Where'd he go?"

"He just got on the bus. The one going to town."

"Don't clean it up," said Sergeant White, frowning. "I'll be right back."

He floored the gas pedal, spewing gravel against the bench. Within a mile or so he brought the patrol car up behind a green-and-yellow city bus, its rear end black from belching diesel smoke. He hit his siren and pulled the bus over. In a minute, the officer was on the bus and off, with a skinny black youth wearing baggy pants in tow. He deposited the kid, who was about nineteen or twenty, in the backseat of the Ford and drove back to the bus stop at Central State.

They got out of the car and stood beside the bench on the shoulder of the road, the kid with his chin down on his narrow chest, the sergeant a full head taller and twice as thick, spiffy in his dark sunglasses, brass, and leather. A few feet away the retarded man from Central State leaned on his shovel, staring at them blankly.

The sun was bearing down now. Sweat had broken out all over the black kid's scalp and rose in his short-cropped hair like little silver beads nestled among the bristles of a wire brush. Perspiration beaded up, too, on the sergeant's upper lip, which was tight across his teeth as he spoke.

"Did you do that?"

"Yes, suh."

"Well, clean it up."

"Yes, suh."

The feces had softened considerably and were covered with flies. The kid looked around for something with which to scrape the pile from the rocks.

"Just pick it up," said Sergeant White.

The kid looked at him with eyes as big as saucers.

"With your hands," he ordered.

Fearing the kid might run instead, the sergeant lifted his right hand and dropped it down casually on the butt of his revolver. The kid bent over and with both hands scooped up the awful load. Then he stood there looking at the sergeant, as if to ask what he should do next.

The sergeant told him, "Now, put it in your pockets."

Grimacing, sweat rolling down his face, flies swarming, he deposited the excrement in the pockets of his baggy pants, filling one and then the other. When he had finished, he bent to wipe his hands on the grass.

"No," said the sergeant, kindly. "Just wipe them on your pants."

Soon, another city bus came along. The sergeant waved it down, put the kid on it and ordered the driver to take him as far as he wanted to go. "And never mind trying to put him off," he said. "I'll be right behind you."

The bus had signs in front and back, designating the seats for "white" and "colored" patrons. By the time the kid got to where the law demanded he sit—the rear row of seats—the bus was already moving and the enforcer of the law was back in his patrol car, his elbow sticking out the open window. Through a blast of diesel haze, Sergeant White could see the other black patrons madly scrambling to open windows and give the new passenger plenty of room. The patient from Central State saw it all, too, and flashed his gap-toothed smile. The sergeant lowered his sunglasses and peered over them mischievously. Then he winked at the patient and returned the grin in gold.

In years to come the sergeant would tell the story exuberantly, as if relating the capture of an infamous bank robber or the escorting of President Harry Truman—with the pride of a job well done. To him what had occurred on the roadside that day was justice pure and simple, the way he had seen it dished out all his life. Neat and clean, and in the case of the bus rider, relatively painless. To the sergeant the punishment had fit the crime. That was the test.

As a twelve-year-old, Dave White had lived on the square in

Lebanon, Tennessee, a small town twenty miles from Nashville, in an apartment above his daddy's grocery store. One morning he got up and looked out the window directly into the face of a black boy not much older than himself. This one had blank eyes that bulged in their sockets, ugly welts across his head, and a purple mouth with flies crawling in and out of it. He was hanging from a tree, lynched by a mob the night before for shooting the county sheriff, who had been his godfather and benefactor.

In 1916, for shooting the sheriff of Wilson County, they hanged you in the public square. Thirty years later, for defecating on the public thoroughfare, the law made you pick it up with your hands and carry it off in your pockets. It seemed to the sergeant they both had gotten what they deserved.

The idea that either black youth was the victim of racism would never have occurred to Dave. To him the lesson of the lynching was the same one he'd just taught the man who'd defiled the public roadway: A wrong done could be righted, by the law, by him. The justice of the last big war had rested on the same principle. The Japanese bombed Pearl Harbor and they got the big one right up the kazoo.

Southern justice had never been color-blind, either—nor would it ever be. A black man was far more likely than a white to be pistol-whipped—or killed—during an encounter with the law. But there were many peace officers and public servants whose level of patience or violence depended more on the offender's attitude than on skin color, men whose racial hatred was tempered by other considerations. Dave White was among such men, who would laugh no harder at the thought of a black man trying to shove his own shit in his pockets than he would a white. The color of a man mattered a lot less than whose side he was on. And whether he could be found when needed—on Election Day.

However humiliated, that black kid would look back on his experience with the highway patrol sergeant as a stroke of good fortune. He could've been arrested, beaten within an inch of his life, or both. He had in reality been done a favor by the law. He had gotten off with only an indignity, for which he could be expected to be grateful. And Sergeant White would know just where to find him when the time for repayment came on Election Day. After all, the boy was from Hopewell near Old Hickory.

Dave had lived in Hopewell back in 1929 when it was just a meadow. His father, Will, a one-legged ex–railroad man, had built a two-family house there just before the Crash. He and Dave's mother, Ovie, lived on the ground floor, while Dave, Sallie, and their baby daughter, Billye, lived upstairs.

Dave was a barber then, though barbering had not been what his parents had planned for him. They had a grocery business, a feed store, and a filling station and wanted Dave to finish high school and go to Cumberland College, a two-year law school, with a marble-shooting pal named Johnny Hooker. But Dave had followed the influence of a slow-as-smoke-off-shit cousin who wanted to go to Nashville Barber College. Faced with such choices, Dave could never tell big wood from kindling. But his mother, Ovie, a dark-complexioned beauty with a bad temper and a history of alley cat inclinations, always saw to it that Dave had a choice. She had allowed him to quit school at thirteen and let him use the family car—one of the few in town—to haul students from the train station to nearby Castle Heights Military Academy.

A few years later when his love affair with Sallie—"the middle Aiken girl from Tuckers Crossroads"—passed the point of no return, Ovie had urged her son to run away rather than marry. She sent him packing to Oklahoma with an Indian chief from a traveling Wild West show and refused to tell Sallie where he was. But not always his mother's son, Dave returned and married Sallie anyway. Ovie promptly hung black crepe on her son's bedroom window and publicly declared her refusal to recognize the union.

Not long afterward, Dave followed suit. In 1924, encouraged by his mother, he left Sallie, then seventeen, and their new baby daughter in Lebanon, Tennessee, and moved twenty-five miles away to the village of Old Hickory in search of hair to cut and for what would be a lifelong pursuit—a new corner to stand on. "Dave was like a piece of paper blowing in the wind," Sallie told her friends. "Wherever he landed is where he stayed until the next breeze."

At Dave's barbershop, haircuts were thirty-five cents, shaves were twenty cents, and shoeshines were a dime. Antics were free, a gift from the proud, wisecracking proprietor cutting the hair of men his own age who'd never been in a barbershop before. "They don't know their ass from a cedar tree," he complained to Sallie. "They sit down on the footrest. If it's called a barber chair, they figure the barber sits in it to cut hair."

The truth was that Dave spotted the country bumpkins when they came in the door and deliberately directed them to sit on the footrest for the amusement of the other barbers. Then he'd pull 'em up in the chair by their ears and tell them the story of his last customer from the country who thought the bathtub he'd found inside his house was storage for coal, or how another had made a biscuit board and a picture frame out of the toilet seat.

By the time they got out of the chair, they knew where to buy whiskey in town and Dave had some more regular customers. But the barber was bored. And once or twice a day, he would glance out the window and see a young man named Herman, spiffy in the uniform of the Old Hickory Police Department, roaring by the shop astride his sleek, fire-breathing Harley motorcycle on the way to some emergency or another. There, he thought, is a man who will be seen and recognized. So Dave bought himself a motorcycle, too. And at every opportunity, he donned a leather jacket and high motorcycle boots and ripped through the village streets.

It was out there in those streets, to the roaring of the twenties and the moans of the Great Depression, that Dave met Garner Robinson and rooted a friendship that would last fifty years.

The Robinsons

Old Hickory was an outgrowth of the first big war. It had risen like magic in sixty-seven days on the bluffs inside a horseshoe loop of the Cumberland River around a powder plant built by the government. One day there was nothing, and a few months later there was a barracks town with its own theme song, "The Du Pont Powder Puff," sung to the tune of "Coming Through the Rye": "Old Hickory Plant is working nights to make the real stuff/To paste upon the kaiser's nose a Du Pont powder puff."

The area was originally settled by men who fought the Indian wars with Andrew Jackson, whose famous home, the Hermitage, was four miles away. Twice the village had been named for him. First it was Jacksonville, but it kept getting mail meant for Florida, so it was christened with Jackson's nickname instead. By 1826, Dr. John Livingston Hadley had amassed an eleven-hundred-acre farm where the town would someday sit. Sixty years later a wild-looking young man named Warwick Gale Robinson floated down the Cumberland River on a load of logs, came to rest on Hadley's land, and married a Hadley girl. Through hard work and ingenuity he gained respect, prosperity, and some land of his own. Through sheer force of personality he became known as "Boss," even to his children.

In 1915, as the Germans grew rambunctious in Europe, a stranger showed up and offered Boss $75 an acre for his land. At first he was suspected of being a German agent. Boss Robinson held out and wouldn't sell until the price got up to $105 and the buyer had been identified as the United States government. People said the government had to pay Boss for the right to build on the land the same way God had to pay him for the right of way to dig the river. And in both instances he supplied the workers.

One of the workers Boss supplied in 1916 was his ten-year-old son, Garner. At first he had literally chained the boy to his bed to keep him out of harm's way, but Garner took the bed apart and appeared outside carrying the headboard. Boss put him to work riding a pony named Easter Girl to and from the jobsite, leading the teams of mules that he was leasing to the plant builders.

At one point thirty-five thousand people, including imported Mexicans, were working on the project. A seven-and-a-half-mile railroad spur connecting the plant to the nearest railhead was laid in thirty days. It carried 32 trains and 275 freight cars a day, mainly transporting workers and raw material. The finished "smokeless" powder was put in waterproof containers and sunk in submerged stockpiles beneath the river to thwart German saboteurs.

None of the powder ever made it into a powder puff for the kaiser. The war ended too quickly, and with it the need for gunpowder. The town almost died. Between 1918 and 1923, the population shrank to five hundred. But in 1923, Du Pont bought the facility from the government and reopened it to make the "silken fiber," rayon.

Old Hickory was soon booming again, this time as a mill-town magnet for young rural southerners ready to leave the farm and pioneer the building of urban America. In Old Hickory they found work at twenty-five cents an hour and refuge from the weather in acres of identical World War I clapboard and tar paper buildings that the government had thrown up for the powder mill workers.

Dave White's father, who followed his son to the little mill village, said it reminded him of the Crib, the infamous tent city San Francisco had walled off at the turn of the century to contain its drunks, prostitutes, and criminals. In 1925, Old Hickory had seventy-five hundred people and two thousand automobiles jammed into a space so small everything was within walking distance. It might as well have been Chicago.

The main street, named after Doctor Hadley, sliced through the village at an angle bisecting the horseshoe and winding through an otherwise perfect gridiron system of single-family "tar babies." Toward the north, they ascended in quality, with the best fronting the river and reserved for plant executives and supervisors. There the streets were paved with crushed stone and asphalt and the gutters shallow and clean.

But to the south—coincidentally no doubt—the quality deteriorated. Beginning at Berry and Bryan streets, there were two open blocks separating the main village from the "colored" or "nigger" section. Between Ninth and Tenth from Merrit to Fowler the streets were rutted dirt and cinder, with ditches alongside deep enough to catch and hold garbage and debris. People dumped coal cinders into them in a futile effort to make them shallower.

Abutting the colored village on the south was the burning ground, where wastepaper and rubbish that had been collected by company trucks were deposited and burned regularly. It was atop this dump that a new black section was built, postponing for a few years the eventual spillover of blacks to Hopewell. A few miles beyond the burning grounds to the southeast lay open farmland whose owners had contracted with Du Pont to collect village garbage as feed for their hogs. It was a convenient and acceptable arrangement except when the wind blew from the southeast, returning the garbage to the village with a vengeance.

The flimsy black cubes in which the villagers lived were designed in 1917 as temporary housing. Ten years later they looked even more temporary, giving the town a makeshift feel and a transient psychology. Many of the workers were young, poor, and rural. Some were unaccustomed to running water, indoor plumbing, and the close quarters provided by the dormitory-style apartment buildings and boardinghouses that were usually their first stop.

To get a room or lease a house in the village, you had to be employed by Du Pont. But you could take meals and get a room at the Farm House, which was run by spindly-legged Ma Sampson, who was Dave White's aunt Ocia.

The only other restaurant was a used streetcar that somebody had bought from the city of New York and had shipped in and deposited next to the community recreation center. The restaurant was named the White Owl but everybody called it the Pie Wagon. It stayed open at night, which was convenient because an ex–pro baseballer named Raggs had started a semi-pro team that played in the park nearby. The Village Confectionery, known because of its specialty as the Popcorn Stand, was around there, too.

FDR had yet to rescue the country from Prohibition, so the only booze was illegal, bootlegged out of the trunks of cars, from behind fake walls in juke joints, and out of supply closets in gasoline stations and nightclubs. With its barracks atmosphere and its young, single population, Old Hickory was a town on the make.

At age twenty, Garner, one of ten Robinson children, was still hard at the Boss's work, which consisted of making money in as many ways as possible. The Robinson family business was a meat and produce market housed in a post office building that also doubled as the bus station. It was described by a 1929 Du Pont evaluation as "old and unsanitary." But this was no deterrent to the crowd of men who constantly hung around, many of them there just to ogle the Boss's daughters, who looked like movie stars to the boys from the country.

"We used to go there just to see them," remembers an ogler named Oscar. "They were always dressed up like they were going out on the town—even in the mornings. They had beautiful faces and long hair and were the only women I'd ever seen who wore eye shadow. Back then, you just didn't see that."

A classic beauty herself, Maude Hadley had imbued all her children with style and grace. No one ever saw her when she was not dressed to the nines in hat and gloves. Although all the other Robinsons, including the daughters, worked like steam engines, Mama Maude was always seen sitting idle, not a hair or a ruffle out of place, a perpetual Scarlett O'Hara on the porch awaiting guests. Her work was apparently confined to having children. And at this she excelled, delivering twelve, ten of whom survived. The five girls lived in one part of the house under the supervision of Boss's sister Annie, the boys in another part under Boss himself, who didn't hesitate to use a buggy whip to keep them growing up in a straight line.

Above all the children, the Boss favored Maude Muriel, who had his work ethic and her mama's looks. She stood six feet tall, had dark olive skin and straight hair the color of coal, which she wore pulled straight back and knotted at her neck. She coated her face with perfect makeup and draped her shapely, angular body with flawlessly tailored outfits, usually in black or white. He put her in charge of the family store.

Of all Miss Maude's brothers, Garner was her favorite. He'd come along after the consecutive deaths of two infants and Maude had been afraid he'd die, too. So she smothered him with attention—and protection. The minute he got old enough to understand the nature of her fear, Garner used it to great advantage. If he didn't get his way, he told his big sister, "I will just go away and die." For the rest of their lives, she treated him like he might.

At the store, she made him her number-one helper, and each day he was dispatched to peddle hot dogs from a cart outside the Du Pont plant's gate. One day in 1925, Garner was waiting for the shift change when Dave the barber roared up on his motorcycle. Convinced that familiarity might breed employment, Dave frequently showed up and requested a pass to visit Sallie, who had become one of Du Pont's first female supervisors, then called a "forelady." That day Dave had augmented his insolent look by clenching a pipe in his teeth.

Visitors' permits had to come from the most senior member of the guard force, a man called Two-Gun Miller, who had once refused admittance to the plant manager because he had lost his pass. "You made the rules, you have to go by them," admonished Two-Gun.

Dave's pipe presented a problem for Two-Gun. "You can't go in smoking," the old guard declared.

"I'm not smoking," Dave replied.

"Well, you've got your pipe in your mouth," said Two-Gun.

"So what? I've got my ass in my pants, too," quipped Dave, "but I'm not shitting."

Two-Gun's sputtering response was buried under a gush of Garner's laughter, and along with it Dave's hopes of getting a job on the guard force. But the frivolity ignited a friendship between the two young men and set off a running feud between them and the plant guards.

Though men of vastly different depth and temperament, Dave and Garner had enough in common to be brothers under the skin. Neither had much formal education. Garner had so hated learning that he'd climb a tree in the schoolyard and sit there all day rather than go inside. At sixteen, tired of the hassle and having been caught by the Boss drinking beer in the cooler at the family meat market, he ran away and got a job at the Ford Motor Company in Detroit, where he lived on cherry pie and learned to hate Italian food and miss Old Hickory.

What Dave and Garner shared most, however, was a propensity for "high-assin'," which is how Dave's mother, Ovie, described the human equivalent of a mule bucking and kicking up its heels. An experienced high-asser in her day, she readily recognized it as the favorite pastime of her son and his friend. While not an illegal pursuit in itself, high-assin' covered some questionable activities, invariably including whiskey, women, and other dangerous pursuits such as racing automobiles.

Garner had a 1927 Chrysler roadster that was always parked outside the Robinson store. It was cream-colored, chrome-plated to the nth degree, with wire wheels and two chrome-topped spare tires set in the fender wells. Centered on the front of the hood was a large chrome radiator cap—with wings. Not to be outdone, Dave bought a hot Ford coupe. Soon, he and Garner were the talk of the town.

On Sunday afternoons, he and Dave made sure each had twenty-eight dollars—the fine for speeding—in his pocket. Then they would roar neck and neck through the center of the village and then directly in front of the rayon plant's little octagonal guardhouse, which also served as the police station and lockup.

At stake was the question of whether the four-man motorcycle-riding police force could mount up and catch the boys before they escaped jurisdiction across the new two-lane bridge over the Cumberland a mile away.

One Sunday Two-Gun's men were lying in wait, and the trailing Garner got stopped short of the bridge. When he didn't show up on the other side, Dave came back for him and got arrested, too. That week's *Old Hickory News* carried a story headlined "White Learns It Doesn't Pay to Beg in His Friend's Behalf."

Garner was as much a dandy as Dave, and in the eyes of some even more handsome. He was bigger, more rough-hewn. He had his father's dark hair, the near-perfect features of his mother, and a gregarious personality that earned him the moniker "Corset"—because "he got all the way around."

At sixteen Dave's wife, Sallie, had been gorgeous and spunky enough to bring him all the way back from Oklahoma and marry him over his mother's objections. But once they got to Old Hickory, he chose to run footloose with Garner rather than stay home with his family.

"Garner still wasn't married," recalled Sallie after she had reached the fiftieth anniversary of her thirty-fifth birthday. "So Dave didn't want to be either. And the way he acted nobody would've known he was. It was all a matter of love. Garner and Dave loved the women. And the women loved them."

One of the women who loved Garner dragged him to the altar—but no farther. One day in the mid-twenties, under strict orders from the Boss, a reticent and reluctant Garner was marched to the courthouse to marry a pretty young village girl who was pregnant. The minute the ceremony was over Garner presented her with a good-bye check for five thousand dollars. It was a handsome farewell but what Boss judged adequate compensation for giving up her claim to the town's most eligible bachelor. Although the girl vowed to name her son Garner Robinson, Jr., Garner maintained until his death that Boss had forced him to take the rap for an older, less eligible brother.

Of all the women charmed by Garner's dash and promise, the toughest and most successful by far was Estelle Neiderhauser, the daughter of a prominent Nashville dairy family who was full of dash and promise herself. She was a big-eyed girl with a model's body so thin she was nicknamed "Skinny." Among her earliest suitors was Dick Jones, an ambitious young man from Old Hickory who worked at her father's dairy. He made the mistake of introducing her to his pal Garner, who promptly stole her away in the roadster with the winged radiator cap.

A striking strawberry blonde, Skinny was as bold as she was beautiful. She dared to wear a pair of skin-tight Navy bell-bottoms in public, raising the eyebrows of the women, taking away the breath of the men, and setting a new standard for popularity. Late one night in 1928 she returned home with her second date of the evening to find a neighbor's house being devoured by fire and a dramatic rescue attempt under way. Among those dashing in and out of the flames to carry three elderly women to safety was her first date, to whom she had bid good night a few hours earlier. Garner's heroism was devastating to his rivals, and soon he and Skinny were talking about getting married.

Initially the Boss had opposed the marriage on the grounds that she was too good for him, meaning that his son could not afford her. At the time, Garner worked for the Boss as the lone full-time employee of the black YMCA in Old Hickory. But Garner had gotten his doting big sister Maude to plead his case. "Estelle is a very frugal girl," he wrote in a note to his sister, "and she's told me we can do fine on $35 a week." Maude was successful and Garner and Estelle were wed in September of 1928.

Like his daddy, Garner had married above himself. The Robinsons talked and ate like farmhands. The Neiderhausers, of Swiss-German extraction, walked and spoke in the manner of the European aristocracy and believed in dressing for dinner. An accomplished equestrian whose boots and jodhpurs turned heads on the Old Hickory village streets, Skinny turned out to be everything Garner had counted on—and then some.

Skinny had a patrician air about her and called her new husband "Gah-na." Soon so did all the other family members, a sacrifice of the *r* in tribute to her having changed her name to Robinson. She taught "Gah-na" the upper-class social graces not commonplace in

Old Hickory or even the etiquette books—sometimes the hard way. Taught to always eat every bite on his plate, Garner was unaware that some young ladies of superior breeding considered it gauche to clean up all their dessert. At lunch one Sunday he refused to call the waiter and pay the check until Skinny had consumed the last bite of her chocolate pie, which she kept assuring him she had finished. When he lifted the final forkful as proof of his point, she pointedly knocked it into the air to prove hers. "Gah-na" paid the check in an ice cream–colored suit decorated with chocolate pie.

Not long after their marriage, they were out for an afternoon drive in the cream-colored Chrysler roadster, which had a phalanx of red and blue lights across the front. Fearful that his straw boater would blow off in the wind, he handed it to Skinny to hold. As they approached Hackberry Corner near Hopewell, she pitched it without a word out in the road.

"What did you do that for?" he asked, incredulous.

"I just got tired of holding it," she said. Angry, Garner stopped to retrieve the hat. A heated argument ensued, which Skinny won by kicking out all the red and blue lights on the Chrysler.

Even after both were married, Dave and Garner refused to act like it. They spent so much time together that people said, "if you gave one a laxative, it worked on them both." And they could usually be found together around the Robinson store, where, according to Sallie, "they hung out at all hours of the night and ran around town like they were shot in the ass with a box of tacks." Once in anger she telephoned Miss Maude there. "I hope you can find an extra closet at the bus station because I'm sending Dave White's clothes up there."

Dave was headed to Robinson's the day his motorcycle didn't make the curve on Hadley Street and ran into the embankment, crashing to the ground with him under it. By the time Sallie got to the doctor's office, Garner was already there, holding Dave down on a table while they tried to cut off his boot. His lower right leg had been crushed. The sight of blood from her daddy biting his lip in pain made four-year-old Billye cry.

The damage was too much for the local physician, so Garner took Dave to a Nashville hospital to be treated by one of the city's premier orthopedic surgeons. A few days later, when ominous red streaks began to appear above the cast, Dave heard the doctors talking about gangrene and became hysterical at the idea of amputation. He knew about life with an artificial leg. As a small boy in the East Tennessee town of Emory Gap, he had watched the railroad men bring in a bloody bundle that had turned out to be his father, Will. A brakeman on the Tennessee Central Railroad, Will had been checking couplings on a train when one failed, crushing his legs between two railroad cars full of coal. There were no orthopedic surgeons in Emory Gap in 1909, so they handed Will White a pint of whiskey and a local doctor cut off his leg with a butcher knife. Dave's mother, Ovie, caught it in a washtub and took Dave with her to bury it in the woods behind their two-room house.

When Dave refused the proposed amputation of his own leg, the surgeon packed it in sandbags and without informing the patient inserted maggots in the wound to eat away the gangrenous tissue. It worked. The leg eventually healed, but wound up a half-inch shorter than the other. Dave was left with a slight limp and a present from his friend Garner—the nickname "Flyblow."

By the time Dave got well, the stock market had crashed and he had lost his barbershop. Sallie was making fifteen dollars a week at Du Pont and Dave's father, Will, had used all his cash to build the Hopewell house. They needed eight hundred dollars to get Dave out of the hospital. At the American National Bank branch across from Robinson's Store, the manager told Will White his railroad pension was not enough income to guarantee such a loan. Will walked across the street and borrowed the money from Boss, who was the bank's largest depositor. "From now on," the Boss told the bank manager, "let Uncle Bill have whatever he needs. I'll stand for it."

His hospital bill paid with Robinson money, Dave went back to barbering at Copeland's Barbershop, where he had started four years earlier, this time sitting on a stool, his leg in a cast. But soon even money for haircuts disappeared. So did the house in Hopewell and the fast Ford. For a few months Will White moved the family, including Dave and his daughter, Billye, to West Nashville, where he managed a grocery store for another Old Hickory family. Sallie kept her job in Old Hickory, although her hours were cut and wages reduced to twelve dollars a week. Dave, meanwhile, was reduced to handouts from Will—a quarter a day, fourteen cents of which was streetcar fare into the city and home again. In between, he wore out the soles of his shoes walking the sidewalks looking for a day's work barbering. Each morning, under the wondering eyes of barefoot Billye, he would cut new insoles from cardboard to patch the holes.

It wouldn't be long, however, before Dave and the rest of the Whites would be back in Old Hickory with the Robinsons. For Boss had found promise and opportunity in a business even the Great Depression could not thwart.

An Undertaking

Unlike Ovie White, Boss Robinson didn't give his children any choices. On the eve of the Great Depression, he decided that Garner ought to become an undertaker. As usual Boss was just trying to put some underemployed Robinsons to more profitable use. He had no idea he was founding a political dynasty.

Dayton Phillips, a young and dapper mortician, had wanted to marry one of Garner's sisters. Dayton worked for a Lebanon mortuary that had opened up a funeral chapel above a furniture store in Rayon City, the community that had grown up overnight around Garner and Dave's racing strip to the Nashville bridge. Dayton and Nora Robinson wanted to marry but the mortuary decided they no longer needed Phillips' services. Rather than watch his daughter leave home with an unemployed son-in-law, Boss took the matter in his own hands. "Well, by God then, let's go into the undertaking business," he declared from under his bushy black eyebrows.

And by God they did—but on Boss's terms. Garner, son-in-law Dayton, and the penny-pinching Miss Maude were each "invited" to put up twenty-five hundred dollars. Though Dayton never came up with his part, Boss went to Ohio anyway, bought a hearse, and called the new business Phillips-Robinson Funeral Home. Garner took up undertaking as if it were his own idea. Like preaching and politicking, the business of burying depends on the marketing of sincerity, real or imagined. And Garner had a way of making people feel he cared about them, that they were important.

The new partners built a small two-story funeral home on the main street in Rayon City. Garner and Skinny lived on the top floor. Boss wanted the undertaking business operated the same way he had run the produce store, with good cheer and liberal credit. No one was refused food on credit during the Depression no matter how far behind he was on his grocery bill. Boss's way of "selling" in the funeral home business was to provide free ambulance service to anyone sick or injured. After all, everyone dies eventually.

This meant a lot of lifting, carrying, and ambulance driving had to be done, requiring large numbers of people for short periods of time. It was the perfect business for a family with ten children, all of whom had friends and several of whom by now had spouses and in-laws. To be members in good standing of the Robinson family, everyone had to put in time at the funeral home. And everybody got a check, including the friends close enough to be considered family.

This included the Whites, who moved back from West Nashville to Dupontonia. Boss gave Garner's old job running the black YMCA to Will. Dave went back to barbering at Copeland's and—because he loved speed and could handle a car with the skill of a professional race driver—to driving Garner's new siren-equipped hearse at every opportunity.

Garner loved the ambulance business, too, for a different reason. It took him inside the homes—and lives—of people in time of their greatest need. His quiet, sensitive nature and confident air became the perfect elixir. For Nashvillians east of the Cumberland River, he quickly became the man to call in time of trouble.

One such call came from Dave's wife, Sallie, in the wee hours one morning in the early thirties. "Blood-curdling" screams from the next-door neighbors, the owners of the Old Hickory Drug Company, had awakened the whole neighborhood. Sallie said Dave had gone to investigate.

For weeks the town had been talking about Dr. Berry's strange behavior. Customers had complained of finding the drugstore locked during business hours, and sometimes the pharmacist could be seen in the window making faces at them. Garner arrived to find Dave and another neighbor, a bootlegger, trying to get in the front door of the Berrys' tar baby. Inside, he saw the pretty young Mrs. Berry struggling with her husband. Through the window he saw the terror in her face and the contorted, almost unrecognizable features of Dr. Berry, who waved a straight razor menacingly.

Somehow Mrs. Berry got the door open. Her husband had his left forearm under her throat, his right hand holding the razor. As Dave and Garner entered, she broke free and ran. Dr. Berry looked at Garner wildly for an instant, then pulled the razor across his own jugular. Blood spurted across the room.

Garner had not come in the hearse, so he and Dave packed towels thick around the doctor's throat and sped him to the hospital in the bootlegger's Hupmobile. He survived.

Like Dr. Berry, many people needing the services of the Phillips-Robinson ambulance also needed blood transfusions. Garner's blood type was O negative, and he gave so much blood to so many people that it became a joke in his family: "As if there weren't enough of us already, Garner's got half Old Hickory claiming kin." The sick wife of a friend of his and Dave's needed repeated transfusions, which Garner gladly supplied. For years the friend told everybody that "Nancy has so much of Garner Robinson's blood, nobody can get along with her anymore."

Such relationships were the treasure of Phillips-Robinson. Garner supplied coffeepots and donuts to hospital emergency rooms, sent country hams to doctors, and buried people sometimes for as little as twenty-five dollars and sometimes for free. Among the most valued relationships were those with the police and firemen, people whose everyday work included summoning ambulances to the scene of accidents.

The business began to make money when it opened a larger facility across the river in East Nashville in an area with an older population. But being a family that never underestimated the worth of roots, they kept the chapel in Old Hickory, too. And by 1932, Phillips-Robinson had made enough money for Garner to build a new house for Skinny in Madison, midway between the two chapels, and to buy back 132 acres of the riverfront farmland Boss had sold to the government seventeen years before.

The recovery of the Robinson land—thirty-five hundred dollars—was an important juncture in Garner's life because it was bought—and later sold for one million—over his daddy's objection. "What the hell you want with a farm anyway?" the Boss asked him. "I'd rather be in hell with my back broke than fool with a farm."

Garner's success as an undertaker had enabled him to begin charting his own course, to be something other than an extension of Boss Robinson. He was becoming his own man, with a reputation outside his neighborhood and, most importantly, beyond his old set of friends. On the wheels of the hearse and the wings of Skinny Neiderhauser's social contacts, Garner Robinson was going places.

His new acquaintances included men of power and position, especially in law enforcement—like Sheriff Bob Marshall. In those days the most important elected posts in the county were those of sheriff and county judge. The sheriff ran the jail and enforced the orders of the courts. He had deputies and court officers, all of whom could be helpful to somebody in the undertaking business. Like the Robinsons, Marshall was from the northern outskirts of the county, the White's Creek area west of Old Hickory. He was an older man and Garner looked up to him in a way common to men with strong-willed fathers, who often look for an alternative role model. Garner courted Marshall and the sheriff was flattered. In return he nourished Garner's interest in politics and encouraged him to run for public office.

In 1936, Garner was elected one of two magistrates representing the Old Hickory district on the county court, which among other things set the sheriff's budget. Marshall was quick to ply Garner with the spoils of victory—patronage. Having ascended to the first rung of Nashville politics, Garner immediately got Dave White the kind of job he wanted—as a motorcycle-riding deputy to Sheriff Bob Marshall.

For a while in the early thirties Dave settled down. In the summer of 1933, he and Sallie, both wearing spectator shoes and matching straw fedoras, loaded themselves in a Packard touring car and drove 450 miles to Chicago for the World's Fair, where they had their picture made with Dave leaning on a cane. He'd given up barbering for a Du Pont job as a lead burner and had joined the Methodist church, where his now dried-out cousin Will Henry was making a name for himself as a preacher. Dave became a deacon and played Santa Claus at Christmas. But Dave's career as a churchman ended when the Methodists insisted he give them 10 percent of his income; his marriage with Sallie failed shortly thereafter over her insistence on his fidelity.

Ten times in fourteen years, Dave and Sallie had separated. Once when he and Sallie were living in a small apartment in East Nashville, he got up one morning, took a look around, and said, "I don't like to live here. I'm going back to Old Hickory." He left and never came back to the apartment. Finally in 1938, during their last separation, Sallie found a postcard addressed to Dave that explained why he had spent so many weekends in Pleasant Shade, Tennessee, bird hunting—in a three-piece suit. The note was from the bird. Her name was Ruby, and she was eighteen. "If you're not up here by noon this Saturday," she wrote, "I'm going to marry Tony."

Sallie'd had enough. This time she filed for divorce, convinced that Dave's sense of loyalty—if one existed—was confined to his relationship with Garner Robinson.

On that question, her insight was correct. Garner could count on Dave when no one else could. In turn Dave did whatever Garner needed done. Hardly a day passed when he did not check with Garner to determine that need. Wherever he went, he served as Garner's ears—a pipeline so direct that what you didn't want Garner to know you didn't tell Dave.

Over the next three decades their political fortunes would rise and fall with the erratic, lurching beat natural to politics, but the steadiness of their friendship would match that of Garner's undertaking business, which proceeded with the relentless certainty of death.

The Robinsons found politics and undertaking naturally symbiotic. Old Boss himself had set the example. He bought himself a black serge suit so he looked the part, wore it every day, and insisted that all employees who met the public dress with similar formality.

In 1938, two years after Garner's election to the quarterly court, one of the jobs filled by the vote of court members came open, that of county coroner. Conveniently, the court had among its members a natural replacement. However valuable the skill of being able to determine the official cause of death, the job of coroner had never exactly been a political stepping stone. Garner didn't necessarily see it as one either. But in politics timing is everything—timing and mutual benefit.

Garner found his business and his politics to be comfortable bedfellows. The driver of a Phillips-Robinson ambulance could roll up to the scene of a crime, site of an accident, or a home where someone had died and assume the authority of the county government. Not only did Phillips-Robinson drivers have more friends among the police, they now also had their own badges. When Garner personally showed up—as he usually did—there was never confusion over where the corpse was headed. Even when the less-imposing brother-in-law, Dayton Phillips, arrived, things proceeded as usual. Garner had appointed him deputy coroner.

When Bob Marshall died in office in 1940, Garner considered

running for sheriff. He had a campaign photograph taken and showed it around the courthouse. He also left some lying around the funeral home. A big, striking man with broad, clean features and a receding hairline, he favored mustaches then and wore a narrow, rakish one that sat under his nose like a postage stamp. At the time, Germany's Third Reich was gobbling up Europe. One day at the funeral home a stranger noticed Garner's picture—and the mustache. "Who is that Hitler-looking sonofabitch?" he asked one of Garner's friends. The mustache was shaved and political ambition shelved until after the war.

At mobilization time, Garner and Dave were already too old for what was then considered a peacetime draft. Dave was thirty-seven with a dependent child, his daughter, Billye, who was about to turn seventeen. Garner was thirty-five, the father of a son named Gale born to Skinny in 1932.

Men with dependent children would not be drafted for two more years. But Dave's deferment disappeared when daughter Billye ran off and married a hawk-faced boy, the son of a tobacco farmer and moonshiner from New Middleton, Tennessee, fifty miles from Nashville. Garner drove Dave around in the ambulance all night long to convince him of the stark consequences of killing a son-in-law.

Upon their return to Old Hickory, Billye took her new husband to an unlikely haven—Garner's funeral home in Rayon City. This unnerved him even more. He had yet to appreciate what all Old Hickorians and many others east of the river now took for granted. Phillips-Robinson was more than a mortuary. The living could—and would—be helped there, too, by the Robinsons.

Billye knew Garner would protect her. For women of all ages, he was definitely a place to take your troubles. He looked at them through big, soft cow eyes, as if they were the only people on earth, and caressed their hands gently in his, like he was consoling the bereaved. Sure enough, when Dave showed up mad all over, Garner stood between him and his daughter, his arm around her. A lot of people were afraid of Dave, but Garner was not one of them. When he talked, he snapped off his words in the sharply nasal fashion of

Grand Ole Opry singers. "Now goddammit, Dave," he twanged, "whatever you have to say to this young lady, you can just say to me."

When Dave took his reclassification physical, he didn't mention his bad leg. Neither did the doctors at the examining station.

"One doctor looked down my throat and the other looked up my ass," he told Garner. "When they didn't see each other, they pronounced me ready to go." Ready or not at age thirty-seven, he enlisted and was assigned to a military police canine unit at Fort Hood, Texas, which earned him a new nickname—"Dog-ass Dave."

A year or so later at Fort Hood, as he stood in his underwear awaiting another physical that would clear him to go overseas, a doctor noticed the leg and said, "Where the hell do you think you're going?"

"Overseas," Dave replied.

"The hell you are," he said. "You've got one leg shorter than the other. Step out of that line."

Declared unfit to fight in Uncle Sam's war, Dave returned home to fight in Garner's. He exercised an option available to noncombat servicemen once they reached at least thirty-eight years of age which provided that they be discharged to work at stateside jobs beneficial to the war effort. All he needed was the job.

In the time it took Garner to dial a telephone back in Nashville, Governor Prentice Cooper hired Dave White as a member of the state highway patrol. He exchanged one uniform for another and his dog for a patrol car.

On twenty-four-hour call in those days, the Tennessee state troopers took their patrol cars home, where they were proudly displayed as symbols of authority and security in the neighborhoods. Dave cared for his car as meticulously as he did his uniform, sometimes seeking out an all-night service station for a wash job before returning home. For the people of Old Hickory to see a muddy patrol car parked on his lawn simply wouldn't do.

But this fierce sense of pride in his position often veered off into the immature antics of a man-child. For instance, the sight of tiny Rayon City resting comfortably and silently on the curve of the road invariably evoked an irresistible urge to run the siren. "These sons-abitches out here in Old Hickory don't need to sleep," he'd say, excusing himself for letting everybody in town know that Dave White of the highway patrol was either coming or going.

While Dave played, Garner worked. When a train transporting troops was wrecked near Old Hickory, Phillips-Robinson became the main preparation facility for the shipping of the bodies. Folding tables had to be set up to accommodate them all. Garner embalmed for thirty-six hours straight. Army morticians were amazed at the speed and skill of the country undertaker. He made friends of them, too; some even applied for work once the war was over.

Dave had returned home from the army in time to preside over the birth of his first grandson, a namesake born in 1943. His son-in-law was headed for the Battle of the Bulge. As expected, Garner, the good Samaritan, was there with the ambulance to take Billye and her new son home from the hospital. A year later, his own Skinny gave birth to twin girls. The day they came into the world, Garner stuck two red feathers in his hatband and went on a handshaking campaign.

Garner's new babies were hardly dry when Uncle Sam decided the time had come for married men with children to do their own fighting. Enlistments soared among the able-bodied, middle-aged courthouse and city hall politicians. A man who missed the war entirely would surely find it a political handicap later. So in 1944, at thirty-eight, Garner left Skinny with three children, including the brand-new set of twin girls, and joined the army tank corps. He left his family in the steady hands of Boss, who was still going strong. But he had been gone less than a year when Skinny's health failed badly. A new set of twins and the departure of her husband had brought on a nervous breakdown.

It also brought Garner Robinson home early from the war, another one of those uncanny, unplanned turns in his life that seemed perfectly timed to award him an advantage in politics.

PART TWO

Politics

I have no earlier recollections than my great-grandfather Will White raising his walking cane and pointing it like a rifle at a neighbor trudging down the railroad tracks by our house in Old Hickory. "There goes old man Thomas," said Pa Will to me, sitting on his knee. "He's a goddamn Republican."

World War II babies grew up hearing such talk. We were children of the New Deal, born with the shadow of Franklin Roosevelt across our faces. My family's idea of the two-party system was wrapped up in a saying of the times. "I am a Democrat. You are a Republican. Let's be friends.

I'll hug your elephant and you kiss my ass." And as in most other southern families, our only choice on Election Day was between Democrats.

For us, the Whites—the families of Pa Will and my granddaddy Dave—the Democrat of choice was whomever the Robinsons were backing. Looking back on it years later, I realized that Boss Robinson was aptly named. He was the neighborhood political boss, a stern-faced old man in a black suit who visited my Pa Will almost every day in a family ritual their sons would carry on their entire lives. Though clearly several rungs higher on the economic ladder, Boss always addressed my great-grandfather respectfully as "Uncle Bill" and treated him like a hero who'd lost his leg in war, rather than in a railroad accident. The Robinsons made you feel like you were special.

When Pa Will would see Boss coming down the lane beside the railroad tracks, he would correct an already ramrod posture. "Well, here comes our politics," he would say proudly, as if politics were a family possession and Boss Robinson power and influence personified—a pipeline of sustenance, which in fact he often had been.

Pa Will was an independent sort, proud that he could keep a roof over his head and bread on his table with veteran's benefits from the Spanish-American War and a disability pension from the railroad. But bread and rent was about all they covered. Anything beyond life's essentials—the new cars, the nice clothes, the trips to Florida, the extra gas ration tickets during the war, and all those cases of hard-to-come-by stuff that had been hauled home in the patrol car and stacked in the garage—were in fact perks of my granddaddy's job on the highway patrol, the booty of politics.

Wealth and privilege existed in Nashville, as it did all over the South, but it was concentrated on the other side of the Cumberland River in tight pockets of aristocrats, the bright and blue-blooded men who had gone north to Harvard and Yale and returned to drive Packards, play golf, and run the banks and insurance companies uptown. They already had money and position, so they left the opportunities of government to the working-class neighborhoods with names like Flat Rock, White's Creek, and Old Hickory.

It was not surprising that my family and other people in the South, which had been deprived of its share of the American dream for seventy-five years as punishment for keeping slaves, now looked to the government and the Democratic party to deliver it. After all, it was government Democrats in Washington who had back-to-back delivered us first from starvation and then from Hitler.

Besides, this was our nature. We were Scotch-Irish, which in itself, it is said, predisposes the women to fits of temper and condemns the men to pursue the precious stone of all Scotch-Irish lusts—politics—the process Plato considered the art of human happiness and the cowboy poet of the day, Will Rogers, referred to as "applesauce."

Tennessee was covered up with Scotch-Irish in the thirties and forties, ambitious, self-reliant people who believed God helped those who helped themselves. Mostly we were the merchants, grocers, and undertakers who earned our way supplying goods and services to the "lintheads" and "bastard barons" sent south by people like the Du Ponts to run their company towns, where everybody lived in the same kind of tar babies, worked at

the same mill, and ate the same kind of food. About all that
distinguished us was whether our wash was hung on the
front or back porch and how big a piece of the New Deal
our politics could command.

This is how it worked. Every time an election rolled
around, the Boss would reach into the pocket of his black
undertaker's suit and fish out the money to pay the poll tax
for every White old enough to vote, just as he did for a lot
of other families in Old Hickory. And in return for this
and other kindnesses like intervention with the law and
extended credit at the Robinson store, the people of Old
Hickory would all go out to work at the polls and deliver
votes unerringly for Boss Robinson's Democrat.

The ability of the Robinsons to deliver the Whites'
and the other Old Hickory votes was the essence of the
democratic system, the way it worked in Tennessee,
the South, and for that matter the rest of the country.
The votes east of the Cumberland River were what gave
them the clout with the bigger boss next up the line and
ultimately with the old red snapper himself, E. H. Crump
of Memphis. For nearly thirty years it was Crump, the
red-haired, blue-talking boss of all bosses, who picked the
senators and governors and handed out local elected office.
And it was Crump's machine that doled out the favors of
government from Washington to Nashville, including tires
when rubber was short, whiskey when it was scarce, and
jobs on the highway patrol.

Industrialization was coming. It would make the rich
richer. But whoever held the political power would be its
escort. And they would get theirs, too, in abundance.

Only a few years earlier, across town in the hallowed

halls of Vanderbilt University, more learned men of the
South, the illustrious Fugitive poets, had taken their
famous stand in defense of the values of agrarian society
and against the evils of the industrial revolution.

And more recently down in north Georgia, the
indomitable Lillian Smith had become the first outright
literary evangelist for the black cause with her publication
of *Strange Fruit*, a novel about miscegenation that had
been banned in Boston because of explicit sex and had
been termed a "literary corncob" by Georgia governor
Eugene Talmadge.

But it would be another twenty years before race became
an issue in the wards of Nashville and the rural precincts of
Tennessee. And to men like my granddaddy and his friend
Garner Robinson, warnings by egghead poets at Vanderbilt about the new urban society were not only
unheeded but unheard, drowned by laughter and the roar
of Oldsmobiles, the clang of slot machines, and the gush
of Jack Daniel's.

Now in the prime of life, having survived both the
Depression and the war, Dave and Garner were hell-
bent on the prosperity that they had discovered comes
automatically with the taking of political ground.

Excellence at politics was what could distance them
from Lewis Mumford's demeaning literary comparisons of
southerners with the Russians of Tolstoy and Chekhov—
"lazy, slow-moving, torpid, imperturbable, snobbish,
interbred, tolerant of dirt, incapable of making effective
plans of organization."

But it did not necessarily exempt them from the
characterization of one of their own, Wilbur Joseph

Cash, who in his landmark book, *The Mind of the South*, remembered the men of the mill villages as being enthralled by a corrupted romantic-hedonist ideal— "to stand on his head in a bar, to toss down a pint of raw whiskey at a gulp, to fiddle and dance all night, to bite off the nose or gouge out the eye of a favorite enemy, to fight harder and love harder than the next man, and to be known eventually far and wide as a hell of a fellow . . . such would be his focus."

From what I remember of those heydays of the forties and fifties, my granddaddy and his friends could have been precisely whom Mr. Cash had in mind.

Boss Crump's Gestapo

The inside of "Crump's gestapo"—the newspapers' name for the state highway patrol—was lined with whiskey and women, both long family traditions for Dave.

Back during Prohibition, Dave could take a pretty girl for a ride in the country, shoot a few quail, and bring back a load of whiskey hidden in his dog kennels, all in a single afternoon. Professional whiskeymakers in Tennessee and Kentucky were flourishing. South of Nashville, the Tullahoma-Lynchburg area was home to the Motlow family of professional whiskeymakers, always a source of high quality liquor. Around Lebanon to the north, the hills and back roads were dotted with stills and the fields rutted from heavily loaded roadsters and touring cars from Nashville and Louisville. Good homemade wine went for two dollars a gallon. Whiskey was three to four dollars depending on the discrimination and thirst level of the buyer.

Long after the end of Prohibition, bootlegging still boomed in Tennessee. Many of its counties would remain dry well into the sixties, but liquor was always available in any quantity. For anyone involved in law enforcement it was both an enduring problem, a continual opportunity, and—in Dave's case—a family affair.

The father of the hawk-faced boy who married Dave's daughter, Billye, was an accomplished moonshiner known as Pappy Jay to his Smith County friends, who included the young congressman Albert Gore. He made his whiskey about fifty miles from Nashville in a hollow on a hilly rock farm, then stored it in barrels a few miles away under his house in the small town of New Middleton until it was hauled to bigger markets like Watertown and Gordonsville. But the nearby creek rose frequently, and once in the mid-forties it washed Pappy Jay's big white house a quarter of a mile closer to town.

When the state highway patrol arrived, they found whiskey barrels bobbing in the floodwaters in all directions. Pappy Jay was arrested and the police threw one of the barrels in the trunk of the patrol car as evidence. A highway patrolman delivered both Pappy and the barrel to the judge at Carthage, the county seat, but when the judge opened the barrel, he found it full of creek water. The charges were dismissed and Pappy Jay went home with a smile, an apology, and one hundred dollars less in his pocket.

Having administered another piece of roadside justice, highway patrolman Dave White gave a gallon of the Pappy Jay whiskey to his friend the undertaker. The rest—and the hundred dollars' cash—he spent on Robi Zeriva "Zoe" Gillum of Yellow Creek, Tennessee, a hairdresser he'd stolen from an Old Hickory bootlegger.

Zoe had already divorced three husbands when she moved next door to Dave and Sallie during the late thirties. The first words Dave ever heard Zoe speak were a yelled threat out of her bedroom window in the middle of the night to kill his barking bird dogs if he didn't shut them up. It was the kind of thing he would have said.

Illegal whiskey was already part of Zoe's life, too. She had been a bootlegger's girlfriend and was helping him haul whiskey into Old Hickory from Kentucky one night when the police stopped his pickup truck. She was driving behind the bootlegger in a yellow convertible, the trunk and backseat loaded with booze. The police arrested the boyfriend and confiscated his load, but Zoe drove the convertible through the backwoods and escaped.

After Dave and Sallie divorced, Zoe and Dave struck up a relationship. It began one night as Zoe was leaving the bootlegger's place, after picking up a bottle. A motorcycle officer pulled her over. She thought she was about to be arrested until she recognized the officer as her neighbor. Dave let her keep the whiskey and said, "You can do better than that, you know?"

"I guess you mean by taking up with you," Zoe replied.

"That's what I mean," he said.

They married in 1942 while Dave was in the army, Zoe says, "just because everybody else was getting married and Dave didn't want to be off to war and leave me home a single woman." The marriage did not get off to a clean start. On the day Dave presented Zoe with her wedding ring, he felt compelled to give his mother a ring, too. And he made both presentations in the presence of his former wife, Sallie, who was at his parents' visiting her daughter, Billye.

"I hugged and kissed him and thanked him for the ring, but I was mad enough to kill him," Zoe recalled. After the marriage, she got a sympathy card from Sallie.

People said they were made for each other. "We had houses, cars, the best money could buy," Zoe remembers. "We went everywhere and did everything and the sex was perfect. Of all my seven husbands, I liked being married to him the best."

When Dave decided to ride the state highway patrol's Harley motorcycle to Panama City, she climbed on behind him. "We just ate, drank, swam, and partied for two days and came back. Of course, my ass was so sore I couldn't sit down for a week."

Zoe always looked like she'd gotten dressed on a dare. At thirty-five she had platinum blond hair, boldly cut short like a man's, and in Garner's words "an ass that would stop a funeral procession." Once a *Vanity Fair* photographer doing a layout on wartime hairstyles got her to model a silk Jean Harlow nightgown for the magazine. And she wasn't shy about flaunting her wares. Frequently she wore no underwear, which brought warnings from Dave about the risk of embarrassment should she become ill and faint or be involved in an accident. "Don't worry," she assured him. "Somebody will just throw an old hat over it."

While Dave was on MP duty at Fort Hood, Texas, he got an anonymous letter telling him Zoe was being unfaithful. He suspected it was from Garner but wasn't sure of the handwriting. Of all their contacts, very little of it had been correspondence.

When Dave finally got mustered out, he told no one but Garner and slipped quietly back into town intent on catching Zoe at the infidelities he'd heard about. He checked into a downtown hotel and telephoned his mother, Ovie, and asked that someone bring him some civilian clothes.

As usual, Ovie took matters into her own hands. She was frightened that Dave might kill Zoe and end up in prison. Convinced that her daughter-in-law had to be warned, she did what the family always had done in times of crisis—called the Robinsons.

This time, however, Garner would not cooperate. Zoe deserved no warning, he said. So Ovie called Boss, who agreed that the situation was dangerous and foiled Dave's plans by telling Zoe to be on her best behavior. She then met Dave at the hotel and convinced him the letter had been the work of a suitor whose advances she'd rejected.

Zoe was as tough as she was persuasive. One cold winter night in the midst of a snowfall, she was shampooing a customer in her beauty shop. The woman commented that she was making so much money in her defense plant job that "I hope this war never ends." At the time Zoe's son from a previous marriage was in the navy and had not been heard from in ten months. Dave's daughter, Billye, and her baby son were in the shop, too. Her husband was fighting Germans in Belgium. Zoe backed away from the woman like she had lice and started drying her hands with a towel.

"Get out of my shop," she ordered.

"Why, what's wrong?"

"My son's missing in the Pacific and this baby's daddy is in the Battle of the Bulge. We don't know if they're dead or alive."

"Well, my hair's wet," protested the woman, suds dripping down her face. "I can't go out like this."

"I don't give a damn if you freeze to death," Zoe said. "If you don't get out of my shop, I'll kick your ass out in the snow."

It was to Zoe that Dave brought home the bad news that he had been suspended from the highway patrol for switching tires on the patrol car. Her reaction was, "Well, you sonofabitch, you sure fucked up the works this time." Dave slapped her and knocked her down. She got right up and said, "What'd you do that for, you sonofabitch?" He knocked her down again. Two more times she got to her feet. Each time she called him a sonofabitch, and each time he floored her. Finally she stayed down, but raised her head and rested it in a hand propped up with an elbow. "You sonofabitch," she said. Dave shook his head in resignation. "Damn, Zoe," he said, with that mean little grin, "I can't kill you."

For them, better or worse was usually just a matter of minutes. They could trade punches and an hour later stop their car and dance in the street to music from the radio.

Dapper Dave and his flashy companion became regulars at the hottest Nashville nightspots. And wherever she went she attracted attention, which she liked and Dave didn't. One night he dressed her down for the way she was dancing with a young sailor at the elite Club Plantation. Not one to take admonition lightly, she slugged him, knocking him into another woman's lap. He grabbed her by the dress, dragged her across six tables, and pitched her out the club's front door. She went home in a taxi with the shredded remains of her slinky gown in her purse.

"She's perfect for a man who doesn't know what he wants," Garner assured Dave. "Now at least you'll know what you don't want."

The only thing Zoe had in common with Skinny Robinson was a bad temper. They were from two different worlds and their husbands kept them there. Although all the other Whites were considered family by the Robinsons, Dave's wives never were, which they all agreed was Dave's doing. In all the time she and Dave spent to-gether, Zoe said she only visited Garner at his home once. "Skinny was out of town. So after she'd gone wherever it was, Garner called up and asked us to come over. As it turns out another woman was there. And Dave and I were just over there as window dressing. You know, so he could say if anyone else showed up that the three of us came together and were visiting. Dave and I stayed in one part of the house and Garner and his friend in the other. It was the kind of thing Dave did for him."

One time Zoe asked why Dave saw Garner so much and she saw him so little. "Why would I want to take you around Garner?" Dave asked. "You got enough men chasing after your ass already." Years later, at age ninety, she spoke her mind about Garner. "The only real friend Dave ever had was Garner," she said. "One thing was sure. It was not an equal relationship between Dave and Garner. Garner was Dave's boss. Dave did what Garner wanted. I've sat in the car for hours and watched them stand outside and talk. I watched money pass between them both ways."

Exactly why they were passing money Zoe never knew. A loan transaction maybe, considering Dave's history of living beyond his means. It might also have been Dave fulfilling his long-suspected role as satchelman for a political boss.

Dave was still hanging around the funeral home as much as ever. But he also had taken to high-assin' with his supervisor on the high-way patrol, a handsome, lanky sergeant named J. J. Jackson, who had also become tight with the Robinsons. One day, Zoe's bootlegger friend, still smarting from the rivalry for her affections, told her that Dave and Jackson were supplying whiskey to rival bootleggers, specifically a Northeast Nashville motel and nightclub called the Eagles Club. Simultaneously, Zoe had struck up a telephone rela-tionship with a dispatcher at the highway patrol, a man she'd never met who clearly did not like her husband. Jokingly, she'd once told him that she'd really like to know "what Dave and Sergeant Jackson were up to."

One night the dispatcher called and told her that Dave and Jackson were "on the prowl," and later that night were due to be picked up at highway patrol headquarters on Capitol Hill by two nurses from St. Thomas Hospital in Nashville. The nurses would be driving a Cadillac, he said, and the foursome was headed to the Eagles Club.

Zoe left Old Hickory in Dave's Buick with demonic intentions and one of his revolvers in her lap. As had been his custom since becoming a policeman, Dave had equipped his private car with a police siren, which he used to clear the road ahead of him, aggravate his neighbors, and amuse himself. Zoe set the siren off full blast, pressed the accelerator to the floor, and raced through the deserted streets toward the city.

It was close to midnight when the screaming Buick pulled up in front of patrol headquarters and screeched to a stop behind a white Cadillac. Two uniformed men, one with a jacket folded over his arm, were just emerging from the office. They were caught in the headlights like startled deer. Two well-coiffured heads twisted around inside the Cadillac. Zoe read the lips of the man with the coat. "Goddamn, it's my wife," Dave said to Jackson. She saw a curse form on his lips as a fifth of whiskey fell from the coat and smashed on the pavement. Then, forlornly, he marched toward the driver's side of the Buick.

"Get your goddamn ass in the car before I blow your brains out," she ordered, waving the pistol.

"Move over," he said, accustomed to driving any automobile in which he rode.

"Move over hell, I'm driving," she said.

In Old Hickory, she dropped Dave at his parents', next door to their own home, and told his mother: "Here, Miss Ovie, I am giving you back your lovely son, and I hope the next time I see you, you will be crawling on your hands and knees in the dirt so I can kick you in the ass."

Then Zoe drove the Buick to the Eagles Club. The place was hopping. She asked the first waitress she saw if she knew Dave White.

"Sure," she said. "We know him, but he won't be here until later tonight." The waitress said he was a frequent customer because he had such an unhappy home life.

"Oh, yeah?" replied Zoe, interested. "Why is that?"

"Don't you know he's married to some big old fat woman out in Old Hickory who gives him nothing but trouble?" the waitress said.

Beside them on the bar were 150 cocktail glasses stacked upside down. Zoe glared at the waitress and raked the glasses off with her stiff hand. They were still crashing to the floor when she turned over a vacant table in the center of the room and picked up a chair by its leg.

"Hey, what's going on?" yelled the waitress.

"Just came by to tell y'all Dave White won't be here tonight," Zoe said, lifting the chair.

"Who're you?" the waitress wanted to know.

"That big, fat, ugly Mrs. Dave White who is so mean to him," Zoe replied.

Then she smashed the chair into the jukebox with all her 110 pounds behind the blows until she was holding nothing but splinters. She gave the place a final dirty look and went home.

When the divorce was final, the property settlement gave Zoe the house in which they lived and Dave the one next door. She immediately made a threatening telephone call to Dave's new highway patrol buddy, Sgt. J. J. Jackson.

"You better send a truck out here and get all this damn stuff that belongs to you and Dave. I don't have a place to park my car."

Along with the house had come a garage full of contraband—cases of beer, whiskey, soft drinks, country hams, automobile tires, and other merchandise taken from overweight trucks by the highway patrol.

"Rather than go downtown and be arrested, they just gave the highway patrolmen some of whatever was on the truck," Zoe recalled. "We had shit stacked everywhere. Some of it we used. Some of it Dave gave away or sold."

The truck arrived promptly, she said, "because he didn't want me calling anybody else to come and get it. That would have screwed up their politics real good. Garner was running for office."

The Public Square

The Nashville public square was laid out on a high bluff overlooking the Cumberland. It was there in its center, in the year after Garner Robinson won his first election, that the politicians, using money from FDR's Public Works Administration, built themselves a new Neoclassical courthouse that looked like a big, fancy shoebox.

The occasion of its opening was notable if for no other reason than it evoked a rare agreement on a matter of public policy by the city's two daily newspapers. Both the owner of the afternoon *Banner*, Maj. E. B. Stahlman, and the rival owner and publisher of the morning *Tennessean*, Silliman Evans, newly arrived from Chicago, viewed the stunning nude murals done for the inside of the building by the New Deal artist as a vulgar affront to public morals. Nudes may have been okay for the ancient Greeks, the newspapers said, but they were not welcome in "the Athens of the South."

Not long after that, on January 2, 1938, the publishers agreed again—maybe for the last time ever—that the death of the city's longtime mayor Hilary Ewing Howse was a step forward for the city.

A former furniture dealer with little formal education, Howse had held office for twenty-nine years, mainly by closing his eyes to vice and aligning himself with the state's evil political dictator, Edward H. "Boss" Crump of Memphis, and the rural county bosses who controlled the state legislature.

By the time the thirty-two-year-old magistrate Garner Robinson and his buddies from Old Hickory showed up on the square in search of their piece of the political pie, Howse was a sick old man and his power was up for grabs. Rival city and county factions were forming, their outlines faintly visible in their choice of lunch spots.

The square teemed with commerce. There were fruit stands, pawnshops, loan companies, drugstores, and one guy still selling harnesses. But none of it was more crucial to the conduct of public business than the two lunch emporiums, both located in the old city hall building across from the new courthouse. Named after their owners—on one side the Smith Brothers' and on the other Frank Underwood's—they were the politicians' hangouts, where alliances were built and deals cut. Friends were made there—and enemies.

Crump's man W. T. "Big Bill" Jones, a leader of the county court and head of the local election commission, ate at Smith Brothers' as did Garner's political patron, Sheriff Bob Marshall. But city councilman Elkin Garfinkle, a former top Howse advisor who had broken away, now aligned himself with the new group of city reformers who gathered regularly at Underwood's.

Jake Winston Sheridan, another city councilman and friend to both Garfinkle and Big Bill, ate at both places. It was a time for flexibility, and nobody was more flexible than Jake. He was a quiet, rat-faced man who wore well-made double-breasted suits and colorful ties and combed his hair straight back like the movie star George Raft.

For twelve years, Jake had labored in the shadows as the Howse machine's man in the Nineteenth Ward. During the thirties he had earned his living in a job Crump had made possible, as custodian for the state capitol building complex on the hilltop around which Nashville grew. Recently, he had given up that post to accept an appointment as court process server and deputy to Sheriff Bob Marshall. With this new employment in the county faction and his continuing membership in the city council, Jake had a foot in each camp. And the betting around the courthouse was that if a third faction developed, Jake could grow another foot.

His clearly rising influence stemmed mainly from his ability to get others elected, which was an asset rooted in being the protégé of the inveterate political scalawag Jones. As election commission chairman, Big Bill set election rules and counted the votes. He had been on the public payrolls for forty years, often holding six or seven jobs at a time. Once, after Jones had been indicted for vote fraud, Boss Crump had the legislature create a new Nashville criminal court and put on the bench a judge who would dismiss the charges.

Two decades after the vote fraud indictment, Jones still exercised power simply by appointing election officers, but he had in recent years turned much of that work over to a younger man—Jake Sheridan, who had a photographic memory for the faces of every worker in every precinct. Jake didn't need any lists. He knew their names and those of their family members. He knew their likes and dislikes, their wants and needs, and the nature of their connections. Most important, he knew what made them work, and he carried it in a wad of small denominations tucked inside his shirt.

Nowhere were Jake's talents more treasured than among the forty-seven members of the Davidson County Quarterly Court, the county policy-making committee to which Garner had been elected. Jake cultivated relationships with each of its forty-seven members, ostensibly on behalf of others—first Jones, then Sheriff Marshall, and later Tom Cummings, a crusading member of the legislature who succeeded Howse as mayor. But Jake had tired of carrying water for others and had seized the opportunity to reassemble the splintered power of Hilary Howse for himself.

His first big step toward that goal came in 1941 with the election of Jake's old Howse administration crony, Elkin Garfinkle, to one of the city's nineteen seats on the county court.

Elkin was a little gem of a man, with an elfish presence and a courtly manner. He had prominent, bushy eyebrows, twinkling eyes, and the habit of wearing his top coat thrown around his shoulders like a cape, as if it had been placed there by his sister Frances on the way out the door, which it often had been. Never married, he lived with one or more of his eight sisters all his life.

One of twelve children of a horse-and-buggy eyeglass peddler, Elkin grew up in a Jewish neighborhood in sight of the state capitol and got a law degree from Vanderbilt University. From that point on the law was his work, his love, and his recreation.

By the time he won a seat on the county court, Elkin was forty-eight years old and had already practiced law for twenty-five years at the Nashville bar. He had been vice-president of the city council, advisor to two mayors, and secretary of the county Democratic party executive committee. Among the planks of his platform that year was a proposal to extend full citizenship to minorities and the indigent by repealing the two-dollar poll tax and replacing it with a system of permanent voter registration. The poll tax had always been a double-edged weapon for the preservation of machine control. On one hand, it discouraged people from voting, especially blacks, which was its original purpose. Yet it also provided an extraordinary opportunity for buying votes cheaply simply by paying the poll tax for people who didn't care how their vote was cast. Favoring the tax's abolition was an unusual position for a machine politician, but then Elkin Garfinkle was an unusual politician.

He never worked the polls, collected money, or sought publicity. Only once in anyone's memory did he try to help anyone get a government job. And when he found out he had earned a city councilman's pension, he declined it. An atypical lawyer as well, he frequently refused to take his share of a fee when he had been associated in someone else's case. Other than books, of which he had thousands, material possessions were of little interest. He was a man of ideas, fascinated by the process of government and the legal basis that supported it. He spent his time building consensus and searching for practical solutions to government problems.

This made him the antithesis of his friend Jake Sheridan, who was a man of neither intellectual mission nor passionate political conviction. A true Scotch-Irishman, Jake saw politics as the road to wealth and respectability. Government jobs were a currency in which to traffic.

But the common ground Elkin and Jake found between them was broad and firm. In Jake, Elkin saw a poorly educated version of himself, someone with both an exceptional mind and an unusual interest in government. He urged Jake to go to law school and become his law partner. For a while Jake considered it, but he never took up Elkin's offer. His love was not the law. To him the ultimate success was winning an election. Even judges had to get elected, he said. But Jake quickly made Elkin's ideas of government his own and spent his time constructing the machinery to implement them. Without conflicting goals or interests, the two men complemented each other perfectly and forged a powerful alliance. No one in the state could match Elkin's expertise in the practical application of government, and for sure no one knew the election laws better, because for years he had been helping to write them. Passing on such expertise in the making and implementation of election laws to Jake was like arming John Dillinger with a machine gun.

The duo suffered only one serious deficiency—a storehouse for their power. Neither had much future as a candidate for higher office. Garfinkle's Jewish name automatically prevented him from running successfully beyond his inner-city district. And Jake simply was not a public man. His style suited a whisper on the telephone more than a speech on the stump, a backroom meeting more than a public debate. Jake realized that the political obscurity in which he had worked all those years had been the strength of his labor. Like Crump, being an anonymous, behind-the-scenes political influence appealed to him.

What Sheridan and Garfinkle needed was a candidate. And in the newly elected magistrate from Old Hickory—smooth-talking, good-timing, likable Garner Robinson—Jake saw the missing part. Here was a man of high energy with an engaging personality who could be talked to, who would listen, and who already knew the secret Jake had learned in his two decades around the courthouse— that politics was a matter of personal friendship.

Garner was cool to Jake at first, viewing him more as a political rival than as a potential ally. But he loved Garfinkle from the outset. Elkin Garfinkle represented the education Garner never had—the cure for a deficiency he feared would handicap his career in politics and one he had sought to overcome by paying special attention to school issues and running for the board of education. But once he heard Elkin Garfinkle explain a bond issue to the quarterly court, he knew there was an easier way.

Garner had gotten to the quarterly court on the street muscle of political patrons like Bob Marshall and boyhood companions like Dave White. To this muscle, he now added brains—Jake Sheridan, a master of politics, and Elkin Garfinkle, a genius at law. Friendship being a natural ambition of all three, their own was inevitable. And it would become the foundation of a bawdy, eye-gouging, vote-stealing political machine—the most efficient ever assembled on the Nashville public square. And that took some doing.

The Democratic primary election of 1945 had Jake's and Elkin's fingerprints all over it. There wasn't supposed to be a local primary until the spring of 1946, but the end of the war meant a massive return of veterans, including many elected officials who had given up their posts to join the war effort. They would all be trying to reclaim their jobs—and to carve up the political power that Jake and Elkin had amassed in their absence. So the local Democratic party executive committee, of which Elkin was chairman, decided to hold a special primary in November of 1945, which meant the veterans would return the following year to find the party slate already filled with machine candidates.

This would assure Jake and Elkin's continued control of the state's legislative delegation, which was important because the legislature was where Boss Crump repaid his loyalists across the state for their help in electing his governors, congressmen, and U. S. senators.

Moving up the primary from August of 1946 until November of 1945 meant fewer qualified opponents, fewer voters, and less chance of being knocked off by a war hero, most of whom were still in uniform mopping up in Europe. More important, it turned all the incumbents into lame ducks, because they had to stand for election a full year before their terms were to expire. The critical job at stake was that of sheriff, where incumbent Claude Briley was an appointed caretaker who was considered unelectable. So after his successor had been nominated, the plan was to force the lame duck Briley to resign. The county court would then appoint the new nominee to fill out the unexpired term and he would stand the general election as an incumbent. In that way the political power of the sheriff's office could be maximized in the general election in 1946 in behalf of Crump's statewide candidates and the county's legislative slate.

In the view of Big Bill Jones, still Crump's top local lieutenant, the newly returned Garner Robinson was just the man to wear the sheriff's badge, which is how Jake and Elkin wanted it. But the county judge, Litton Hickman, and Mayor Cummings wanted an older man named Charles Smith, who was incumbent sheriff Briley's chief deputy and had been the chief of the Old Hickory Police Department when it was being tormented by Dave and Garner.

So few Republicans were registered that Davidson County didn't even bother to hold a primary for them. This meant that the nominees selected by the Democrats were shoo-ins for the general election the following August.

Elections had become the personal preserve of Boss Crump, the wealthy former Memphis congressman who had become a dictator the likes of which the state had never seen. In Memphis, the state's largest city, he repeatedly stole elections with bribery and intimidation. His thugs attacked opponents' supporters at the polls. His police jailed any witnesses to the attacks—even newspaper reporters. Sometimes the attackers were the police themselves. Elsewhere in the state, Crump used his influence with the rural-dominated legislature to put puppets like Big Bill Jones in charge of local elections and to send in the highway patrol on Election Day to strong-arm voters.

It was precisely this kind of election stealing and political bossism that the new publisher of the morning *Tennessean*, Silliman Evans, abhored. Before coming to Nashville, Evans had done all his newspapering in Texas and Chicago, where he'd seen plenty of both. Being the editor Marshall Field brought to the Chicago *Sun-Times* for the express purpose of taking on Colonel Robert McCormick's mammoth Chicago *Tribune*, Evans was not a man of feeble opinion or lame spirit.

Evans' purchase of the powerful *Tennessean* had pumped new life into opposition to Crump and the political reform movement. Since his arrival, the reformers had succeeded in implementing a system of permanent voter registration, suspending the poll tax in certain local elections, and replacing the paper ballot with mechanical voting machines. They planned to swell the voting rolls further in 1946 with returning war veterans and then field war heroes against the Crump machine candidates in both the summer and fall elections. At stake were the offices of sheriff, county judge, congressman, governor, U.S. senator, and the all-important state legislative delegation, whose votes could revise the Nashville city charter at will.

In the thirties and forties, the political power of cities, especially in the South and West, was still only a dream in the minds of mayors. Yet the cities were where the action—and the problems—were concentrated. Each day more people jammed Nashville's streets searching for jobs and housing. Population of the city and county combined was already 275,000, half of it inside the city limits. But the city's share of taxes were disproportionate. Civic improvements were largely dependent on voter-approved bond issues, so the power to raise taxes and provide services remained with state legislatures and county courts. And all across the state, political bosses of one stripe or another controlled the county governments, which in turn controlled the courts, the elections, and thus the power to tax.

The bosses perpetuated their power with exactly the kind of election manipulation that was apparent to Silliman Evans in the plan to stage the "early" 1945 primary. And the publisher had no doubt who was responsible for the chicanery—Jake Sheridan.

Jake had been stuck in Silliman Evans' craw since the 1942 mayoral election—the first time he'd attracted the attention of either the publisher or the public. It was then that prominent Nashville attorney Jack Norman, who represented the *Tennessean* and was one of incumbent Tom Cummings' campaign managers, saw Jake in the office of the county trustee with what appeared to be a handful of poll tax receipt stubs. Being in possession of more than your own receipt suggested vote fraud, the very brand of election thievery that the death of Howse and the election of reformer Cummings was supposed to end.

When Jake saw that Norman had noticed the receipts, he promptly stuffed them in his mouth. As Norman approached, he chewed and swallowed them. Twice Norman tried to have Jake indicted but twice the grand jury refused for lack of evidence. Nonetheless, in the minds of Jack Norman and *Tennessean* publisher

Silliman Evans, Jake was guilty. And from that point on, Cummings was never comfortable with Jake as part of his political organization. By the time the 1945 primary rolled around, the discomfort had grown to an intense feud between the county and city factions of the Democratic party, with Jake at its center.

In the January session of the legislature, Jake's county group had forced a revision of the city charter, dividing the power of Mayor Cummings among five city commissioners. As was often the case, Jake had personally overreached by getting the legislature to create a special six-thousand-dollar job for himself as deputy commissioner of public works. Mayor Cummings, however, had gotten the city council to refuse to fund the position and was working to get the old charter restored.

It was as part of this feud with Cummings that Jake Sheridan had held up the county machine decision on whom to field in the sheriff's race. Although he had no intention of doing so, he threatened to run himself, in effect giving him the deciding vote.

Big Bill Jones, unaccustomed to such outright rebellion, traveled to Memphis and laid the dispute at the feet of Crump himself, who quickly settled it. If Nashville expected any more help in the legislature, the Boss decreed, Garner Robinson had better be the sheriff and Jake Sheridan the chief deputy. Jake had always intended to support Garner, but by playing the recalcitrant, he had gotten himself a new job in the process.

Jake immediately became Robinson's behind-the-scenes campaign manager and his presence a bone of contention to be gnawed on by Silliman Evans' *Tennessean* for years to come.

The Hopewell Box

On the morning of November 12, the *Tennessean*'s political writer, an eagle-eyed, bald-headed man named Joe Hatcher, whose words carried the weight of the publisher's opinion, issued a front-page warning to the citizens of Davidson County.

In a column sandwiched between composer Jerome Kern's obituary and a report of King George VI honoring England's war dead, Hatcher explained that a vote for Garner Robinson and the county "gang" ticket would keep the city under the thumb of the machine. Which meant, he said, that county bosses would control the elections the following year when the city voted on its new charter and selected a new delegation to the state legislature—a disgraceful circumstance "that no thinking citizen condones."

Despite the presence of five other names on the ballot, the sheriff's race had narrowed to a two-man contest between Garner and the city administration's candidate, John Cole, a former city and county policeman who had served during the war in the merchant marine. In personally declaring his support for Cole, Mayor Tom Cummings had made it clear why he preferred him over Robinson. "John Cole," he said, "is the candidate who has pledged that he will not seek to interfere with the city government." There would be no such pledge from any candidate backed by Jake Sheridan, and Cummings knew it.

The large number of candidates in the sheriff's race was evidence in itself that the two machines had squared off. Machines do best when they hold down the vote and split the opposition forces, so each side had fielded phony candidates in an effort to draw votes away from the main opponents. While Garner ran positively on his record as a businessman and a soldier in World War II, Jake had recruited a former chief of the state highway patrol, Joe Boyd Williams, to campaign negatively against Cole by challenging his war record. Meanwhile, the Cummings crowd countered by pushing a fourth candidate, pear-shaped Raymond Cannon, a commissioned deputy sheriff who ran a private police and fire service in Garner's East Nashville stronghold.

Gentlemanly Walter Stokes, Jr., a leading reformer and head of an election watchdog group known as the Citizens Protective Association, was quoted by Hatcher as saying the sheriff's race was so close it might well be determined by how many people went to the polls. Less than twenty-six thousand, he said, would make it difficult to beat the machine. But a turnout of thirty-five thousand or more would certainly guarantee its defeat.

In an effort to encourage voting, Stokes had elicited promises from all the sheriff's candidates that they would not follow their normal practices of sending out large numbers of supporters to the voting places as "poll watchers," leaving the task to members of his independent Citizens Protective Association.

The need for independent election monitoring was apparent. A local grand jury had already been asked to investigate rumors that police officers had been shaking down lawbreakers and legitimate beer and whiskey dealers for campaign funds. In an apparent effort to provoke a public confrontation, John Cole had deliberately rammed his car into Garner's one day, but Garner recognized the ploy, smiled, and drove away.

Still, Stokes was publicly optimistic that a fair election could be held. An increase in the number of voting locations and the repeal of the two-dollar poll tax had clearly extended the opportunity to vote beyond all previous boundaries and—theoretically at least—had decreased the chances of thievery as well. And because all the major candidates had waived their rights to have poll watchers, there would be less chance of confrontation and disruption at the polling places.

Most encouraging of all, Governor Jim Nance McCord, although a Crump man, had ordered his state highway patrolmen—the feared gestapo—to stay away from the polls. In previous elections the head of the patrol himself had led the packs of state troopers who showed up at the polls in plainclothes, carrying guns and blackjacks. Ostensibly, they were there to keep order, but invariably they turned out to be election terrorists, there to intimidate Boss Crump's rivals.

Early on Election Day, across the Cumberland River in Rayon City, within sight of the Du Pont plant and just around the corner from

Garner Robinson's funeral parlor, state highway patrol sergeant Dave White read Walter Stokes, Jr.'s, plan for clean elections. He was sitting at his breakfast table in his uniform pants and a sleeveless undershirt that revealed a tattoo below the elbow on each arm, one a heart with an arrow through it and the other a small American flag. As he read the paper, a little smile curled across his lips, revealing a flash of gold.

"What are you grinning at?" asked his father, Will.

"Oh, this pee-willy Stokes running off at the mouth."

"About the election?"

"That's right."

"What are you doing today?"

"Same thing you are. Working for Garner."

"I thought they said the patrol couldn't poll-watch this time."

"That's what they said."

"Well, where are you going to be?"

"Me? In the highway patrol car."

"Doing what?"

"Rounding up voters. This pee-willy Sillyman Evans says we need a big vote."

A few minutes later, he backed the patrol car out of the yard and headed for Hopewell, where the night before Deputy Sheriff Lewis Hurt, another member of Garner's inner circle, had spent the night doing road work.

Hurt had gone to Hopewell late in the afternoon on election eve to line up votes. He was packing promises. At the end of one row of dilapidated shacks, the residents had gathered around deep ruts in the dirt and asked him, "What are you going to do about the road?"

"Fix it," Hurt declared.

"When?" they wanted to know.

"By tomorrow morning."

"It's already getting dark now," they said.

"It'll be fixed by morning," he promised.

Then the Hopewell residents all went back inside their shacks, wearing dubious smiles. In the morning the road had been fixed. Lewis and his brother had commandeered a piece of state road equipment they had seen parked on the side of the highway, hot-wired it, and graded the road overnight.

The next day the shack dwellers concluded that Lewis Hurt was the most powerful man in Tennessee. And all day long they lined up to be driven to the Hopewell voting precinct. Carload after carload were delivered, all by a lone, uniformed state highway patrolman with tight lips and darting eyes.

By the afternoon some of the voters being hauled in began to look familiar to the minister who was monitoring polls for Mr. Walter Stokes and the Citizens Protective Association. One man the preacher was sure he'd seen earlier in the day wore a white uniform like a painter or hospital orderly. He grinned a lot and was missing some teeth in front. Another repeat voter was a thin young black boy who always kept his chin on his chest and never looked anybody in the eye. Finally, the minister began to ask questions.

"Where do you all live?" he asked.

"Lebanon," several of them said.

"But that's in Wilson County, not Davidson," said the minister.

"Lebanon Road," said the highway patrolman. "They work in Lebanon but they live on Lebanon Road at Hopewell." The patrolman's lips relaxed a little when he talked, revealing a gold tooth. But it was not a friendly smile.

Almost all the voters the patrolman hauled in were poor blacks unable to read or write, which was still a legal requirement for voting. The minister protested that also. But the officer in charge of elections, Deputy Sheriff Lewis Hurt, had consulted his election rule book, which had been prepared by Elkin Garfinkle, and replied, "But the law says the judge of the election can cast the vote for the physically handicapped. These people are just physically handicapped, so I'm voting for them."

When the polls closed at 7:00 P.M., the highway patrolman came back to the polling place in civilian clothes with a bottle of whiskey for Hurt, who already had one in his car. Then they drove around, stopping now and then to telephone Hurt's girlfriend, who worked at the election commission, to find out how Garner was doing.

Only 21,340 ballots were cast, less than 40 percent of those registered and far fewer than Joe Hatcher, the bald-headed antimachine columnist, had prayed for in print. This kept the sheriff's race close as a barber's shave. Even though all of the former highway patrol boss's supporters suddenly had switched to Robinson, Big John Cole had a thousand-vote lead when all the city returns had been tallied. As the count proceeded, Garner went through the precincts in East Nashville thanking people he figured had been for him. He stopped at Fire Hall Eighteen in the district next to the one where Raymond Cannon operated his fire and police force to thank the firemen for support they actually had thrown to Cannon. When he drove away, the firemen laughed behind his back. "What's wrong with that damn fool?" one said. "Doesn't he know he's lost already?"

In the Eleventh District, which was home to both Cannon's private police force and Robinson's largest funeral parlor, Cannon beat Robinson 728 to 598. Cole ran third with 345. The city organization's strategy was working.

Out on the sidewalk behind the Davidson County Courthouse, word of the latest count circulated through the crowd of candidates' supporters. Among them was Robinson's thirteen-year-old son, Gale, unanimously regarded by all sides as an annoying little shit. Some of Cole's men began to celebrate. They began to sing out, "Big John wins . . . Big John wins." A pistol was fired into the air. Whether in revelry or protest, no one knew for sure.

But then Old Hickory Community Center, the district's first precinct and its largest, reported. The vote was 921 for Robinson to 110 for Cole, with Cannon getting only 20 votes. Cole's lead dropped to less than 100. All that remained uncounted was the Fourth Precinct, the tiny hamlet called Hopewell where much of the population was black, and where about a hundred votes was the routine.

Rumors spread through the crowd that the election commission official in charge, Hurt, a chancery court officer, was reportedly on his way to the courthouse with the tally. Inexplicably, he was delayed beyond all predictions. This was an embarrassment. The reporters were anxious. Walter Stokes, Jr., began to fret. Only sixty-seven votes separated the candidates in the most important election of the day, the one in which both political machines had big stakes. And there was no sign of the Hopewell box.

Big Bill ordered police guards posted at the door of the election commission. Outside, the number of pistols suddenly visible in the crowd unnerved Garner's supporters, including his son Gale, who stared at the guns bug-eyed. Fists were clenched in tension.

As the night wore on, the dawdlers from Old Hickory eventually became drunk but never imprudent. Hurt did not plan to count and report the votes of Hopewell's registered dead and missing—those whose votes had been cast by Dave White's haul-ins from Lebanon and Madison—unless, of course, they were both sufficient and necessary to affect the outcome. After all, such a large vote with such a lopsided Robinson margin would surely cause a stink. When most of the whiskey had been consumed and enough time had passed for all votes to have been counted except those on the official tally sheet locked in the trunk of his car, Hurt made his last call. This time he didn't even bother to ask for vote totals. He just wanted to know, "How many votes do we lack?"

Very late in the evening, there were rumors that Hurt had called in. Election commission officials counting votes for the Democratic primary board had talked to him, once for sure, maybe twice. He sounded drunk. Walter Stokes, Jr., demanded to know what was going on. Finally, Hurt, with no explanation for his tardiness, showed up with the official tally sheet.

Hopewell voters had cast 4 votes for Raymond Cannon. To Big John Cole, they gave 18. But for their clear favorite, their neighborhood undertaker, Garner Robinson, they had cast a record total of 304, thereby giving him a claim to the Democratic nomination for sheriff by 219 votes.

Cole's campaign manager immediately cried foul. Noting the unusually large turnout in the tiny hamlet, he said, this "certainly doesn't appear as a logical vote."

The returns were placed under armed guard until they could be recounted officially the following day. The morning *Tennessean* reported the tight finishes on the front page along with pictures of all the "apparent winners," making sure that Robinson's photo was the one from 1939 with the Hitler mustache.

Later that day an attorney representing the losing candidates attended the official primary board vote canvassing to ask for a delay in certification of the count until the names on the poll lists in Hopewell and Old Hickory could be compared with the registration. But Garfinkle's primary board certified the returns in spite of the protests.

A stunned Walter Stokes, Jr., who had sent three members of the Citizens Protective Association to the official counting, was amazed by the board's decision.

"It appears," he said, "that the community of Hopewell has cast more votes than it has citizens." Which had indeed been the case.

Lawyers for Cole and the other losers later filed a petition with the primary board alleging that "large numbers of unqualified voters were herded to Hopewell," where they had cast "illegal ballots." It asked that the Hopewell box be thrown out and the nomination given to Cole.

They might as well have asked for public confessions and acts of contrition from Dave White and Lewis Hurt. The board ignored the petition. In the scheme of things the number of votes stolen for Garner Robinson in his first big election was trifling, and the nature of the thievery was, in the minds of the thieves, more mischievous than nefarious. It was to them simply part of a game played by opponents of equal opportunity with a common set of values and virtually no moral compass. To American politicians of the forties, cheating in elections was like cheating on your wife. Not everybody did it, but those who did viewed it as perfectly okay as long as you didn't get caught. Unlike adultery there wasn't even an applicable commandment. Politicians were more likely to spend a sleepless night over having lost an election than for having stolen one.

Eventually a lawsuit was filed in circuit court challenging the validity of the election—but not on the obvious legal grounds that the Hopewell voters were fraudulent. A successful court test of the Hopewell vote on grounds of election fraud would have required proof that the people who voted were not the ones who had registered. Since many of them were illiterate it would also require proof that Lewis Hurt had knowingly allowed enough unqualified voters to cast ballots to change the outcome. More important, the overwhelming majority of those voters were black. To unseat Garner Robinson as sheriff, the reformers would have had to disenfranchise the very voters for whom they had worked so hard to suspend the poll tax.

So rather than try to document fraud in Hopewell, the Cummings faction and Stokes's Citizens Protective Association decided to challenge the primary election on entirely different grounds. In doing so, they made the mistake of matching legal wits on the intricacies of election law with Elkin Garfinkle. It was fatal.

As a lawyer Garfinkle had won many cases over the years on the basis of technicalities such as opposing lawyers' having decimal points in the wrong place when citing statute numbers and subparagraph designations. He was also an expert on matters of court jurisdiction and knew how overworked judges loved to discover they had no legal authority to listen to the complicated case before them.

For him the primary board challenge was duck soup. It ultimately had been filed not by the losing candidates but by seventy-seven reform-minded taxpayers in a class action. Instead of charging Hurt with irregularities, they claimed the primary was not held in accordance with provisions of the 1927 state primary law.

Garfinkle responded by rounding up seventy-five distinguished members of the Nashville bar, including the district attorney general, J. Carlton Loser, to defend the primary board. Rather than file an answer to the suit, the lawyers filed a demurrer. This was the kind of procedural strategy at which Garfinkle excelled. It had the effect of forcing the judge to rule on whether the reformers' petition ought to be dismissed, rather than on the issues raised by the lawsuit. Garfinkle found all kinds of good reasons why the case should be dropped: since it was only a primary no one had been elected yet so no taxpayers could have possibly been damaged, and no candidates had been listed among the plaintiffs; the petition contained no allegation that any of the nominees had failed to receive the most votes; and the 1927 primary law had specifically provided that legal relief be sought elsewhere than circuit court. The judge quickly agreed with Garfinkle and so did the supreme court of Tennessee.

Having lost in Garfinkle's backyard, the reformers had little choice but continue the fight on Sheridan's territory. Backed by the Cummings faction, Big John Cole ran as an independent against Garner in the general election of August 1946. Aided by the Crump machine's statewide push for its candidates, Garner won both the city and county precincts and beat Cole by a scant seventeen hundred votes.

Again less than twenty-five thousand people voted in Davidson County, which the *Tennessean* attributed to a "machine slow-down." Indeed there were mysterious goings-on at the Glenn School precinct in the city's Sixth Ward, where Jake Sheridan was in charge. During the early morning rush, a voting machine failure forced a line of two hundred people to leave for work without getting to vote. And at the lunch hour, another peak voting period, an electric power outage that the Nashville Electric Service said lasted only four minutes shut down all of Jake's voting from noon to 1:30 P.M.

In Hopewell, independent poll monitors nearly outnumbered voters. This time Garner won the box by only 6 votes, 155 to 149. Joe Hatcher, the *Tennessean*'s front-page columnist, suggested that Garner's dramatic drop in popularity might have had something to do "with the absence of one state patrolman who was very anxious over the previous contest in which he might have become involved as an industrious car operator, some say not always in Davidson County. But Hopewell must be a big place to vote so many, it seems."

On his front porch in Rayon City, highway patrol sergeant Dave White read the newspaper's account of the election sitting in a swing in his undershirt with a straw Panama on his head. He felt a surge of smugness when he read about the plans for the new sheriff's swearing-in ceremony. How appropriate that ceremony chairman Garfinkle had arranged for Dave and Lewis Hurt to present their friend Garner with a nickel-plated inauguration pistol and Jake with a gold badge—symbols of the victory they had assured months earlier with their theft of the Hopewell box.

There was no way to know then that their routine acts of roadside justice, overnight road-grading, and Election Day shenanigans had begun the rise to power of what the *Tennessean* would call "the Sheridan-Robinson-Garfinkle machine," and that for the next twenty years it would win election after election by similar tactics and similar margins for mayors, governors, and United States senators.

But the first taste of victory could not have been sweeter. There they were on the front page, Dave and the other Old Hickory boys from the wrong side of the Cumberland being reluctantly acknowledged for their success. They had whipped the mayor of the city, outfoxed the election detectives of blue-blooded Walter Stokes, and shoved it in the face of the morning newspaper that clearly hated them.

But what the newspapers had to say was now of keen interest to Dave for reasons beyond the election. Each day he searched their columns for clues about his chances of going to federal prison. Not for election theft—for murder.

Mink Slide

That Dave White and his buddy J. J. Jackson ended up doing the killing was not surprising, considering their temperament. In view of their political clout, this turned out to be fortunate for the gestapo.

Jackson was the state highway patrol's rising star, a political protégé of a judge Boss Crump had recently gotten appointed to the federal bench. On the basis of past performance, he was the man

Crump called on to handle troublesome Election Day precincts. A strapping six foot five, he was a fearsome sight. In the 1944 elections he had shown up at a Nashville polling place, announced himself as a representative of "the People's Ticket, by God," and pulling a pistol from his coat said, "Here are my credentials." He promised to "blow this place full of holes. There'll be plenty of smoke if it isn't fair." When the *Tennessean* photographers later caught him rousting voters with his pistol, Jackson had thrown his coat over his head and said, "The boss told me to duck." Crump liked that.

Jackson had been promised the job of chief deputy to new sheriff Garner Robinson. But when Crump gave it to Jake Sheridan, Jackson was instead promoted to captain and made chief of the Nashville highway patrol division. This created a sergeant's vacancy lower in the ranks, which Jackson gave to his sidekick Dave White. The two were reveling in their good fortune one Monday night in late February when the telephone rang at the patrol station.

It was Governor Jim McCord himself, calling about "the most disastrous and regrettable thing that has ever happened in Maury County." In what proved to be a harbinger of the racial strife that would fracture the nation twenty years later, black snipers in nearby Columbia had ambushed the city police chief and some of his officers. Maury County sheriff J. J. Underwood had called McCord requesting highway patrol assistance.

Earlier that day a black man, James Stephenson, had gotten into a dispute over a radio repair and pushed the repairman through a plate glass store window. Stephenson's mother, Gladys, who had attempted to help her son by hitting the repairman with a shard of broken glass, got cracked with a city patrolman's nightstick and was pummeled by a passing white man who joined the fray. But no one had been seriously injured, and Stephenson had been arraigned for assault and released on bond.

But by nightfall, there was talk that a lynch mob was coming for Stephenson. It hadn't been just any repairman whom Stephenson had put in the hospital. It was William Fleming, twenty-eight-year-old brother of Flo Fleming, a decorated war hero who was a member of the state highway patrol and who had only recently defeated incumbent sheriff Underwood.

At about 6:30 P.M., the three thousand residents of the Mink Slide (or Black Bottom) area of the town of eleven thousand, turned off their lights on cue. A hundred or so gathered what weapons they could find and began to congregate in and around James Morton's undertaking parlor, Sol Blair's barbershop, and Patton's Restaurant.

About the same time, Stephenson had driven his girlfriend around the square, dropped her at her home, and returned to Mink Slide. There he got a haircut and a shoeshine at Blair's and had a few drinks at Patton's. Then he joined the crowd at the barbershop, selected a rifle from the weapons piled there, and climbed up on the roof with about twenty-five other armed men. Several among them had also served in the war and were comfortable using the weapons they held. About the same time, Sheriff Underwood telephoned James Morton at his funeral home and asked if the crowd was still armed and building. Informed that it was, he warned Morton that if the men did not go home, the police would disperse them.

By 8:00 P.M. the crowd around the edge of Mink Slide had grown to around two hundred. Some black businessmen who had refused to extinguish their lights saw them shot out. At least one automobile was riddled with buckshot. A few blocks away at the county jail, a crowd of about thirty whites, mainly teenagers, showed up demanding to know Stephenson's whereabouts. All they got was Sheriff Underwood armed with a machine gun. He promptly arrested two of their leaders who were drunk and dispersed the rest.

Meanwhile, Columbia's chief of police, J. W. Griffin, and three uniformed officers entered Mink Slide, responding to intermittent gunfire. As they walked through a lighted intersection, the "entrance" to Mink Slide, they were met by shotgun fire. All four were injured, one critically shot in the mouth. Without even unholstering their weapons, they withdrew to seek medical attention. That's when Underwood had called the governor.

Dave White and J. J. Jackson arrived within an hour as part of the first contingent of sixty-seven state highway patrolmen and fifty-nine national guardsmen from Nashville and other neighboring towns. State safety commissioner Lynn Bomar, a towering former Vanderbilt University All-American football player even bigger than Jackson, came soon after and assumed command of the state forces.

At 3:00 A.M. Jackson, armed with a sawed-off shotgun, and Dave, brandishing a .30-caliber semiautomatic army carbine, led a patrol force that raided James Morton's house and emptied it into the street. Morton and thirteen other black men in the house were arrested and charged with attempted murder in connection with the earlier shooting of the city policemen. There was no resistance, which was fortunate because Dave and several others had itchy trigger fingers.

During the night a crowd of white men intent on taking weapons and ammunition from the state armory was turned back by a highway patrol sergeant. A carload of armed blacks was stopped at the city's edge; a woman was captured but at least two men escaped in an exchange of gunfire. By dawn one hundred state patrolmen and five hundred guardsmen, mostly young boys, had been deployed. Columbia was virtually occupied. Martial law had been declared.

At the first crack of light, Bomar led a systematic shakedown of Mink Slide and the residential area nearby. Where there was not immediate surrender, there was gunfire. The men atop Blair's Barbershop fired two shots. One of them struck patrolman Ray "Slick" Austin. Dave and the rest of the patrol shot the place to pieces. One black man was hit in the shoulder. Everywhere they went, the slightest resistance was met with the maximum force tolerable to Bomar, who never left the scene. A crack marksman who could uncap Coca-Cola bottles at one hundred yards, Dave shot at anything moving or breakable. By dawn his carbine was generally regarded as a nuisance and the fact that no one had been killed as a miracle.

The huge Bomar was suffering from a crick in his neck and he had it bundled in a large yellow scarf against the cold. At midmorning, he mounted an open military command car with newspaper reporters hanging off the back and rode through Mink Slide with a bullhorn like an Allied general after the Normandy invasion.

"We're going to give you folks the same protection as people on the other side of town. That's all the trouble we're going to have. We had it back there where four policemen were wounded last night and which was cleaned up by the state highway patrol this morning."

Not many residents were visible, but a few frightened black faces could be seen peering out from behind curtains in their unpainted shanties. On East Eighth Street, Bomar encountered a few knots of people who'd gathered outside.

"Let me see you smile," he bellowed on his bullhorn. "You people go ahead. We're gonna get things straightened out."

Several "Hallelujahs" arose from the knots. One man yelled, "Can we go to work?" And another spoke for many when he called after the command car, "You better stay down here for a while."

The following day, the Columbia *Herald* reported that "to war veterans, the scene was reminiscent of American troops going through a captured town in Europe." By Thursday morning, arrests totaled 103, all but two of them blacks. And the entire episode was headed for history as a "Negro uprising."

"The Negro has not a chance of gaining supremacy over a sovereign people and the sooner the better element of the Negro race realize this, the better off the race will be," proclaimed the *Herald*. Then it breathed a sigh of relief. "We understand that the prime leader of the Negro uprising has been captured and is in the hands of the law."

The undertaker James Morton and the barber Sol Blair had been branded the ringleaders and were among those now jammed into the county jail. All day long on Thursday, March 28, they and the others seized in the shakedown were questioned two and three at a time at the sheriff's office. The office also served as the temporary headquarters for the visiting highway patrol, and as a result the place was severely overcrowded.

The prisoners fell into three categories. Some like Morton and Blair would be charged and released on bond. Others were simply being questioned and released. The third category—those who would be charged and held because they were unable to make bond—

looked to be largest. A decision was made to transfer forty-two of the prisoners to the Davidson County Jail in Nashville for at least one night.

Meanwhile, three prisoners who had been arrested in the Tuesday-morning sweep were brought to the front of the building. They were told that after questioning they would be able to make bond. One of the three, a farmworker named William F. Gordon of Franklin, was fearful and agitated. While awaiting his turn to be questioned, he had canvassed his cellmates for a pocketknife or some weapon that had been overlooked when they were searched. Unable to obtain one, he had handed his wallet and other personal belongings to his brother before he left.

"Somebody's going down when I get out there," he declared. "I may get killed or hung before I get back."

The others being questioned with him were James "Digger" Johnson, the son of prominent black leader Meade Johnson, who had also been jailed, and Napoleon Stewart. Together they were waiting in a room occupied by two deputies. One was talking on the phone. The other, the sheriff's son-in-law, was lying across a bed. In the room were three caches of unloaded weapons that had been confiscated, part of the store of 550 rifles, shotguns, and pistols waiting to be cataloged. One stack was behind Johnson's chair, a second was in the corner near Gordon, and a third was behind the sheriff's son-in-law.

Out in the hallway a contingent of state troopers had arrived, among them Captain Jackson and Sergeant White. As was customary, all were being asked to check their weapons before entering the jail and were waiting in a double line to do so. Seated at a table just outside the deputies' office was a photographer for the Nashville *Banner*. He looked up just in time to see the prisoner Johnson pointing a rifle at the deputy on the telephone. The deputy didn't see Johnson but noticed that Gordon had picked up a weapon, too, and was attempting to load it. He dropped the phone and wrestled for the rifle in Gordon's hand. As he did, Johnson fired a .30-caliber rifle at him from across the room, grazing his arm and piercing the table where the photographer sat.

At the sound of the shot, the highway patrolmen in the hall re-acted violently. Jackson and White, who had been in front of the line, reached the doorway first and emptied their pistols into the room. Three other officers fired from behind them. Others passed loaded weapons to the front of the line to Jackson and White, who took second turns firing until Johnson and Gordon were both down and no longer moving. Outside the jail Patrolman T. G. Fite saw dust flying from the walls as the fusillade went off inside. By the time Commissioner Bomar retrieved a pistol and raced into the room, it was all over.

The official report said that the prisoners died en route to a Nashville hospital. But witnesses said there were so many bullets in Gordon and Johnson that some rolled out on the ground as their bodies were being lifted into the ambulance. Miraculously, the third prisoner, Napoleon Stewart, who had raised his hands and backed into a corner, was not hit. From the outset the public questioned how the prisoners could have armed themselves inside a jail, why they were even in a room with a cache of confiscated weapons, and why the patrol had responded with such a show of force. Stewart had been an eyewitness to it all.

The killings created a furor, focusing national attention on the eventual indictment and trial of the black Mink Slide residents who had been arrested in the crackdown. While charges were brought against the officers, thirty-one blacks and four whites were eventu-ally indicted by a Maury County grand jury in connection with the ambush of the city policemen and charged with attempted murder. The NAACP sent its best legal minds to represent them, including a white lawyer from Chattanooga, Maurice Weaver, and two black attorneys who would later become legends in the civil rights strug-gle, Z. Alexander Looby of Nashville, and Thurgood Marshall of New York. Then thirty-seven years old, Marshall refused to accept Tennessee officials' offer of police protection, telling the New York press that he "did not trust the state police."

A national defense fund committee was established, with Eleanor Roosevelt, Senator Wayne Morse, and Representative Adam Clay-ton Powell among its members. Writer Carl Van Doren wrote an appeal for funds so incendiary that the pamphlet itself became the subject of a federal grand jury investigation. Van Doren accused the police of murder, rape, destruction of property, unlawful search and seizure, and violating the civil rights of those arrested.

Attorney General Tom Clark assigned his special assistant James E. Ruffin to look into the matter, and an FBI investigation was ordered. Clark's statement the day of the shootings, directed to all U.S. attorneys, was one of the first signs of a changing national attitude regarding the oppression and political disenfranchisement of blacks in the South.

"Human rights and civil liberties will be protected to the full extent of federal provisions whenever they are infringed," he said. "We have come thus far in the unsettled postwar period without disorder. However, symptoms of increasing intolerance have been noted recently. It is my desire that you immediately devote special attention and investigation to protection of all Americans in their civil liberties, regardless of race or color. Special attention should be paid to laxity or inefficiency of peace officers of any category."

The need for such vigilance could not be overstated. State and local officials, including Governor Jim McCord, who had visited the area shortly after Bomar's triumphant ride through Mink Slide, defended the highway patrol and the guard. And many of the complaints about the harsh crackdown in Mink Slide, among them protests by the American Communist party and rambunctious labor groups such as the CIO, were generally dismissed in Tennessee as the work of outside agitators.

Three days later, as the Sunday burial of the two dead prisoners approached, a representative of the sheriff's office visited the white family on whose farm William Gordon had worked. "It would not be wise," he told them, "for anyone from this family to show up at that nigger's funeral." None did.

On March 29, the first day that Thurgood Marshall appeared in a Maury County courtroom, U.S. District Judge Elmer Davies, the political patron of J. J. Jackson, ordered a federal grand jury probe of possible civil rights violations in connection with the arrests and the killing of the prisoners at the jail.

Both the federal probe and the state court trial of those charged would drag on for months, and considering the political climate, toward not wholly predictable conclusions. The system of justice in Tennessee, as elsewhere in the nation, was still a white preserve. The jury that tried the black defendants was all white, a situation that the Tennessee Supreme Court, to the dismay but not surprise of defense lawyers, deemed constitutional. The federal grand jury investigating the civil rights violations was also white.

Meanwhile, rumors spread that the grand jury had been told that the highway patrol and sheriff's deputies had intentionally made sure there was just enough ammunition available to provoke the prisoners to attempt a prison break. What else explains why they acted precisely when the hallway was filled with armed patrolmen?

Government agents showed up at Dave White's home in Old Hickory and wanted to know how he came into possession of an army carbine, which he told them he had acquired in a trade with some of the troops who had been on maneuvers in Tennessee during the war. Dave told his family that he and Jackson might be indicted for murder. Early each morning he sat on the front porch searching "Sillyman" Evans' newspaper for clues to the grand jury's intention and his own fate. Then he would go by Garner's funeral home, and then on to the courthouse to see Jake, searching for news or rumors about the grand jury deliberations. Usually, there was none.

In the end, two factors swayed the grand jury's decision. The two-hundred-page FBI report, prepared by agents based in Memphis, Crump's political stronghold, gave state troopers and sheriff's deputies the benefit of the doubt at every turn. It was not customary then for law enforcement agencies to be at one another's throats, and relations had always been good between the FBI and the state patrol. And more important, the additional testimony by a surviving witness to the jail killings was in itself proof that the incident had not been staged just to kill Negroes, as critics charged.

Like a handful of votes in the Hopewell box, Stewart's grand jury testimony on the events that day constituted the slim difference between winning and losing. In its final report on Friday, June 14, the grand jury said, "We consider the killing of the Negroes Johnson and Gordon justifiable homicide. The testimony of eyewitnesses, including Napoleon Stewart, admits of no other interpretation."

The jury concluded that "the Negroes of Mink Slide" had been partially responsible for the destruction of their own property and that the force used in the shakedown had not been excessive. Further, the jury said, "We have found during the course of our investigation that the events transpiring at Columbia have been the subject of nationwide misrepresentation. Falsehoods and half-truths have been widely publicized by letter and pamphlet under the sponsorship of various organizations. . . . Many of such accounts concerning these events are wholly lacking in factual foundation, and the conclusion is inescapable that they have been manufactured and circulated with the malicious intent and desire to incite racial discord and intolerance and to cause further racial strife."

To the grand jury, the whole thing smelled of a communist plot. "In disseminating such propaganda—the avowed Communist Press of the country has been especially active, having carried a series of inflammatory articles on the racial disturbances of Columbia," the report said. "This technique is characteristic and dangerous and manifestly is designed to foster racial hatred and to array class against class. . . . In the opinion of this Grand Jury nothing is so likely to erode and ultimately destroy peaceful and friendly relations between the races as the dissemination of half-truths and falsehoods such as have been so freely circulated in relation to the events occurring at Columbia."

Having done its duty and delivered fair warning, the jury was dismissed. The state court's actions, however, were less predictable. Looby and Marshall put on an extraordinary but tedious legal defense that eventually overwhelmed state prosecutors. Ultimately twenty-five black defendants were tried in the ambush of the four Columbia city police officers on the night of February 25. Their trial, which had been moved to nearby Lawrenceburg on a successful change of venue motion, ended with twenty-three acquittals and two convictions. The convictions were quickly overturned and the cases were later dismissed altogether.

One night after the Columbia trial a group of state troopers, sheriff's deputies, and city policemen fell in behind Looby's Buick as he and Marshall headed out of the county. Near the city limits, Looby recalled, "three cars drove up with their siren open, one pulled in front, one on the side, and the third in the rear.

"Eight officers jumped out and notified us that they had a search warrant for my car; they searched the car thoroughly and found nothing.

"We started off, they stopped us again and asked Thurgood for his driver's license, and on inspection found it satisfactory and as we proceeded to start they stopped us again for the third time and said they would have to arrest Thurgood for driving while drunk.

"They put him in one of their cars and started off a byway; I followed them and after certain suspicious turns they drove back to the highway and to the magistrate's office."

After concluding that Marshall had not been drinking, the magistrate released him. He and Looby, still trailed by officers, eventually switched cars with a local resident and drove out of town undetected. All his life Looby believed that by persistently following the police car he had saved his friend from a lynch mob.

Fifty years later, one of the officers suggests that Looby might have been right. "We thought Thurgood Marshall ran off at the mouth and deserved to be taught a lesson. It just might be that something like that was planned for him. But Looby, now, he was a good nigger. We wouldn't have wanted to do anything to him."

The Columbia uprising eventually would come to be seen as a seminal event in the political life of the nation. In no small way it was a harbinger of inevitable change. While the altercation over the radio repair was but a minor incident, it was nonetheless a moment to be seized, first by whites who had been complaining that the town's young black war veterans needed to be put back in their place, and then by the black veterans themselves who were fearful, and yet so emboldened by their war experience they would climb atop a barbershop with shotguns and ambush the symbols of white authority.

The lessons of swift, streetside justice doled out by Dave White would no longer be universal among blacks or whites. Even as the grand jury was clearing Dave of civil rights violations, U.S. Attorney General Clark was publicly reminding federal prosecutors of the need for vigilance against the abuse of police power. More important, he pledged an extensive Justice Department fight to help blacks vote in the upcoming primary and general elections. Of all their civil rights, none were "under greater threat" than their right to vote.

The era of urban voter empowerment was beginning. All over America, there were signs of an awakening to the need for a more inclusive democracy. The postwar years would see a growing realization that elections had been closed contests for far too long, and a new awareness that what seemed like a harmless struggle for supremacy among equal participants was in reality a private game of exclusion. In some states poll taxes still made voting a class advantage. Three states—Arkansas, Mississippi, and South Carolina—still conducted virtually all-white elections. Poll taxes, though partially dropped in some counties for primaries when it suited those in power, would stay on the books in Tennessee until 1953. And even in states where poll taxes had been abolished and blacks were being recruited to cast votes, democracy was far from a square deal. Not only was one man's vote worth more than another's, the opportunity to steal an election—and thus steal the power to rule—was the sole prerogative of a handful of white political activists within the Democratic party. With the power of theft—regardless of how minute the scale or benign the intent—went the privileges of making and enforcing the laws, of serving on court and grand juries, and holding public office.

Elections, which had been the locks for preserving the status quo, would now become the keys to change. That very year, the United States Supreme Court had refused to review an Illinois reapportionment case, narrowly missing its first opportunity to empower thousands of disenfranchised voters. One of the lawyers in America who appreciated the importance of that case was Jake's and Garner's friend, Elkin Garfinkle, who noted the development and filed a brief history of it in his private law library.

And within a matter of months, Z. Alexander Looby would become the first black man since Reconstruction to hold elected public office in a major American city—Nashville. There in the Tennessee capital, in the precincts and neighborhoods where Jake Sheridan and the machine controlled the voting process, the black vote would first rise as a voice of protest and a clear path to power.

Whatever their opinion of blacks as human beings, Jake, Garner, Elkin, and friends pioneered community recognition of their full worth as citizen-democrats. To the Old Hickory political machine, the votes of black people were to be courted, won, and lost—or bought and sold for that matter—just like those of whites.

Make no mistake. In the minds of these urban political pioneers, the blacks had not yet approached social equality. But neither did the men around the sheriff's office and the funeral home ever consider that color disqualified anybody from voting. Because political equality always precedes social equality in a democracy, this self-serving political egalitarianism was, despite its paternalism, the opening through which progress would pass.

The same political machine that sprang into action to put down the Columbia uprising and administered raw roadside justice in the interest of its own preservation would ultimately open up Nashville as a training ground and launching pad for the civil rights movement. From that city's streets came the legions of Martin Luther King's Freedom Riders and nonviolent foot soldiers to wage the second great war of emancipation. And the city itself would play a crucial role in the legal revolution that realigned political power nationwide by shattering rural white control of the state legislatures and eventually the United States Congress. This led to the one-man, one-vote principle, to the concept of single-member districts that produced all the black elected officials in the land, and—ultimately—to the civil rights and voting rights acts of the sixties.

PART THREE

The Colemere Club

The only way to see out was to sit on the edge of the front seat with my chin resting on the dashboard. From there, I could tell the neighborhood was different from Old Hickory, where we lived. The houses were brick, not shingle and clapboard, and they were bigger, sitting back off the road under great trees whose limbs hung out into the street sheltering the smooth pavement. No cinders crunched under the tires of the patrol car; there was no smell of coal in the air, no sight of people or laundry on the porches.

"Where are we now?" I asked Granddaddy.

"Belle Meade," he said.

"Who lives here?"

"Guys with good luck. You know, big shots."

But the only people on the streets were blacks, "jigaboos" my granddaddy called them. I had seen them in Old Hickory, too. They lived in Hopewell and in the village, changed the tires at the filling station, bought meat on credit at Robinson's Store in the same line we did, and on Saturday nights sat out in front of the recreation hall in straw hats and black and white shoes.

"Are the jigaboos big shots? They live here?"

He shook his head and smiled, showing his gold tooth.

"Why are they here then?"

"To work. Belle Meade has the best bus service in Nashville just so the jigaboos can get to work."

The blacks were clumped at the bus stops or trudging on the side of the road, mostly women in white dresses like I had seen at the doctor's office.

"Are they all nurses?" I wondered out loud.

"No, they're wearing their work uniforms," my granddaddy explained.

My understanding would become complete years later when a Belle Meade woman recounted the story of a childhood friend who while on a trip by car to Florida accompanied her mother inside a Georgia grocery and saw for the first time a black child about three years old. Once back in the car, she asked excitedly, "Mommy, Mommy, did you see that little bitty maid?"

My granddaddy had to explain to me what a maid was and why they wore uniforms. I had never seen one in Old Hickory.

Sometimes the women smiled as we passed. Now and then, we would see a black man in a yard pushing a lawnmower or clipping a hedge. But they were unsmiling and watched us warily, like they might a snake.

One day on the grandest street of them all, Woodmont Boulevard, a black man working in a yard raised his hand in salute to the patrol car as it passed. My granddaddy screeched on the brakes. "What the hell is that nigger wearing?" He stopped and backed up.

The man walked up to the curb. He looked old to me. His skin was blue-black, glistening with sweat. Around his neck was a woman's necklace.

"You're dressed up pretty fancy there, boy. What in the hell is that around your neck?" my granddaddy asked.

"Them's nat'chel pearls. Belongs to the missus heah," he said sheepishly, pointing to the big house.

"She know you got 'em on?"

"Oh, yas suh. We do it reg'lar. Missus says nothing like human sweat to keeps them pearls nice."

"You mean she puts them on you to shine 'em up?"

"Yas suh."

"Goddamn, I declare," my granddaddy said, shaking his head and driving off fast.

"Can we blow the siren now?" Sometimes he would when I asked him, especially if we were going fast.

"Not now."

"When then?"

"Somewhere the other side of Murfreesboro Road."

I didn't understand that then. But I came to.

The state and county police didn't patrol in Belle Meade as part of their regular duty; Belle Meade had its own private police force. But Murfreesboro Road to the southeast was the main route from Nashville to Chattanooga and Atlanta. The land alongside it was soaked with the blood of Civil War combatants in Nathan Bedford Forrest's final and futile attempt to repel the Yankees. The highway eventually became home to the airport, which in turn spawned industry all the way to the big bend of the Cumberland River at the city's edge. Together the road and the river formed a sort of buffer zone between haves and have-nots, a dividing line in the city's soul.

The airport property itself, which had been owned for years by the prominent Weaver family, whose fortune was made in banking and insurance, came to be divided in a similar fashion. Sandwiched between the onslaught of modern air traffic and the city's only mental institution, where Dave White had administered roadside justice to the bus-bench shitter, the land was sold by the Weavers to the city in 1940. They then fled west to Belle Meade, a proto-type for the wealthy, blue-blooded, lily-white, purely residential suburb of the twentieth-century American dream. And there they joined the Belle Meade Country Club, which would become the citadel of big money and social status in Nashville.

But a mansion the Weavers left behind on Murfreesboro Road became a citadel of another kind. The house had been built before the Civil War by Mrs. Weaver's family, the Coles. The place was called Colemere, and she'd had it restored in 1930, ten years before it was purchased by the city. After the elections of 1946 and 1947, Jake, Garner, and my granddaddy's friends took the house and occupied it like a conquering army. And in the next few years it became a symbol of their power and their rising social and economic status. In the late forties and early fifties my granddaddy would pull his patrol car off the road in front of it so we could sit and watch the airplanes take off and land.

Huge and white, bathed in lights, the mansion looked just like the houses we drove by in Belle Meade.

"What is that?"

"The Colemere Club."

"Can we go there?"

"You bet."

I didn't believe him when he said we could go to such a place. But one day we did. And it looked like I imagined the Belle Meade houses did. The twelve rooms were an obstacle course of cream-colored sofas and big wing chairs that were deftly negotiated by courtly, white-coated black waiters, balancing trays of delicate china. In the kitchen we saw a smiling, bowing Negro man named Leslie, the manager, whose wife, Juanita, gave me the world's greatest fudge brownie with sugar on the bottom.

And then Jake and Garner met us, wearing suits with pistols under their coats. We all walked the grounds while they talked about the mayor and the governor and put down little flags to mark where to park cars when President Truman came the following Sunday. My granddaddy had on his police uniform and I walked beside him, his pistol swinging in a holster on a brass swivel near my ear.

Not long after that, my granddaddy got a green-and-cream-colored torpedo-back Cadillac and a new wife named Verna with long red fingernails, and we went back to the Colemere Club on an Easter Sunday afternoon. They watched while I played on the thick green grass with other boys in bow ties and long white pants and with snaggletoothed little girls in frilly lacy dresses that bobbed up and down and showed their underwear when they bent over to pick up the colored eggs. Garner's pretty blond twins were the only kids there I knew, but they just smiled and ran off.

All afternoon my granddaddy stood on the edge of the crowd talking to Garner and Jake, about President Truman, I suppose. And I spent a lot of time thinking about how I was the only kid there who knew they had guns under their coats.

Advancing the Art

Shortly after buying the *Tennessean* in 1937, Silliman Evans was invited by James G. Stahlman, who had succeeded his grandfather as publisher of the *Banner*, to attend the Sulphur Dell Club, a monthly dinner meeting of the town's movers and shakers named after the old minor-league ball park.

There Evans met round-faced, cigar-smoking Jack Norman, a crackerjack criminal defense lawyer, rising political power, and Skinny Neiderhauser Robinson's first boyfriend. He would become the newspaper's counsel and Evans' confidant. Also among the guests introduced to Evans that day was dignified, courtly Walter Stokes, Jr., a man typical of the families who lived in stately mansions in the city's West End and owned sprawling antebellum estates in the beautiful Tennessee countryside. He was from a family of lawyers whose wealth went so far back even the descendants had trouble pin-pointing its beginnings. He dressed elegantly, carried himself rigidly in the manner of the well-to-do, and spoke with the soft, precise vowels of southern aristocracy.

Both Stokes and Norman, a man of more modest beginnings from a section of South Nashville, were do-gooders, paragons of cit-izen concern about good government. Norman had worked his way to prominence and had courageously backed the campaigns of several reform-minded political candidates. Stokes had formed the Citizens Protective Association in the interest of preservation of a nearly extinct species—an honest Tennessee election.

Like the other rich, well-educated men who gathered regularly as the Sulphur Dell Club, Evans, Stahlman, Norman, and Stokes had high aspirations for the future of their city. Every day the *Tennessean* had a line under its masthead calling Nashville the "Inner Citadel of the Nation." And in his afternoon *Banner*, Stahlman authored a reg-ular front-page editorial called "From the Shoulder" in which he dispensed advice on how the city should conduct itself. Not unlike committed city fathers elsewhere, the Sulphur Dellers felt they should have the power to chart the direction of their town. The problem was they didn't.

The real decisions affecting the future of Nashville were not the prerogative of the well-intentioned businessmen of the Sulphur Dell Club. They belonged to the political wheeler-dealers on the public square.

Ten years later, nothing had changed. Garner's election as sher-iff in 1946 had solidified the machine's control of the county court. The old county judge Litton Hickman, who had opposed Garner's election, had made a fatal mistake when he attempted to block the sheriff's first budget appropriation. "There will be no compromise," the judge declared. And there wasn't. Between them, Jake, Garner, and Elkin had already lined up twenty-seven of the forty-seven mag-istrates behind their proposal. The appropriation passed, and from that day on Jake, Elkin, and Garner had firm control of the court. They later punished Hickman by throwing out his friend and Jake's old mentor, Big Bill Jones, as county party chief and replacing him with their own man, an East Nashville hardware dealer named W. Y. "Booty" Draper.

Draper's rise to prominence was typical of the way the trio worked. When Garner was running for sheriff, he had gotten a Nashville hardware supply executive to come out to the suburb of Madison where he lived to escort him to the local hardware store, which was operated by Draper and his brother. While Garner mingled with Draper's customers, the supplier offered Draper a deal. "You and your brother know a lot of people out here on this side of town," the supplier said. "If you help Garner get elected, he'll make you a court officer."

Draper helped and Garner kept his promise. After Draper became a court officer, Jake came by and offered to support him for a city council vacancy in his home district. The council job also carried with it membership on the county court. Within two years, Draper, who was already a well-off businessman, had two paying government jobs. And when Jake and Garner wanted Booty Draper's vote for anything, they got it.

People liked to deal with Jake because he was a nice fellow—a man of moderate feelings whose limberness of philosophy and principle automatically moved him into position as bargainer. He listened to what others wanted, then figured out what was negotiable and ultimately possible under the circumstances. Thoughtful, pleasant men always made the best fixers.

As a precinct worker for Hilary Howse and Boss Crump, Jake had learned the basic lesson of politics—that it was personal, that success depended more on acquaintance and friendship than anything else. Delivering a friend's vote required less work than that of a stranger, bribing a friend was easier, stealing from one less risky. Jake's deals were based on knowing the players. He was as comfortable talking to the uneducated bootlegger Charlie Riley from Varmit Town in South Nashville as he was the brilliant uptown lawyer Elkin Garfinkle. He knew how much money meant to Riley, how little it meant to Garfinkle. He could be on the opposite side of either man one day, then join up with them the next—an art he quickly taught the neophyte Robinson. You never quite knew exactly where Jake stood on an issue, only that in the end you wanted to stand beside him.

But when Jake found someone who would not make a deal, he instantly targeted them for removal from office. As the 1947 election approached, that thought plagued Mayor Tom Cummings. He and the reformers had hoped to get the 1947 legislature to revise the city charter again and restore the power of the mayor's office. Not only could Jake and his crowd block that, they were now in a position to defeat Cummings for reelection as well.

The mayor's feud with Jake had been counterproductive. Nashville needed rebuilding. It was soot-stained, dilapidated, and short of jobs and housing. Cummings knew he could mobilize the business community, but he could not build and sustain a political coalition in the county court and state legislature behind any of the progressive programs he proposed. Until he could do that, his dreams for Nashville—and those of Silliman Evans, his chamber of commerce backers, and do-gooders like Walter Stokes—would remain just that.

The mayor was a farm boy from the gently rolling hills of McMinnville east of the city. He had been a successful grocer, earning enough money to pay his way through Vanderbilt law school. A respected lawyer, he once brought a lawsuit to force an audit of city books in an effort to expose thievery in the Howse administration. As a legislator he had been courageous enough to take on Boss Crump. None of this had been accomplished without compromise here and there. Cummings knew that Jake could make the system work, and that he invariably made it work for his friends and for himself. As pragmatic sometimes as he was hardheaded, Cummings decided the best way to deal with Jake Sheridan was to buy him.

As chief deputy to a new sheriff who was having budget problems, Jake's salary was only four hundred dollars a month. At that price, Jake saw himself as a seriously undervalued commodity, a man in the market for a better offer. Cummings made him one. They had split in the first place over a six-thousand-dollar-a-year job Jake wanted in the city public works department, so Cummings had the

post funded and hired Jake as city director of public property reporting to the mayor.

As soon as Jake went on the city payroll, the Robinson-Sheridan-
Garfinkle combine made the kind of quick, slick turnaround that
would become their trademark. Splitting with many of their county
friends, Sheriff Robinson publicly endorsed the reelection of the
same man who had run John Cole against him twice in the last eighteen months. Jake went a step further. He added Ben West, a former
assistant DA, state legislator, and one of the mayor's worst political
enemies, to Cummings' ticket as vice-mayor.

The new alliance split the reform movement down the middle.
The blue-blooded Stokes and his Citizens Protective Association
convinced a respected judge, Weldon White, to step down from the
bench to run for mayor against Cummings. White drew the support
of the *Tennessean*'s politically astute lawyer, Jack Norman, and the
district attorney, Carlton Loser. But *Tennessean* publisher Evans
could not abandon the political investment he had in Cummings.
Despite the presence of Jake Sheridan in the Cummings administration, Evans swallowed hard and endorsed the mayor.

This produced what may have been the most incoherent of all
Nashville elections and ushered in a remarkable new development in
southern politics—the power of the black vote.

After representing the Columbia rioters, Z. Alexander Looby, the
brilliant black lawyer, had returned to Nashville a hero. As the 1947
city elections began to shape up, something called the Solid Block
organization appeared out of nowhere in an effort to get him elected
as the city's first black city councilman. Solid Block aligned itself
with the reformer White. Jake saw this not as a threat but as an opportunity to organize the black vote for Cummings. In his personal
dealings, Jake was an equal-opportunity politician. He'd pay as
much for a black vote as he would a white and just as quickly.

Absurdly, the reformers, including District Attorney Loser, work-
ing as a poll watcher for the liberal and progressive reform candidate
White, found themselves challenging the credentials of black voters.
At Twelfth Avenue North and Jo Johnston Street, the precinct with

the heaviest black vote, both Loser and Jack Norman showed up to guard against shenanigans, which was smart given the presence of Lewis Hurt there as a poll worker for Jake and Garner. But Hurt prevailed. That box went 440 for Cummings to 60 for White, and the mayor ended up winning the ward by 1,000 votes—close to the final margin of his citywide victory.

From that day on, voting among Nashville blacks would increase with each election, and for the next decade could be counted on by Jake as certainly as the Hopewell box.

In the wake of this unusual election and largely because of it, the middlebrow Colemere Club was born in a spirit of political unity and hope. The club was soon the envy of the highbrow Sulphur Dellers, and its members were imbued with political power even big Belle Meade money could not buy.

The newly reelected Mayor Cummings was the club's first president, and among its founders were a notorious election thief, a real estate salesman, a machine-owned judge, and one Jew—Elkin Garfinkle. Two of the most prominent and powerful of its original one hundred members were the East Nashville street hustler Jake Sheridan and the Old Hickory undertaker Sheriff Garner Robinson.

Both newspaper publishers, Stahlman and Evans, felt obliged to join, if only to avoid being left out. And with them as members, the club's activities were suddenly of extraordinary interest to Nashville newspaper readers.

The Colemere was chartered for "the advancement of arts and sciences," the *Tennessean* reported confidently, "and a large segment of the club's membership meets there daily to discuss community and welfare problems and to relax and enjoy the club's spacious facilities."

But the presence of Garfinkle, Sheridan, and Robinson implied a threat that the Colemere's president felt obliged to address publicly. "No citizen should consider lightly the spirit in which the club was organized," said Mayor Cummings. "This organization is bigger than any individual or any group of individuals."

Both the newspaper's description and the mayor's assurance belied the reality that the Colemere Club had become the seat of government. Advancement of arts and sciences may have been Colemere's theoretical dedication, but the massing of political power was its practical aim. No organization with Jake Sheridan as a member ever operated beyond his influence. Initiation cost only one hundred dollars and the monthly dues were only five dollars. In keeping with his faith in a stacked deck, Sheridan recruited dozens of machine loyalists as members. Soon Jake had the Colemere organized as well as one of his elections. As its first "civic endeavor," the club threw an autumn barbecue for seventy-five hundred Democrats in honor of the party's statewide nominees in the 1948 election. Jake ordered up three tons of barbecue and arranged entertainment by a barbershop quartet—Will Nussbaumer and his Swiss accordion players and yodelers—recommended by Skinny Robinson.

Over the next few years, the three "endeavors" for which the Colemere Club would become best known were two events for children—an annual Easter egg hunt and a turtle race—and "Jake Sheridan's political dinners."

Once each quarter prior to the regular meeting of the county court, Jake hosted a dinner at the Colemere for his working majority and their friends. Political strategy, once plotted on cigarette-scarred desks in the back room of the sheriff's office or among the corpses in the basement of the funeral home, was now the topic of conversation over sterling and Waterford on the linen-draped banquet tables at the cavernous Colemere. Blue-collar politics had become a black-tie affair, complete with attendant publicity from the city's two newspapers.

No one benefited from this more than Garner, who switched from a fedora to a Texas Stetson. He wore it with light gray or cream-colored double-breasted suits, with belly and pistol often bulging underneath. Now he looked like the marshal of Dodge City instead of a Mafia hit man. The new look helped him with *Banner* publisher Stahlman, with whom he shared an interest in the local Shriners' organization, the Al Menah Temple. The two became friends, although the stiff-necked *Banner* owner frequently warned the sheriff never to forget that "I am a newspaperman first."

Relations with *Tennessean* publisher Evans remained personally icy, but Garner got around that by making friends with *Tennessean* reporters and midlevel editors. He started by giving the *Tennessean*'s enterprising city hall reporter, Wayne Whitt, exclusive access to two drifters who'd killed an entire family in Kentucky, even claiming to Kentucky authorities that the newspaper's photographer was on an official mission from his office. Some time later the city editor on whose watch Whitt had reported his exclusive repaid the sheriff by refusing to print a picture of the normally kind sheriff backhanding a sassy black prisoner.

"Garner has been good to us," the editor said. "We can't do that to him."

Now the *Tennessean* and *Banner* reported when Garner and Jake fished together in Florida, or took their families to the Colemere on Wednesdays to play bingo and on weekends to see Bob Hope and Doris Day. The beautiful Robinson twins and their spotted walking horses rated the cover of the *Tennessean*'s Sunday magazine. And the once-hostile morning newspaper even took note of the depth of political loyalty inspired by Sheriff Robinson with a detailed report of how his Old Hickory buddy Dick Jones had dived into icy water to recover a billfold containing fourteen hundred dollars that Garner had dropped while crossing a stream on a midnight coon hunt.

Similarly, the previously pilloried Elkin Garfinkle enjoyed a new public stature as an admired constitutional lawyer and public figure of growing power never before afforded a Jew in Nashville. People even began to drop his name in an effort to exact favors from those in authority. A lifelong bachelor, Garfinkle dated a woman called Harris one night a week for fifteen years. Once the couple was accosted by a policeman for being in Centennial Park, site of Nashville's famous replica of the Parthenon, after closing hours. "But Officer, I'm Elkin Garfinkle," the little lawyer told him.

"Oh yeah? I've heard that before," the officer said. "Let me see some identification."

Garfinkle assumed the job of peacemaker at the highest levels of local government, a role he would share with the *Tennessean*'s hard-charging lawyer, Jack Norman, for decades to come. In their first joint effort, they pushed through an urban renewal project to wipe out a black shantytown nestled between the new courthouse and the state office complex on Capitol Hill.

Perhaps most important of all, Jake Sheridan's deal with Tom Cummings ended Boss Crump's hold on the voting apparatus in Davidson County. For the first time in the century, the reformers and those in control of the election apparatus were on the same side. In the August primary of 1948, Estes Kefauver and Gordon Browning, candidates for U.S. Senate and governor respectively, led a re-form ticket to a statewide victory over Crump's men. This was the famous "coonskin cap" campaign in which Crump labeled Kefauver "a coon." Kefauver in turn started campaigning in a coonskin cap. He might be a coon, Kefauver acknowledged, but not a pet coon of Boss Crump's.

The Crump effort that year was but a pathetic shadow of its former self. Crump and his main ally, U.S. Senator K. D. McKellar, had never been able to agree on which candidate to support against Kefauver. And Governor McCord had been hurt badly by his decision to impose a one-cent state sales tax that Crump had warned him against. At a meeting in Nashville, Crump had said, "If you put that tax on, the people will run you out of office." Which they did. Reading the handwriting on the wall, Jake and Garner abandoned McCord. He got less than 9,000 votes in Davidson County, compared to 22,540 for Browning.

In West Tennessee, the best the Crump machine could do was break even, despite unusually aggressive Election Day strong-arming by Crump's state highway patrol. One West Tennessee patrol captain had been so brutal in McCord's behalf that he became the new governor's highest priority on Inauguration Day. Immedi-ately after taking the oath, Browning marched to the state highway patrol headquarters on Capitol Hill, seized the microphone from the dispatcher, and got the captain on the radio. "Wherever you are," he said, "park your car. Leave your badge and the keys in it. You are fired."

It was a joyful day for reformers and do-gooders. The fearsome highway patrol was finished as an election gestapo. Boss Crump had finally lost a statewide election. More important, he had been trounced decisively in the state capital. The Walter Stokes crowd hailed the end of bossism. And on their editorial pages the newspapers pontificated about the "dawning of a new era of political leadership" for the city. What they envisioned, of course, was the blessed unity and camaraderie of the new Colemere Club spreading over all levels of local government in the interest of reform.

Jake and the boys saw it a little differently. To them politics still rolled on the wheels of slick, quick deal making, the down and dirty double cross, and the delivery of votes—one by one.

The demise of Crump's gestapo after the 1948 election deprived Jake and Garner of one of their most effective political tools—guys with guns and badges to collect tribute and work the polls on election days. For this they couldn't count on the Colemere Club. They needed guys they could trust—like Dave White.

A blazing shootout, a near indictment for murder, and the Hopewell box scandal hadn't been enough excitement for Dave. Tired of being called Buglemouth, a name he earned on the patrol for yelling at a motorist, and fresh off the carpet where he'd been called for feeding Ex-Lax to Captain Jackson's pet monkey and ruining a patrol car, he quit his job as sergeant, got married for a third time, and went to Florida. At forty-five, he found managing a motel on Daytona Beach more appealing, even though his new wife attributed the sudden move to "a wild hair in his ass."

The root of Dave's wild hair may well have been nothing more than the promise of relief from the relentless stress on anyone whose work requires him to buckle on a loaded gun every day and accost hostile strangers. Looking down the barrel of a .30-caliber deer rifle in the cramped hallway of the Columbia jail, Dave White had seen his own mortality. When the adrenaline shut down, he was still alive, but his own bullets had helped kill two men. His father, Will, while working as a guard at Brushy Mountain Prison in East Tennessee at the turn of the century, had shot and killed a fleeing escapee. Taking another man's life was enough to end his gun-packing days and send Will off to do railroad work. Dave soon discovered that his similar experience had driven him to night clerking in a dump with roaches big enough for him to shoot with his .38. And when he began contemplating shooting the motel owner instead, he and his new wife, Verna, shook off the sand and headed back to East Nashville. Naturally, he went to Garner for a job, but the appropriation to the sheriff's office had been temporarily suspended by the county judge after a political squabble. At the moment, Garner had only "voluntary patrolmen." He made Dave a turnkey at the jail, one of the few paying jobs he had.

A high roller even when the chips were down, Dave was driving a recent model white Cadillac, which soon created a problem for Garner. With county judge Litton Hickman having put the sheriff's office on bread and water, having a turnkey flaunting a flashy new Cadillac would not do. Friendship or no, the Cadillac had to go. The next day Garner called Dave into his office and told him to get rid of it.

"Why?"

"Because of what people will think. A turnkey at the jail can't afford to drive a Cadillac. They'll think we're stealing."

The Cadillac soon disappeared, replaced by a 1949 green Ford coupe.

When the county appropriation finally came through, it contained money for an additional sergeant's job. Dave, of course, wanted it, but appointing a sergeant was not as easy as it sounded. In his first year in office Garner had picked a sergeant so controversial that four patrolmen up and quit rather than work for him, resulting in a spate of negative publicity. This time Garner checked with the magistrates and the patrolmen about their preferences. There was definitely some skepticism about Dave White.

But Garner and Jake agreed on the qualities they wanted in their ranking officers. Dave's experience in politics was every bit as valuable as his experience in law enforcement. And he possessed the one trait they valued more than any other: his loyalty was unmitigated, matched only by that of the wallet-retrieving Dick Jones. Politics being what it is, Dave's ability to speak for the sheriff, especially to the law violators with whom the sheriff couldn't afford to be personally too cozy, was invaluable. From them Dave could raise money and other election booty such as whiskey, which was routinely handed out as enticement to vote—and to vote right.

The sheriff had the dispatcher summon Dave to the courthouse. Dave was wary; such calls usually meant Garner wanted to chew him out about something. The sheriff opened the conversation as usual. "You sonofabitch," he said. "I've been talking to the magistrates and I didn't find anybody that likes you worth a damn."

"Goddamn, Garner," Dave said. "Did you call me all the way in here just to tell me nobody likes me?"

"No. I called you in here to tell you that I was gonna make you sergeant the first of the month but . . ." Garner paused and shook his head. Dave figured the sergeant's promotion was out of the question. "But by God, after talking to all the magistrates who hate your ass, I've decided I'll just make you sergeant today."

Considering the plans Garner and Jake had for the patrol, they couldn't have picked a better man.

The Colemere cabal's first political act was a daring double cross of the *Tennessean*'s candidate for county judge executive, Beverly Briley. After helping Briley to defeat Litton Hickman, Garner and Jake then quietly fielded their own slate of magistrates to oppose those being put forth by Briley.

A week before the primary in which the new county magistrates were to be chosen, Garner assembled his deputies and patrolmen in a criminal courtroom on the sixth floor of the courthouse. He wore a light-colored suit, a summer Stetson, and a serious look. The sheriff had already told Jake and Elkin what he would say. But first, the roll had to be called by Hudepohl Buck.

A former deputy and part-time ambulance driver from Old Hickory, Buck Overton was not a man for the Colemere Club. He had to be pulled out of wrecked cars and dried out at the Madison Sanitarium from time to time. But he had the same invaluable tie to Jake that Dave had to Garner, a record of loyalty that made for the perfect political lieutenant. While Buck answered to Jake, Hudepohl Beer now paid Buck's salary, a reward for Hudepohl being one of two brands of beer "officially recommended" by the sheriff's office.

As Hudepohl Buck called the roll, Garner noticed that some of the names produced no response, which he didn't like. Of all the meetings his men were asked to attend, none was more important than the election planning sessions. This was what government and politics were about. People should register to vote and go to the polls. And people who had public jobs had a responsibility to get people to vote—the right way.

Garner looked around. Dave White was there, with his eight-year-old grandson at his elbow. And so was Lewis Hurt, and Seth Mays, a longtime friend of Jake's who was the city police commissioner. Garner looked upon those assembled before him as more than law enforcement officers. They were the government, the faces of the sheriff's office, gun-carrying, badge-wearing ambassadors of his own idea of public service. Yes, they had been hired to arrest criminals and keep order. But they had also been hired to reach into the community and do the work of politics, which to Garner meant helping people. That's why all that free food and beer that came naturally to the sheriff's office was put into the patrol cars, so it could be distributed out to people found hungry and destitute. That's why at the beginning of every shift in the winter the patrol cars went by the coal company and filled their trunks with bags of coal to be handed out to people found cold and without fuel. And why those red, black, and white patrol cars were used the way Boss had taught him to use the ambulances—as free transportation to get people on foot to where they were going.

Just like his ambulance attendants, Garner's patrolmen sometimes didn't know whether they were cops or taxi drivers. But that was the way Boss had run the grocery store and the way he and Dayton had run Phillips-Robinson. And that's the way Garner would run the sheriff's patrol. An investment in goodwill was profitable politics. An easy credit policy produced dividends with interest, especially on Election Day. And there was not a damn thing wrong with collecting what was owed.

Garner took the floor from Buck. It was time to "get on the ball," he said matter-of-factly, to work for the "Taxpayers" magistrate ticket. And while they were at it, they should work for the legislative ticket he had already endorsed and for the reelection of Governor Gordon Browning. "Make your stops. Call your friends. Have your wives call their friends—you know how to do it."

Then a bevy of councilmen, magistrates, and city and county officeholders assembled by Jake and briefed by Elkin took the floor one by one and spoke positively about the people the sheriff was endorsing. But Garner's machine was far from being all talk. On Election Day the state highway patrolmen stayed away from the polls just as the reform governor, Browning, had promised. But in Davidson County, they were replaced by Garner's deputies, dispatched to the districts where magistrate and constable jobs were in dispute. By this time state election laws prohibited city or county employees from serving as election officers. But Elkin and Jake had found a way around it. As a constitutionally elected officer, they concluded, the sheriff was not technically a county employee, so his deputies, who were compensated from fees, or in some cases from Garner's own pocket, were installed where needed.

On election morning, jailer Tommy Dolan showed up in North Nashville's First Ward's Fifth Precinct with a card entitling him to be a machine operator. Someone complained that he was a county employee. No, Dolan protested, "Garner Robinson signs my paycheck personally." Conveniently, a member of the county court, local magistrate John T. Nolan, was on hand to swear Dolan in over the protest of the Briley ticket's poll watchers. "You can have him arrested tomorrow after the election if you want to," Nolan assured them.

In nearby Precinct Three of the same ward, reformers tried to displace the election officer who was also a commissioned deputy sheriff, but to no avail. They had the same success out in the Twelfth District, where the election officials at both precincts were relatives of the incumbent magistrate and constable, who were on the machine slate. At the grammar school building where voting was heavy, the law prohibiting Election Day campaigning within fifty feet of the polls was widely ignored. And instead of the state election authorities the reformers had requested to insure a proper vote count, there were a half-dozen sheriff's deputies, some of whom gave away soft drinks in the school driveway.

And, as usual, another irregularity was reported at the Hopewell box. One of those aggravating electric power failures shut down the voting machines during the morning rush period. Fortunately, Dave White and Lewis Hurt, still the election officer at Hopewell, were there to handle the matter.

Two months later at the October meeting of the quarterly court, the new county judge Beverly Briley tested the election results. Jake and Elkin summoned the faithful to their usual "premeeting meeting" in Jake's office to finalize what had already been decided at the Colemere Club.

When the court convened, twenty-five magistrates—one more than needed for a majority—banded together to deprive the new county judge of the power to appoint committees, an indignity they had not even sought to inflict on Litton Hickman. Then they named their own committees and made their own appointments according to the plans they had laid earlier.

Jake celebrated by throwing a big dinner at the Colemere Club. The *Tennessean* had been right. The defeat of Boss Crump in 1948 and the new prominence of the Colemere Club in civic affairs had indeed advanced the art of politics.

Jake and Sillyman

One piece of Elkin Garfinkle's advice that Jake persistently ignored was that he try to make peace with Silliman Evans and his *Tennessean*. Jake knew that doing so would entail trying to charm the old publisher, which he figured was useless.

Jake was right.

A man of small stature, Evans was, according to his rival Stahlman, "small of brain, too, sometimes." But he had giant self-confidence and a lifelong immunity to the charm of politicians, as Big Jim Folsom, the colorful giant who served as governor of Alabama in the late forties, would attest. Folsom was six foot eight, weighed 250 pounds, and wore a size-fifteen shoe. He had a correspondingly sized ego and appetites of similar proportion for sex and bourbon, which he indulged to the extreme one night at a party aboard Evans' yacht, the *Tennessean Lady*. As the boat chugged down the Tennessee River somewhere in the wilds of north Alabama, the little publisher finally had enough of the big governor.

"Pull up to the bank and put the sonofabitch off," Evans ordered.

The startled crew began scrambling around to determine the nearest town. One scanned the bank with a searchlight looking for a landing but illuminated only a dense forest. "Where are we?" he wanted to know.

"Looks like Treeville to me," said one of Evans' front-page columnists, who was only a few sheets in the wind behind Folsom.

"That'll do. Put him off there in Treeville," the publisher ordered. And they did, along with his Alabama highway patrol escort.

Later in his life Folsom remembered Evans as a "high-tempered little bantam rooster always looking for a fight." In those days, wagering on fights to death with roosters was common in the South. And in between the fatalities, the more faint of heart could play a less exciting game of chance called "Rooster Bingo" in which a single cock ambled about nonviolently in a wire coop suspended above a numbered board, with betting conducted on which number would catch the next plop of excrement. The most vulgar and memorable features of both games were often the hallmarks of the other main recreational pursuit of the time—politics. Nowhere was this more evident than in the two-decade-long power struggle between Silliman Evans' *Tennessean* and Jake Sheridan's political machine.

Jake's double cross of the new county judge Beverly Briley at the fall 1950 meeting of the quarterly court sent Silliman Evans into orbit.

On a Thursday morning, October 30, Mayor Cummings went on a matter of considerable urgency to Jake's office two doors away. Jake wasn't there, so the mayor asked his secretary, Mrs. Elizabeth Iverson, about the progress of the property inventory Jake had been hired three years earlier to complete. It was two years overdue, he told her. Mrs. Iverson said she believed the inventory was near completion and would soon be filed.

When Jake came back that afternoon, he telephoned the mayor's office and Cummings returned. This time he found Jake huddled with Elkin and Booty Draper, city councilman, court officer, and party executive committee chairman. Politely, as was his style, Cummings asked when the property inventory would be ready.

"I don't have it yet," replied Jake in a loud voice, which was uncharacteristic. "And I'm not going to be in any hurry about finishing it."

One word led to another, with Jake finally offering to quit "if you write me a letter asking me for my resignation."

Cummings went back to his office and wrote a letter of dismissal, which he released to the *Tennessean*.

"Dear Sir," wrote the mayor. "Differences of opinion have come up between us concerning the policy of this administration, which are impossible of solution. In view of this, I consider it for the good of the service that you be relieved of your duties as director of public property of the City of Nashville.

"This is, therefore, to advise you that effective Nov. 1, 1950, your services as director of public property of the City of Nashville will terminate."

The *Tennessean* splashed the story all over the front page. Sheridan's firing, the story claimed, was a surprise to political observers. The paper predicted that "with his ouster he is certain to lose command of the controlling bloc of the county court. . . . The majority are bound either to the city administration of Mayor Cummings or the state administration of Governor Browning. . . ."

For days, the newspapers wrote and rewrote Jake's political obituary. And in doing so they made the mistake that all undertakers fear. They buried the wrong man.

The *Tennessean*'s prediction that Jake's firing would loosen the machine's hold on the county court turned out to be just more wishful thinking. With the help of Garner and Elkin, the coalition had held firm. Jake and Elkin had immediately begun plotting what seemed to Garner a dubious endeavor—the defeat of the incumbent Cummings in the 1951 election race against Vice-Mayor Ben West. At first Garner balked at actively opposing Cummings. He was uncomfortable turning on the man who had supported him only a few months earlier. But his friendship with Jake ultimately overrode those reservations and the sheriff's office went all out against Cummings. So did the weather.

In December and January, the city was hit with its worst blizzard in modern history. Subzero cold, snow, and a crippling ice storm shut down the city for two weeks. Many of its residents were without heat and electricity. While Garner and Jake had the sheriff's patrol hauling coal and groceries to the afflicted, Mayor Cummings had been caught in Florida on vacation. With all transportation into the city halted, he was depicted as helpless in the sunshine. Jimmy Stahlman's *Banner* fried him for it. Political cartoonist Jack Knox caricatured Cummings on the beach in dark glasses, bathing suit, and Hawaiian shirt. "Where was Tom when the lights went out?" asked the caption. "Down in Florida with his shirttail out."

Jake of course reproduced the cartoon as a West campaign poster. Meanwhile, Rafael Benjamin West had turned out to be a helluva candidate. Ben was cut from the same blue-collar cloth as Jake and Garner. The middle child of seven, his father was a railroad telegrapher, and when the family had lived alongside the tracks in rural Lewisburg, Tennessee, south of Nashville, their next-door neighbors were John and Fannie Hill, whose family was both large and black. Ben grew up with soot on his face and a fire in his belly that everybody interpreted as burning ambition. While in high school, he waited tables and worked as a newspaper copy boy and through college he worked as a reporter for Jimmy Stahlman's *Banner*. He made friends and enemies with equal ease and never minced a word in the process. After receiving his law degree from Vanderbilt University, he became a prosecutor and gained a reputation as a tough, thorough lawyer with a glib tongue and an eye for publicity.

Always regarded by the *Tennessean* as a loyal disciple of the county machine, West had no use for Cummings, and during his tenure as leader of the city council he had openly challenged his leadership, often with the blessing of Jake and Elkin. West was a natural to oppose the mayor as the machine "revenge" candidate. West had shed the histrionics of his 1943 campaign and attempted to talk about issues, promising better schools and improved fire and police protection. This pleased Stahlman's *Banner*, and the newspaper endorsed him with editorials and favorable reports.

But the fight became tough and ugly. The *Tennessean* succeeded in making Jake and Elkin the issue. Because Garner was now in his third term as sheriff and could not succeed himself, the *Tennessean* didn't name him in their daily attacks. They substituted West instead, calling him "a front man for Sheridan and Garfinkle," the same label they had given Garner.

As the 1951 election approached, no one gave West much of a chance. Joe Hatcher's front-page column in the *Tennessean* beat the drum for a big turnout, proclaiming that "all odds favor Mayor Cummings' return to the office for a four-year term."

Two weeks before the election, Garner had agreed to implement a goodwill policy of having deputies and patrolmen refuse to show up in court as witnesses against drunks and other petty offenders. Every one of the defendants would walk, Jake reasoned, and owe the sheriff's office a favor that could be collected on Election Day. Dozens of offenders went free, which provoked a howl from the district attorney's office and a front-page story in the *Tennessean*— "Sheriff's Officers Halted in Pre-election Strike—Deputies Say Failure to Prosecute Ordered by Sheridan."

A black minister maneuvered by Jake into signing a West endorsement advertisement publicly recanted and accused Jake of "trickery"; the gambler Goodjelly Jones was photographed carrying voters to the polls in a car bearing a West bumper sticker; and an unpredictable rogue constable was accused of harassing a black woman and threatening to arrest her because she was for Mayor Cummings.

On Election Day, the front page of the *Tennessean* reported that the state's most famous politician, former secretary of state Cordell Hull, lay dying of old age in Washington. Also imminent that day, the paper said, was another demise. The certain reelection of Mayor Tom Cummings would put the final nail in the political coffin of the Colemere Club's most powerful member, Jake Sheridan.

But despite all the negative publicity, the machine had quietly laid a minefield along the road to the mayor's reelection. In the 1949 legislature West had successfully sponsored a major change in election laws long advocated by Garfinkle. City council candidates would no longer run citywide, but would be elected from within a single geographic district. For the first time, people had to vote at precincts located within the district where they lived.

This caused Cummings two major problems. Confusion over where to vote would hold down overall voter turnout. There would be delays and long lines as poll workers checked precinct records for the names of those wishing to vote, and unassisted voters turned away at one spot might not have the time or inclination to seek out the correct precinct. On the other hand, for the first time black candidates had a chance of getting elected to the city council. There were black candidates running in several districts, and the possibility of their success had heightened tension and interest among blacks and whites alike.

For a well-oiled political machine, it was the best of all worlds. Old hands like Jake and Elkin knew exactly how and where to slow down voting or expedite it in their interest. And they had in their hands the most potent lever—the intimidating presence of the county patrol. Garner had sent two uniformed officers to every precinct where blacks voted in large numbers. They stood over the shoulders of the election officials, glaring at some voters, smiling and assisting others. At Dudley Park in West Nashville, two deputies went into the booth with voters who looked like they needed assistance.

Cummings had tried to offset the effect of the patrol by fielding poll workers of his own in record numbers. Seventy-seven candidates were vying for the twenty-one city council seats. They all had poll watchers, too. In all, more than sixteen hundred election workers had been dispatched to forty-one polling places. The law requiring them to stay fifty feet away from the voting machines might as well not have been on the books. Some precincts resembled mob scenes; voters couldn't even locate the election official keeping precinct records. At the sight of the turmoil, many voters simply kept driving. Others stopped but couldn't shoulder their way through the mob. At one precinct, nearly fifty voters were turned away.

Patrol Sergeant Dave White, whose official duties did not include patrolling inside the city limits, was nonetheless placed in charge of mob-building at the Second Avenue fire hall in South Nashville, where Jake wanted the vote kept down. About 2:30 P.M. God weighed in on the side of the machine when He blessed Dave's efforts with a rain shower, which in turn sent his mob of sixty-one poll workers scurrying into the tiny fire hall for cover and leaving no room for voters.

After the rain stopped, an election-machine operator named

Jamie went behind the curtains on the voting machine to help a voter whose professed preference was for Cummings; Jamie was immediately tackled by a West poll watcher. The city police arrested the West man on the spot, but Sergeant White called a sheriff's car to bring him back after he posted a fifteen-dollar bond.

After the polls closed at 7:00 P.M., Jake, who was back in his old job as chief deputy sheriff, loaded his family into a new black Buick sedan and drove through his East Nashville neighborhood toward the Davidson County courthouse, where the votes were being counted.

As they neared the Woodland Street Bridge over the Cumberland River, the Buick fell in behind a clunky Hudepohl beer truck, which made a right turn at the old shoe factory and headed into the Bottom, home to the city dump and three hundred black families. The Buick followed. The Bottom was in Jake's old city council Nineteenth Ward and Jake Jr. had spent the day there ferrying voters to the polls.

The truck stopped in the center of the road for a barrel-shaped man in crisp starched overalls. He had hamlike forearms and a row of piano keys for teeth. Old Lyge had been Jake's friend for twenty years. Jake got out of the Buick and the two talked for a moment. Then Jake told the beer truck driver, "Twenty cases." When they had been unloaded, the truck moved on down into the Bottom and stopped at Sonny Boy's, where the scene was repeated. "Ten cases," said Jake.

This was an election night ritual, part of the dogma by which the machine lived. Jake had accepted it on faith from his father-in-law, the detective Sam Giles who'd seen him in his twenties trying to make a go of it in a grocery store with his mother and brother as partners. "You gotta quit that store and run for the city council," Sam had said. "Get out and walk the streets. Knock on doors. Talk to everybody and get to know them all by name." Eventually Sam took Jake down into the Bottom where he'd met Lyge and Sonny Boy, and when they came out, Sam said, "Now, those boys don't do nothing but work and get drunk and fight and have babies. You've gotta take care of 'em and keep 'em out of jail and workin'. And if you do, they'll work for you and keep you in office forever."

Jake had believed Sam, and from that day on had been religious about taking care of the people in the Nineteenth Ward. He'd take calls from the boys in the Bottom in the middle of the night same as if they were white, and get up from his card game at the fire hall to go help them on Sunday afternoons. And on Election Day, he sent drivers in cars donated by the used car dealers and delivered them all to the precinct to vote.

As soon as the polls closed and the votes were counted, the beer showed up. Along with the cash, it was distributed on the basis of performance. Jake's democracy worked just like Crump's in Memphis and Curley's in Boston and La Guardia's in New York. The tribute levied on those who had been favored during the year—the truckers and saloonkeepers, pimps and the owners of dice tables and one-armed bandits—was spread around on Election Day where it would do the most good. Only participants were rewarded. Jake was like a church preacher splitting up last Sunday's collection among those who came to this week's service.

Once the beer had been allocated, Jake drove to the courthouse and parked the Buick next to the door behind the sheriff's office and waited. He was eager, like a man about to taste revenge. Jake usually didn't take his politics this personally, but Mayor Cummings and Silliman Evans had wanted it this way. They had precipitated it with Jake's unceremonious sacking. They'd meant to kill him politically. But Jake was not dead—not yet.

The long day of mutual suspicion had its effect on the people who gathered that night at the courthouse for the vote count. Ben West's brother, Wilson, tight as a drum, complained when one of the election commissioners was late, delaying the beginning of the count. Only Jake seemed immune to the tension. He sat placidly outside in his Buick with his arm resting on the open window. Every few minutes, his friend Booty Draper, the party executive committee chairman, would bring the discouraging news down from the city council chamber where the election commission was counting votes.

Mayor Cummings had jumped out to a sixteen-hundred-vote lead. Each subsequent report from Draper had Cummings' lead narrowing but tempers boiling higher inside the council chamber. A tough-talking county patrolman named Paul Terry, one of fifteen the sheriff had stationed in the chamber, was antagonizing almost everyone. He had shoved a newspaper reporter and had nearly come to blows with a Cummings man who resented his manner. An actual scuffle had broken out between one of Garner's deputies and a voting-machine operator who was for Cummings. Seven or eight blows were exchanged, leaving the machine operator with a bloody nose.

Jake was more interested in the unreported precincts. With twenty-seven of the forty-one precincts counted, the mayor's lead had been cut to five hundred. But with only four boxes out, Draper believed the margin would hold.

"It's over, Jake," Draper said. "Cummings is going to be reelected."

Jake was unfazed. "Just hold tight," he said. "It's not over. The Bottom is still out."

More than the Bottom was still out, and Jake knew it. As was always their style—no matter what the election—the last boxes to report were all machine strongholds. But Jake had not been above learning lessons from the Hopewell box fiasco. Never again would the final vote be reported from a machine-controlled, heavily black precinct. So he brought the Bottom in early, 208 for West to 137 for Cummings—a margin of 71 votes.

The North Nashville High School box was the next to report. Here, Jake had sponsored a black city council candidate, whose presence had spiced up the race and increased voter participation dramatically. Four years earlier, the precinct had voted only 226 people in the mayor's race. With Jake's backing, Cummings had lost it to Weldon White by 32 votes. This time 753 voted in the precinct with surprising results. West carried it 494 to 198—wiping out all but four votes of the mayor's lead.

Cummings' forces knew they were done. The last box to report was Hillsboro High School on the Southeast Side, an upscale neighborhood the mayor had lost to the reform candidate White by a two-to-one margin four years earlier. This time White, who lived in the area, had supported West. Cummings ran better but still lost the box by thirty-nine votes, giving West an election night lead of twenty-seven votes—the closest in Nashville election history.

Outside in the Buick, Jake relaxed, but inside the courthouse Garner was up to his ample belly in bedlam. When the final numbers were announced in the council chamber, both Garner's deputies and Cummings' city police force assumed responsibility for protecting the ballots until an official canvass could be completed the following day.

At the news of his brother's hairsbreadth victory, Wilson West went ashen and nearly fainted. But he revived instantly when he saw City Police Inspector Oly T. Boner leading a phalanx of officers toward the election commissioners, who were already surrounded by an escort of Garner's men. Saying that the city police had as much right as the county to protect the ballots, Boner elbowed his way through the press to the side of the commissioners. West blocked his path. "Over my dead body," he shouted.

Then the troublesome Terry, the pugnacious county patrolman who had been girding for battle all night, came out of nowhere and grabbed Boner around the neck. Boner pulled away and cocked his fist. Terry gave him a shove and the other officers squared off with Boner's men outnumbered two to one. Before a blow could pass, the city's elderly police commissioner, Jake's old friend Seth Mays, stepped in between them. Right behind him was the hulking Sheriff Robinson, his lantern jaw set squarely under the Stetson, a nickel-plated pistol in plain view under his open coat. "Nobody's taking these ballots," he growled. No one wanted to hit the old commissioner—or test Garner Robinson. What was left of the city's reputation for civility had been saved. Together they had stopped what Silliman Evans' newspaper would call a "near riot."

The official canvass the following day would correct a number misreported to the newspapers and increase West's official victory margin to fifty-five votes. This of course came as no surprise to Jake Sheridan. He had known how many votes were needed when the Bottom reported its seventy-one-vote margin for West.

Over time, nothing the machine ever did would be more important

to the future of the city of Nashville and the state of Tennessee—
and indeed the political landscape of the entire nation—than the
election of West. For Ben West was the prototype of the sixties'
liberal politician, a classic, blue-collar Democrat, a man from the
wrong side of the tracks committed to change.

Under other circumstances, he would have been a natural ally
of the *Tennessean*. Like its publisher Evans and its tough editor
Coleman Harwell, West was a social liberal and political progressive. Like the *Tennessean* editorial board, he believed in an active
government that would both tax and spend in quest of improved
quality of life for all citizens, especially the disenfranchised blacks
at the bottom.

Most important, considering what lay ahead for the city, no
politician in the South was more comfortable with the full empowerment of black Americans than Ben West. On the strength of the
single-district legislation West had sponsored, the first two black
city councilmen in Nashville's history had been elected. His top
legal advisor and most respected political backer, Elkin Garfinkle,
had championed the egalitarian provisions of the law at every turn,
especially in their government applications. And he would bring to
West's side another politician from Old Hickory, a young lawyer
named Z. T. Osborn, Jr. Together they would make legal history
in the cause of equal rights.

Yet Silliman Evans' personal dislike for Jake's local replica of Boss
Crump's election machine and his rivalry for Jake's power would
come to be the overriding factor in determining the city's political
alignment. It would split the city's social progressives between the
two warring factions, each represented by a newspaper, driving the
political leaders personally most comfortable with the prospects
of integration into a decade-long alignment with the reactionary
Banner and its publisher Jimmy Stahlman, a political neanderthal
and committed segregationist.

Over the next twenty years, this split would give the city a blurred
perspective on the issue of race that in the long run would prove as
fortuitous as it was incongruous.

PART FOUR

Booze and Bones

The enduring nature of race as a cutting issue in American life was lost on me until the civil rights movement of the sixties, after I had become a man. But the politics of whiskey and gambling were ingrained in me as a small boy watching my granddaddy smashing roulette tables with a sledgehammer and loading cases of confiscated booze into his car trunk.

It was illegal to sell whiskey by the drink in Nashville in the forties and fifties, and some Tennessee counties are still dry today. Back then, gambling was to Nashville what country music would become, the lucrative business at the heart of the tourist trade. It had flourished in the city since before the turn of the century when white-vested riverboat gamblers stepped down on the docks of the Cumberland and heard the click of rolling bones from behind the walls of the nearby restaurants. Though strictly prohibited by an ironclad state constitution, gambling remained an unwritten menu item at the honky-tonks and roadhouses, which were as crowded on Saturday night as the churches were on Sunday morning.

On the weekends, the bones rattled and the booze flowed, and the excitement of going on patrol with Sgt. Dave White was heightened by the prospect that we would take part in a raid. One Friday night at a Cumberland River honky-tonk, I saw him delicately remove a case of Jim Beam bourbon whiskey from atop a gambling table before smashing the table to pieces with an axe. I later saw him transferring the whiskey from the patrol car to his Ford.

"Why did you tear up the gambling stuff?" I wanted to know.

"So they couldn't gamble on those tables anymore," he explained.

"Why didn't you smash up the whiskey, too, so they can't drink it?"

"Oh, they won't be able to drink the whiskey," he said, smiling. "Unless they come to my house."

A year or so later I was with him when he sought Jake Sheridan's guidance on what to do with a disabled pickup truck we'd come across blocking a thoroughfare. The truck was loaded down with contraband whiskey, and the driver had claimed close friendship with Jake.

"Give him a ticket for something and let him keep half his load," Jake said. "Pass out the rest in the Fifth Ward. We can use some help over there."

Jake's advice, a model rebuke to the hypocrisy of the state's gambling and whiskey laws, was a blueprint for political expediency. Laws that had been written to suit the moral predilections of a churchgoing public were enforced to suit the sizable majority that wanted them relaxed when they were honky-tonkying.

Men like Garner and Jake and my granddaddy, all of whom had grown up gambling and drinking whiskey in violation of the law, could never take very seriously the idea that people who gambled and sold whiskey illegally were enemies with whom they were at war. To the contrary, these "criminals" were members of their own families, their neighbors, and their friends on whose political support they counted in every election. Their common roots ran deep.

During the Depression my granddaddy had worked in a barbershop in the uptown Arcade with another skinny boy from the country named James Tubb Washer, who in 1917, at the age of fifteen, had come to Nashville from the hills of Dekalb County to seek his fortune.

By the time Ben West became the mayor of Nashville at midcentury, Jimmy Washer was already known as the Mayor of Printer's Alley, a famed row of plush nightspots uptown between Third and Fourth avenues. Washer's Uptown Club, at the corner of the alley and Church Street, was the city's most notorious illegal gambling house, which made Washer one of the town's premier criminals.

Yet I never saw Washer treated as anything other than a member of the tight circle of friends and family around the Robinsons. For years my grandfather, wearing civilian clothes, would take me with him to the uptown Arcade where we invariably met Washer, a man with a friendly hound-dog face and fancy clothes. He would be standing on the corner near his club wearing an expensive cashmere overcoat, a gray homburg, and horn-rimmed glasses. A five-carat solitaire glistened on his left hand and a diamond horseshoe stickpin sparkled at his throat. Since my granddaddy always had a big diamond ring and lots of new hats, I thought Washer was just another off-duty policeman.

They would put their heads together, conversing in laughs and grunts that I could never seem to hear. Then invariably we would walk through the Arcade, where someone dressed up like a Planters' Mr. Peanut handed out tiny samples, and a blind black man named Cortelia Clark sang the blues with a cup attached to the head of his steel-string guitar. Cortelia didn't wear the usual dark glasses, and you could see only the whites of his eyes.

This obviously disturbed my granddaddy, who asked him, "Why don't you get some sunglasses like Ray Charles?"

"So folks will see me blind and tell I ain't jiving 'em," Clark said.

Washer always stuffed cash in Cortelia's hand, not his cup. And sometimes, if it was late in the afternoon, we would lead the bluesman down through Printer's Alley, where a driver waited for him in a new red Pontiac. They would kid Cortelia about how good business was and how they were gonna get themselves a tin cup, too, and go into competition with him at the other end of the Arcade.

No matter how late I stayed out on Saturday night, even when on patrol with my granddaddy, my mother, Billye, dragged me to mass on Sunday mornings at Holy Name Church, an inner-city parish in East Nashville just across the river from the Davidson County courthouse. And there in the back of the church with a cross around his neck would be my granddaddy's buddy Jimmy Washer.

He was there with such regularity that my mother used him as bait in an effort to lure my granddaddy into the Catholic church. "If the biggest gambler in town goes to Holy Name every Sunday, so can a policeman."

It was the first time I ever knew what Washer did for a living.

Garner's daughters knew Washer even better than I did. They called him "Uncle Jimmy." And as high schoolers together, still too young to drink or gamble, our biggest thrill was to go to the Uptown Club. Jimmy's doorman Sam, who always seemed to know when we were coming, would park us at the end of the bar so we could pour down alcohol-free Shirley Temples and Virgin Marys and watch the dice-table action at the same time.

Nashville was beginning to make a name for itself as a recording center then, and it was not unusual to see New York and Hollywood entertainers like Gene Autry and Tex Ritter among the patrons.

Seeing the diminutive Autry at the Uptown in a white ten-gallon cowboy hat and glittering Nudie suit signing autographs for a group of visiting disc jockeys was as unforgettable to me at age nineteen as going on a police raid had been at age eight.

Gambling and whiskey were crimes all right, technically speaking, and Jimmy Washer may have been—as was widely rumored—a big-time criminal. But you couldn't prove it by the policemen's children.

Stickmen and High Rollers

Tennessean publisher Silliman Evans was anything but a self-righteous moralist concerned about corruption of his community by unscrupulous underworld gamblers. When he bought the newspaper, it was housed in the old Southern Turf building on Fourth Avenue, previously the city's most famous downtown gambling house. It had expensive frescoed walls and ermine toilet-seat covers and shook like an earthquake every time the presses ran. Gambling, he knew well, was as integral a part of the city's life as whiskey was of his own.

The newspaper's attorney, Jack Norman, was no antigambling crusader either. As lawyer for the leading distributor of one-arm bandits, he had obtained one of the illegal slot machines as a present for Evans' youngest son, Amon Carter. The favor had cemented his relationship with the publisher and resulted in the newspaper's becoming his client.

But both Evans and Norman understood the advantage of the moral high ground, and they seized it frequently in their long struggle to evict the election thief Jake Sheridan from the public square. Evans realized that to the Bible-thumping fundamentalists who dominated Nashville's pulpits, gambling walked hand in hand with whiskey and whores. This was a three-headed evil against which voter fury could be whipped up. Simply branding a man a gambler left him with a stigma that was hard to shake. They would hang illegal gambling around the necks of Sheridan, Robinson, and Garfinkle and flog them in the public square to the amens of churchgoing voters.

On the books at least, Tennessee was hard on sinners, with laws on whiskey, gambling, and sex tough enough to please the most righteous of the rural fundamentalists and moralists who dominated the state legislature. A dry state from 1909 to 1939, Tennessee passed laws in 1917 levying even stiffer penalties than those of the national

Prohibition. Yet the successful urban politicians of the time—machine bosses like Crump and Howse—were those who quietly promised to wink at any laws attempting to legislate morality, the same way the whole country was winking at Prohibition. Howse first won election on a pledge not to enforce Prohibition and was returned to office by the voters for nearly three decades. His success set in stone the resulting political commandment: Leave the bootleggers and gamblers alone. They will appreciate it. And unless there is a huge turnout of voters, the coalition of gamblers, bootleggers, honky-tonkers, and police will be enough to carry Election Day.

From the minute he won the sheriff's office in 1946, Garner Robinson, like his predecessors in law enforcement, stood on the gallows of this hypocrisy. And over the years he was given enough rope to hang himself.

A few days after taking office, his nickel-plated, engraved inauguration pistol in his pocket, Sheriff Garner Robinson knocked on a locked door at the Orange Inn on Dickerson Road. A peephole opened, revealing the big, kind eye of card player James F. "Slo" Barnes. "Well, well. It's the new sheriff, boys," said Slo, fumbling with the lock. "Come on in, Garner." Garner marched in, took one look at the cards and money on the table, and arrested Slo and his three friends.

"Slo, what in the hell were you thinking?" Barnes's partner wanted to know. "Why didn't you wait until they got the money off the table before you unlocked the door? That is the dumbest god-damn thing I ever heard of."

Barnes was called "Slo" because of the pace of his feet, not his brain. He had been completely surprised, not by the visit so much as by the arrest. And who could have blamed him? It may have been the first time in years that one of the city's big-time gamblers was visited by the police without advance warning. And it would not happen again for many more years to come. For, as Dave always said about Garner, "he knew when he had stepped on his pecker."

The raid had not been an act of law enforcement as much as one of political necessity. Earlier that day, four of Garner's new deputies, trying to serve a warrant on a man for carrying a pistol, had stumbled upon a nickel-dime poker game with nineteen dollars in the pot, clear evidence that some crime doesn't pay much. They confiscated the money, arrested eighteen black men, and hauled them before a sharp-nosed young judge who wanted to know why they had bothered with such a penny-ante crime. Of course, the judge already knew the answer: because the sheriff's office operated on the fee system, the salaries of the sheriff and all of his deputies were paid out of the court fines. The more arrests, the better the earnings.

Nobody liked the fee system but everybody had to live with it. Clear-thinking, well-intentioned judges feared it took the common sense out of law enforcement and encouraged fee-grabbing by the easy arrest of backyard card players and jaywalkers. John Draper was one of those judges. He not only refused to issue warrants against the men but made a big deal out of the arrests for the benefit of the newspapers. He wouldn't charge small-time gamblers, he declared in open court, as long as the big-timers were running wide open. "Start at the top. Not at the bottom. That's my attitude. If you really want to raid some gambling places, I'll give you the names of several uptown where dice games and slot machines are."

When Judge Draper challenged his commitment publicly, Garner responded by pulling the politician's weapon of choice for self-defense—lip service. He would raid anybody violating the law, he declared dutifully, and he asked for the judge's list of names, even though he (and every other law officer in the county) knew the gamblers and their haunts as well as he knew wrecker operators and beer license holders.

On the morning after Judge Draper's diatribe, the *Tennessean*'s Pulitzer Prize–winning cartoonist depicted a rotund Garner Robinson wearing a fedora and blindfold. The caption underneath read "See no evil," and on his chest was a sheriff's badge upon which the word DEPUTY had been crudely scrawled. The newspaper's message was clear: Garner was no more than a puppet of Jake Sheridan, and a blind puppet at that.

One thing was sure about Nashville's gamblers. They had never been hard to see. The city's first illegal "dinner club" was Doc Mannion's Pines, which opened in the twenties. Doc was a friend of the sheriff, Gus Kiger, who raided the Pines but generally let the well-to-do and well-connected go without charging them. The Pines' competition was Sam Borum's Camp, run by a former sheriff who insisted that his waiters and bartenders wear loaded .45s. Neither was as legendary as the notorious Ridgetop Club, a huge two-story colonial house that was situated squarely astraddle the line separating Davidson County from its northern neighbor, Robertson. Police using warrants from one county used to raid the place, only to have patrons run across the line to the other side of the room. It was such a headache that a bill was once introduced in the state legislature to straighten the county line, putting the house in one county or the other. The bill failed and the inn remained a legal oddity until somebody burned it down in 1955.

Whatever the charms of the stellar betting parlors of their time, none was as luxurious or lucrative as those that dominated the Middle Tennessee landscape at midcentury. Al Gus Alessio's Automobile Club north of the city was simply the biggest, fanciest illegal betting parlor in America.

Big and friendly Al opened his Automobile Club on a Cumberland River bluff in the depths of the Great Depression and ran it on the wrong side of the law for thirty-five years. From the late forties until the mid-sixties, the Kansas City steaks and pepper-pot soup made it the city's finest restaurant and the favorite haunt of some of Nashville's most respectable and powerful citizens. It was routine to see a man like Rube McKinney, fund-raiser for the state's most popular and often-elected governor, Gordon Browning, rolling the dice at three or four thousand dollars a crack.

A square man with an engaging smile, Alessio established both his good-citizen credentials and his friendship with the law in the Great Flood of 1937. The restaurant, which sat high above the flood plain, was turned into a community shelter, with Alessio himself picking up the stranded in a small boat and ferrying them to safety. Among those helping Al pull his Bordeaux neighbors from the muddy waters were Sheriff Bob Marshall, his motorcycle-riding deputy Dave White, and their buddy Garner Robinson.

From that day until he was shut down by the federal government in 1966 for violating interstate commerce laws, Al never fretted a minute about police raids. He would welcome the officers through the heavy mesh screen door like returning children and usher them through two swank dining rooms to the back room. There they would find two long, green Las Vegas–type gaming tables with casino odds painted in gay colors along the side, and a small group of guests and restaurant employees engaged in a spirited game of no-payoff bingo. The minute the police left, the games returned to craps and blackjack and bingo that paid.

When Alessio died people talked about his uncanny ability to know when there was a cop at the door. Actually there was a little more to it than that.

Old Mayor Howse's definition of good politics—and accordingly Jake Sheridan's—was the trading of favors in a way that would produce the most votes. Illegal whiskey and gambling were calculated as either assets or liabilities depending on the time and place. They were to be trafficked in constantly with the idea that come election time, the gamblers, bootleggers, and honky-tonkers rounded up by police would outnumber the Bible-thumpers who came out to vote voluntarily.

Understanding this personal exchange of favors, Al the gambler cultivated friends among the police just as Garner the undertaker had done. And his business benefited the same way. The more and better the friends, the more likely he was to get the warning call.

Alessio ran a class joint. Rather than seeing him as a nuisance or a threat to the quality of life, Nashville law officers believed the opposite. And Al himself provided the evidence with his good humor, his unstinting support of any church or charity that came to his door, and his own personal brand of philanthropy. At Christmas, he bought clothes and toys for kids, food for the hungry, and all winter long he bought coal and heating oil for anybody he knew who needed it. And he never forgot to reward those who made the telephone calls.

"Come by before Christmas," he would say to Sgt. Dave White,

"I'd like to see you. I have a little something for your mother." It was always a case of whiskey or an envelope full of cash.

Like the politicians he cultivated, Al was especially skilled at picking his friends. Other than on the *Tennessean*'s editorial page, the loudest outcries against gambling sounded from the city's pulpits. Smack in the middle of the Bible Belt and the country's leading center of religious publishing, Nashville had more churches per capita than any city in the country—637 congregations in fifty-six denominations in 1958. That was one for each 256 people, enough to earn the city the title of the Protestant Vatican. Always in hot pursuit of the purveyors of sin, the preachers agreed that the city could not possibly be big enough to be home to both gambling and the Southern Baptist Convention. As a result Alessio found it advantageous to become a one-man fund-raising drive for the churches. All a concerned pastor had to do was telephone a complaint that one of his hard-working parishioners had lost his rent or car payment at the Automobile Club. Al would return the amount lost forthwith to the pastor, along with a generous contribution to the ministry.

Alessio was such a stalwart member of St. Pius Catholic Church that its aging, arthritic pastor, Father Dan Richardson, testified from his wheelchair in Al's behalf when the federal government came down on him in the sixties. Those ten thousand poker chips Al had bought through the mail in violation of interstate commerce laws, the pastor testified, were indeed bought as Christmas presents for the men's club at St. Pius and for other Knights of Columbus chapters in the city to which Richardson was the spiritual advisor. It was simply a typical Alessio response to a request for assistance, Father Dan told the court. He had asked Al "for some of your old poker chips"; instead, the club operator had surprised him on Christmas with ten thousand new ones.

Alessio gambled illegally for thirty-five years and survived countless FBI bribery investigations. During all that time he served a total of only six months in federal prison for an interstate commerce violation and tax evasion.

If Al had been like the backdoor bootleggers and black numbers runners—nondescript men who stayed submerged in the under-world—he could have nestled quietly in Jake Sheridan's asset column, his existence of no concern to big-mouthed preachers, blue-blood re-formers, or Silliman Evans' minions. All the sheriff would have to do was leave him be and then reap the returns at election time.

But that was not Al's style, nor that of his contemporary and downtown counterpart, the legendary James Tubb "Jimmy" Washer, partner of Slo Barnes and friend of every cop who ever knew him. Undisputed king of the city's gamblers for three decades, Washer gambled illegally for over fifty years. He was arrested dozens of times. Yet he served only three weeks in jail—during the federal crackdown in the sixties.

On more than one occasion mobster Mickey Cohen was an Up-town Club guest, and his friendship with Washer eventually brought them both unwanted publicity. In 1960, a California grand jury sub-poenaed Washer to explain how a revolver registered to a Nashville policeman had gotten into Cohen's possession. It was one of three weapons found at the scene of a gangland slaying of a West Coast bookie. The policeman, Morgan Smith, a friend of Washer's, was also called before the grand jury. He said he had sold the gun to an-other policeman who had passed it to Washer, from whom it was allegedly stolen in a burglary.

Associations with people like Cohen notwithstanding, Washer shared Alessio's reputation as a gentleman. He, too, excelled at anonymous philanthropy and was a soft touch for anyone in need or trouble, two conditions with which he was intimate. He paid the hospital bills of strangers, sent abandoned children to school, and kept an open account at a Nashville heating oil supplier so lawyer Norman could order warmth for the needy.

Like Alessio, Washer also cultivated the church as a defender. A priest from Holy Name who worked among ghetto blacks once wrote a letter to a U.S. attorney on Washer's behalf.

"I have known Mr. Washer for the past five years . . . ," wrote the Rev. Charles Brown. "I have found him to be kind and charitable. Although he is not a member of the Roman Catholic Church, he has assisted us financially in order that our work may progress among members of the Negro race. I have come in personal contact with individuals whom he has assisted.

"He does not seek publicity in so doing. No questions are asked. No red tape is involved. From a heart filled with a sincerity comes forth assistance, regardless of race, color, or creed. . . ."

Because the sheriff's office never made a big case against either Al Alessio or Jimmy Washer during Garner's three terms in office, rumors of organized payoffs to public officials were routine. The *Tennessean* hinted as much in its editorials, and at election time ran front-page stories about how Garner and Jake winked at illegal gambling.

This was neither unfair nor unusual, but simply part of the hypocrisy, which had become institutionalized. Politics was like a children's game of cat and mouse, played instead by reporters, publishers, and politicians. Everyone knew that Al Alessio and Jimmy Washer had been gambling every day as sure as the sun rose, but outrage over it surfaced only in response to the need for an election issue. It was a ritual signifying the approach of another vote, another round of battle.

Governors, mayors, and sheriffs had played the game by staging the precursor of the modern-day photo-op. Back then, the official standing for reelection—on whose watch the gambling had occurred—would lead a band of axe-wielding lawmen into the gamblers' den and destroy everything in sight. J. J. Jackson and Dave White had swung axes regularly on behalf of Boss Crump's puppet governors, Jim Nance McCord and Prentice Cooper. It served both as stimulation for the church vote and as selective punishment for law violators who were dragging their feet on contributions or had ties to the opposition. In what may have been a miscalculation stemming from overconfidence, Jake and Garner refused to play the game. Garner thought that axe-wielding was a waste of energy and perfectly good equipment that would only be replaced. "The furniture hasn't violated any law," he'd say. Anyway, how could he explain to his children why their father had his picture in the paper busting up things that belonged to Uncle Jimmy, as Washer was known inside the Robinson family.

Jake also knew Washer and the other gamblers well, far better than he knew Walter Stokes or the newspaper publishers or any of the Belle Meade reformers. They'd all come up together on the streets, like onions and potatoes floating to the top in the same East Nashville stew. Politician, gambler, cop, or ex-con were the same stock, separated like vegetables by a thin broth called luck. Jake had been fortunate enough to marry the daughter of a city detective and had been talked into politics by his father-in-law. He'd come to appreciate the value of property by finally owning some and saw the transformation of bars and pool tables into kindling as a counterproductive political exercise. Watching the destruction of property by policemen might create hard feelings that could not be overcome at election time. For certain it reduced the resources of the people from whom he collected tribute.

When sudden awareness of illegal gambling sent pangs rippling through the conscience of the community and the political heat began to rise, Garner and Jake did not terrorize the elite crowds with door-busting raids during the dinner hour. Instead they picked up the telephone and called their friends. "It's time for you-all to take a vacation," they'd tell Washer, Alessio, and associates. "Go on down to Florida and do some fishin' until I get back to you." During these intervals Washer's partner, Slo Barnes, would sometimes move his private game for professionals and trusted regulars into a local hotel, where they wrote the odds on bedsheets with laundry markers and played unmolested until breakfast.

If a more structured corruption of the sheriff's office by the gamblers existed, the details passed with the players, a folded hand never revealed by any grand jury investigation or any of the many court trials of Washer and Alessio. But these men—Sheridan, Robinson, Alessio, Washer, and Washer's partner Slo Barnes—all knew one another for half a century. And their relationships were flush with arrangements of one kind or another. Some were quite unusual. At least one was extraordinary.

As a by-product of Garner's years as coroner and his roots in law enforcement, his undertaking parlor ended up with many of the city's homicide and accident victims and a lion's share of the John

Does, the unidentified dead destined for a pauper's funeral at public expense. This was not normally profitable business for the morticians involved.

But both Alessio and Washer, it seems, had a common and rather peculiar manner of expressing their charitable feelings toward the less fortunate: They paid Phillips-Robinson to bury strangers. Washer subsidized funerals regularly, among them several John Does, a waitress at the Maxwell House dining room who had drowned, and a woman who had lost both hands and her sight when a vindictive lover sent her a letter bomb. When Alessio himself died in 1983, Garner recalled how it worked.

"Al would call up and say, 'Garner, what'll it cost to bury that old man?' and I'd say, 'Whatever you want it to, Al.' Al'd say, 'Well, I want him to have a decent funeral.'

"And we'd bury them and send him the bill and he'd send us a check. For people he didn't even know."

While the practice could have qualified as an ingenious bribery technique, it continued long after Robinson left law enforcement, suggesting that the burials were never anything other than expressions of goodwill. Over the years many underworld figures have concocted a public image of philanthropic activity and good citizenship to cover their criminal behavior. But Washer and Alessio generally acted anonymously, giving cash or paying bills through intermediaries. Washer habitually kept cash reserves for this purpose with his lawyers, who said they doled out thousands over the years to people who never knew the source of their good fortune.

Shortly before his death in 1981, Washer delivered a shoebox containing seventy-five thousand dollars to the wife of Jack Norman, the lawyer who had given away a lot of Washer's money over the years and who had successfully defended him in his one serious legal battle with the federal government in the sixties. Washer said the money was simply a thank-you to Carrie Norman for the personal kindnesses she had shown him over the years. Some of the cash eventually had to be used to pay Washer's debts, but the rest was given away.

Good guys or bad, whatever the basis for the arrangements

between Garner and the law violators, the end result was that gamblers and bootleggers operated free of harassment except when some politician or freelancing police officer sought publicity or a share of the protection money.

"Thanked" or not, the Robinson-Sheridan sheriff's office tolerated whiskey and gambling violations of the law in the belief that the political realities of the time demanded it. That decision carried with it a stark political reality of its own—that Jake and Garner would be branded corrupt politicians and would eventually have to fight for their political lives on the high moral ground staked out by their toughest opponents, Silliman Evans and his morning newspaper.

Back in 1944, when the war forced Garner Robinson to abandon his first countywide political office, he had left the job of coroner in the hands of the master of the Hopewell box—Lewis Hurt, who graciously relinquished it when Garner returned from the war. Eight years later, when Garner had reached the end of the three-term limit on being sheriff, Hurt was standing there again with his hand out. After all, the machine simply wanted a stand-in for a single term, until Garner could run again and take the job back for another six years. To Lewis Hurt the machine appeared strong enough to elect anybody it wanted.

But Jake knew better. The machine's opposition to the new county administration of Judge Beverly Briley had made Jake a marked man at the *Tennessean*. He and Elkin were still exercising mastery over the city council. And this, combined with his control of the county court, made Jake the single most powerful politician in the county. With Robinson no longer eligible to succeed himself, Jake figured that Judge Briley and Silliman Evans would go all out to strip the sheriff's office from the grasp of the machine. He was right.

As their candidate, Briley and the *Tennessean* settled on Tom Y. Cartwright, the popular farm equipment dealer who had run a good race against Garner in 1950 and whose father had once been sheriff. Last time out the younger Cartwright had been defeated by only thirty-five hundred votes out of thirty-three thousand cast. This time he would have the backing of Judge Briley's county faction—and, more important, the firepower of Silliman Evans' newspaper.

Jake was too smart to run Lewis Hurt, who had added a reputation as a heavy drinker to his notoriety as an election officer. To find a man with a squeaky-clean record acceptable to all factions of the machine, they turned at the last minute to the number-three man in the sheriff's department, a young captain named Oscar Capps, who was only twenty-six years old and had been to the FBI training academy. He was an unknown, but so what? The *Tennessean* wouldn't find a thing about him to criticize. Besides, the machine was flying high.

Picking Capps was a mistake. Hurt had a public temper tantrum and accused his longtime friend Garner of reneging on a promise of support he'd made six years earlier. The *Tennessean* loved it and ran a story calling Hurt a revenge candidate out to defeat his old bosses. And that he did—but not as a candidate.

Hurt pulled out of the race. He buried the hatchet with Jake and Garner and continued in his job as a deputy sheriff. But in the end he became the glue that would stick the *Tennessean*'s charges of gambling corruption on the sheriff's office and bring the Sheridan-Robinson-Garfinkle machine its first election defeat.

Since endorsing Robinson's second reelection in 1950, the *Tennessean* had made an abrupt turnaround. In the two subsequent years the newspaper had pummeled him at every opportunity. Evans' editor, Coleman Harwell, a tough and gifted journalist who believed newspapers existed to serve as a critic of government, saw clearly that Jake Sheridan stole elections the way Boss Crump had always done. Discrediting Jake became a front-page obsession, and Jake's political affiliations with known law violators offered plenty of cannon fodder. The most obvious were the gamblers.

Since the thirties illegal slot machines had been routine furniture at honky-tonks and roadhouses. They were usually kept out of sight in back rooms, or behind false walls. Before 1951, when a federal law was passed regulating their interstate shipment, hundreds of machines were in use in Davidson County. In 1950, two sheriff's patrolmen had run across two slot machines at the Negro American Legion Post Six and smashed them to bits. The next day the sheriff had called the commander of the post and told him it would be all right to put the machines back in as long as "you let me know what's going on out there."

Little was said or done about the slot machines until, as the 1951 and 1952 elections approached, the *Tennessean* began to portray them as evidence of a vile and corrupt sheriff's office. And their exposés got a response.

The federal government conducted a series of statewide raids and confiscated 327 machines. Judge Chester Hart and District Attorney Carlton Loser ordered Garner to investigate the fifty Davidson County residents who had purchased federal gaming stamps, most of which were for slot machines. The *Tennessean* obtained the list of stamp holders, and prior to the 1951 elections sent reporters and photographers to the home of the undisputed king of the Nashville numbers racket, Bill James. There they found pictures of the machine-endorsed candidates displayed on his front porch and from his windows. They looked up the notorious black bootlegger Henry "Good Jelly" Jones, who had a record of sixty-one arrests by city police, and found bumper stickers promoting Jake's candidates on his car.

Under pressure, Jake and the sheriff abandoned their previous policies. Garner ordered his first raid on Al Alessio's Automobile Club, and a contingent of sheriff's deputies led by young Capt. Oscar Capps showed up in time to halt a roaring bingo game. The next day the *Tennessean* reported the raid had been conducted without even a search warrant and demanded to know why. Replied the sheriff, "They didn't need one."

Candidate Cartwright was primed to seize the issue. Capps' FBI training, he declared, must not have included any classes on search warrants. Cartwright wanted to know why none of the fifty-eight members of the highway patrol had bothered to raid Alessio earlier. And why was Alessio so well prepared? "Could it be, Captain Capps, that someone called to let him know you were coming?"

Using the list of federal-gaming-stamp holders, the *Tennessean* found another numbers racketeer, a man named Chuckie Flandell, driving a car with Capps' bumper stickers on the back. One of the paper's top reporters, Nat Caldwell, surprised Capps with the revelation on a radio talk show, and asked why he accepted support from "men like Flandell."

"I'll accept the support of any citizen," Capps replied.

"Even if that citizen happens to be licensed as a gambler by the federal government?"

"I don't know Mr. Flandell," said Capps, retreating, "but if he's what you say he is I don't need his support and I don't want it."

Up against a clearly superior candidate, Jake and the machine again turned to their most reliable and successful election strategy— manipulating the process. First, in an effort to avoid a long election campaign, which would give the *Tennessean* time to whip up public interest, they had stalled the setting of the primary date until the last minute. Finally, it was set for May 28, with the qualifying deadline for candidates thirty days earlier. Elkin's primary board then authorized a special voter registration drive targeting the county suburbs only.

The sheriff's department was put to work hauling in prospective voters, mostly black, to be registered. This time, to avoid newspaper stories about the political use of the sheriff's office, an effort was made to disguise the cars with phony license plates. One set of plates had been obtained from A. H. Richardson, a member of the county court, a machine loyalist, and head of the state agency that sold license plates. But the *Tennessean* discovered Richardson's involvement and he was forced to confiscate the plates. The same week another car with a single unusual license plate and a Capps bumper sticker was spotted by the *Tennessean* hauling in black residents to the courthouse to be registered. The driver was Good Jelly Jones, the ex-convict. And when the *Tennessean* checked out the plate number, they found that it was registered to Chuckie Flandell.

All of this was front-page news, but ironically the newspaper missed the best story of all. Garner had stopped going home and had been sleeping around, including in the sheriff's office. After a few days Skinny had had enough of it. She conducted a violent midnight raid on the sheriff's office, which included terrorizing the court officer, Booty Draper. The next day Garner told Dave it was a good thing Booty had forgotten to wear his gun to work. "Skinny would have shot me with it."

Skinny's assault on the sheriff's office did not make news. But Garner's old friend Lewis Hurt did. Five days before the vote, the *Tennessean* ran an eight-column headline in huge black type: "SHER- IFF OFFICE, SLOTS LINKED." Under it was an exclusive report of how one of the men closest to Sheriff Robinson had provided an East Nashville tavern owner with two slot machines and split the take with him fifty-fifty. The portrait of a serious and sober Lewis Hurt, which he had hoped to use as his campaign picture, was in the middle of the page.

The details were all there, along with the complete text of a signed affidavit from the tavern owner, S. P. Vaden, who said that two years earlier Hurt had come to his tavern and told him the sheriff's office wanted to put in the machines. Hurt had soon returned with a carpenter and built a false wall to hide them from view and then came back regularly to service the machines and collect his half of the take, which amounted to about fifty dollars per week.

The deal had lasted four or five months, Vaden told the *Tennessean,* until two other sheriff's patrolmen had come by and asked how business was. When told it was pretty good, Vaden said the officers told him they figured it was good enough that he could afford to ante up one hundred dollars a month so they "could have a little party every once and a while." Vaden said he refused and ordered them to take the slot machines out of his tavern.

So as to leave no doubt about who was responsible, the *Tennessean* reported that the retiring sheriff denied that he planned to stay around as chief deputy if Capps got elected. Garner, whose picture was also on the front page, was quoted as saying Vaden's allegations were "a damn lie" and that he had no knowledge of what Lewis Hurt had been up to. The message was clear: either the sheriff was an accomplice or a lousy administrator who tolerated graft among his closest aides.

Meanwhile, Lewis Hurt was reported ill and confined to a local

hospital, where he was unavailable for comment. Hurt would recover quickly, but Capps' campaign never did.

The columnist Joe Hatcher finally got his wish. Davidson Coun-
tians turned out in record numbers—52,768 voters—in the 1952
primary. And he was right about what that would mean for the
machine. Tom Y. Cartwright buried Oscar Capps by a two-to-one
margin.

After six years of living his dream, Garner Robinson would now
be forced to give up being sheriff and return to his funeral home
business full-time. For days after the election, the *Tennessean* boasted
of "the utter defeat of the Sheridan political axis." But by now burying Jake prematurely had become a bad habit.

The Gorgeous Little Stooge

Failure to elect Oscar Capps in the spring primary of 1952 meant
machine control of the sheriff's office would end with the August
general election, in which the nominees for local office were running unopposed or faced only token Republican opposition. But
Garner would remain sheriff until the August vote, which coincided
with the most important election of all, the statewide Democratic
primary for governor. Never a man to waste a drop of power, Jake
Sheridan knew this situation held the makings of a deal. So one hot
day in July he and Garner drove two hundred miles to Memphis and
made one—with the old political devil himself, Boss Crump.

Crump was nearly eighty then and on the ropes as an election
power as a result of the double-barreled defeat of candidates for governor and senator by his one-time protégé Gordon Browning and
Estes Kefauver. Now Browning was up for reelection again, seeking
a fourth two-year term, his third consecutively, and Crump, never a
man who knew when to quit, was out to get even. The huge Memphis

vote was still under his thumb and with a little help he could regain control of the governor's mansion. The state's population spread and voting patterns were such that one good deal could do it. A candidate for statewide office could carry ninety-three of the ninety-five counties and still lose—if Memphis and Nashville went heavy enough for his opponent. And that's exactly what Jake and Garner had in mind for Crump—a deal with Nashville, which had voted over fifty thousand in its spring county primary.

Jake and Garner had been Browning supporters, but by now past alliances meant little to Jake. It was the future he fretted over. Garner was still perhaps the most popular politician in Davidson County. More important, he would have control of the county highway patrol and court officers through the primary. And Jake, as the new public works director for the Ben West administration, had control of a huge chunk of city patronage. Jobs fixing potholes made valuable election currency. It was too big a card not to play. Even though he and Garner couldn't carry the day for young Oscar Capps, they now promised to deliver Nashville voters to the man the *Tennessean* had called Crump's "gorgeous little stooge"—Frank Goad Clement.

A handsome, sleepy-eyed lawyer and ex–FBI agent from Dickson, a little town southwest of Nashville, Clement was only thirty-two years old, but he had been groomed by the Crump crowd almost from boyhood. He had an actor's face, a big booming voice, and the brashness of a daylight burglar.

People in Dickson remember a sixteen-year-old Clement stopping at their homes just to introduce himself, shake hands, and inquire about their health. By eighteen, he had learned to compliment mothers on the beauty of their babies, and by twenty-two he had gotten a law degree from Vanderbilt. Then he persuaded the FBI to slice a year off their rule that agents had to be at least twenty-three years old. He left the FBI in 1942 for a stint in the army as a lieutenant in charge of a military police unit; in the mid-forties he returned home to be appointed general counsel of the state utilities commission. Clement had been trained politically by a notorious machine operative named Willie Gerber, Crump's messenger to the legislature, and had been brought to the attention of *Banner* publisher Jimmy Stahlman as a man capable of being governor, or even president of the United States. Clement was one-third cop, one-third evangelist, one-third con man, and 100 percent slick.

Like Nashville mayor Ben West, Frank Clement was a new breed of southern politician, a philosophical moderate, progressive on integration and in tune with the urban and industrial character of the emerging modern South. But in April of that year, Crump had thrown an extravagant open-house party for Clement in Memphis and there they had had their picture taken together. In it Clement posed with his toothpaste smile fixed on the camera, while reaching backward—almost surreptitiously—for a handshake with Crump, a grinning old tomcat under a fedora.

This photo graced a two-column front-page editorial of condemnation in the *Tennessean* entitled "All Out for Frankie," in which the newspaper branded Clement as no more than a puppet of Boss Crump and Jake Sheridan. Browning's defeat of the Crump machine four years earlier had made the governor virtually a folk hero at the *Tennessean*. To Silliman Evans, a Clement victory would be like turning back the clock. With Crump and Sheridan among his backers, Clement would be trapped in an affiliation with the reactionary *Banner* and forever condemned as a machine politician by the progressive *Tennessean* with which he had so much in common. By making a deal with Crump, Jake had handed publisher Evans a stick with which to beat him—and Clement.

Clement campaigned largely against excessive taxation under Browning and corruption in his administration. And when the Browning crowd fielded boys wearing campaign posters made from the picture of his handshake with Crump, Clement said, "There's one thing I can promise you: you'll never see a picture of me handing over a million dollars to a couple of my friends, for a deal like the sale of the Memorial Hotel." He was referring to the state's acquisition of a Nashville hotel from Browning supporters at twice the price at which it had been offered to a previous administration. It was part of his "ten-count indictment" of Browning's governorship, whose charges ranged from broken promises to outright thievery of state funds.

But to the *Tennessean*, whose readers would most likely decide the election's outcome, the major campaign issue was Crump's meeting with Jake and Garner. In exchange for their support of Clement, the newspaper charged, the two had been promised important jobs in the new administration. Jake would again be a rabbit guarding the carrots—"a state democratic party official involving the handling of party funds"—and Garner would head the highway patrol assisted by his failed captain, Oscar Capps.

Clement denied that Crump ever promised Jake or Garner state jobs. But it was not jobs that the two Nashville kingmakers were in search of that day: it was a new political home. Clement's candidacy had attracted a powerful new coalition in Nashville, including important members of the financial community. Jimmy Stahlman's fondness for the young lawyer had brought the Belle Meade Country Club crowd into the local Democratic party at unprecedented levels. One of the city's leading banks, Third National, whose president, Sam Fleming, was among Belle Meade's leading citizens, had allowed a senior vice-president to become Clement's Nashville fund-raiser. One of the state's leading trucking companies had contributed over four hundred thousand dollars to Clement's campaign. Though Clement was not one of their own, the elite shared a common view of his future: the Tennessee governor's mansion would be only a stopover on his way to the White House. This was a crack in the door to a rich and Republican world so tightly sealed that even Silliman Evans himself couldn't have penetrated it, had he wanted to. When the *Tennessean* publisher had hinted at joining the Belle Meade Club, he had been told he would be wasting his time. That was Stahlman's preserve.

Still, Clement faced tough going in Nashville. Browning was still popular, and the *Tennessean* would do everything possible to reelect him. But Jake and Garner knew they could still produce on Election Day and that once again they might control enough votes to make the difference. No matter how slight the margin, Jake figured, Boss Crump and his new governor would be grateful.

Out on the hustings, Clement's oratory was an awesome arsenal of political weaponry, which no less of an authority on eloquence than Big Jim Folsom himself had described as "guttin', cuttin', and struttin'." Clement could preach, pray, quote the Bible, and sing gospel songs. He could speak so softly, tenderly, tantalizingly that he could spellbind an audience. Or he could rain hellfire and damnation down on political enemies and bury them under rhetorical avalanches the likes of which hadn't been seen in Tennessee since William Jennings Bryan, the Boy Orator of the Platte. Beside him on every podium was his pretty wife, Cille, a childhood sweetheart, and two small boys, Bobby, nine, and Frank Jr., three, wearing T-shirts that implored "Vote for My Daddy." Like Garner, Clement was a glad-hander and a club-joiner who courted the American Legion and the Shriners. And he would prove to be the best campaigner for whom the machine ever bought or stole a vote.

Persuasion was what Frank Clement was all about. That he was bought and paid for with the wallets of bankers and truckers, and had been packaged, addressed, and delivered by Crump, Sheridan, and the Nashville *Banner* was of little consequence in light of the illusion he could craft—that he had been anointed right there on the stump by the Good Lord himself.

Clement turned out to be way too much for Browning. He won six of the state's nine congressional districts and was elected by fifty-seven thousand votes. None of those votes were more satisfying, however, than the thirty-five hundred by which he won Nashville and Davidson County. Clement had whipped the incumbent governor and the *Tennessean* in their own backyard. Although no one could have known it at the time, the deal cut by Garner and Jake with Boss Crump had assured that in Nashville the patronage and power of state government would continue to belong to the Sheridan-Robinson-Garfinkle machine for the next eighteen years.

Having elected the mayor of Nashville one year and carried the county for the new governor of Tennessee the next, Jake was riding highest just before his fall.

The *Tennessean* had been hard at work for months investigating his personal finances, which it found fascinating. While holding a series of low- and middle-level government jobs—the best of which paid nine thousand dollars a year—the backstage manager of the West administration had amassed a real estate fortune in the city alone worth approximately five hundred thousand dollars. The *Tennessean* laid it out in a series of front-page stories. The bulk of Jake's holdings were in two apartment complexes built while he was Garner's chief deputy with two hundred thousand dollars in loans from the Federal Housing Administration.

While no laws had been violated, the newspaper suggested that Jake had gotten favorable loan treatment from a mortgage company official who had been appointed to several government boards and who was considered part of the machine.

The newspaper suggested that another machine politician, who headed up the county board of tax equalization, had given Jake preferential treatment by cutting his tax assessments in half and that a third officeholder, the city tax assessor, had deliberately failed to reassess Jake's property in his 1951 tax assessment canvass.

All this was true. Jake did favors for his friends and benefited from their favors in return. And the *Tennessean* didn't know the half of it. There was the real estate partnership in High Locust Inn, a Dickerson Road motel. Jake, Garner, and another member of the county court, A. H. Richardson, had bought the motel anticipating that the road would be widened and they would make money on the condemnation of the property's road frontage. Jake had also bought an interest in a second Dickerson Road motel in which two of the city's most notorious gamblers, Jimmy Washer and Raymond Berryman, were his partners. For Jake, politics had turned out to be a very good business. When he died thirty years later, his net worth was over a million dollars—all of it from real estate investments made while a public official.

Mayor West quickly came to the same conclusion that Mayor Cummings had: Jake drew strikes from the *Tennessean* like a lightning rod, and the strikes would continue as long as he held a public job. Silliman Evans had been right in his preelection editorials:

Giving Jake the public works department had been too big a price to pay. It was a direct patronage-rich link to the public, where Jake could trade government favors for political power. As boss of public works, he had advance knowledge of road building and both public and private construction—the best opportunity in government for a real estate developer like Jake to make money. As publisher Evans had reminded the mayor privately and in print, West had given away his administration.

Jake, meanwhile, had failed to build the kind of personal friendship with West that was the foundation of his political alliances with Garner and Elkin.

Whatever Jake Sheridan did, he assumed control of it one way or another, even when control officially belonged elsewhere. Garner and Elkin tolerated this. They could suppress their egos in the interest of success. But West could not. Jake still controlled about a third of the council's twenty-one votes, which along with a similar number of West loyalists would have constituted a clear working majority for the administration. But West could never fully count on Jake's support. And when a seat on the council opened up, Jake looked to fill it with someone whose first loyalty was to him. As an irritant to a political sore, he had no equal.

Unlike Cummings, West was an impatient and combative man. His first two years in office were rife with internecine warfare. He argued with all his top aides, including his brother, Wilson, whom he banished for a short time. Aware that Sheridan and the fire and police commissioner, John B. Milliron, were in a position to undercut him, West regularly usurped their powers. He gave direct orders to their subordinates and assumed the major decisions involving their departments.

This did not set well with Jake, who believed that usurpation of power was a one-way street. As was his habit, he had cultivated friendships and built alliances underneath the mayor that challenged his leadership. Among those whose loyalty Jake had pilfered was Z. T. "Tommy" Osborn, the young, politically ambitious Old Hickory lawyer whom Elkin had convinced West to make city attorney.

Early in the administration, Jake had enlisted Osborn to intercede with the mayor to stop bypassing him in favor of a subordinate in the public works department. Jake asked Osborn to bring back a written vote of West's confidence. Brilliant and persuasive, Osborn returned with a letter from West assuring Jake that he was "still in charge of public works," and things cooled off for a while. But soon the mayor went back to his old ways and Osborn was caught in the cross-fire again when he tried to mediate a dispute over the filling of a vacancy caused by the death of a city councilman in the Third Ward. The mayor had put his brother, Wilson, in charge of selecting an administration candidate, taking away what Jake had seen as his window of opportunity.

Frustrated in his efforts to get West and Jake together behind a compromise candidate, Osborn, who was then only thirty-three years old, threatened to resign. "I think you ought to," said the quick-tempered West. And he did.

Osborn's resignation incited the *Tennessean*, which blamed Jake. The paper began to beat the drum again for West to fire him. Somebody sent Jake some flowers on the occasion of his political death. But Jake held on. Mayor West was stubborn, too. He didn't like Jake running his business, but he didn't want Silliman Evans running it either.

In 1954, the *Tennessean*, with the help of County Judge Briley, put together a new political coalition for the sole purpose of stripping Sheridan-Robinson-Garfinkle of control of the county court. A unified slate dedicated to that purpose was put forward.

The *Tennessean*'s pounding was relentless, depicting the "Sheridan-West" machine as a corrupt roadblock to city progress. Crumplike control of the county court by two unelected city political bosses became the only campaign issue. Thirty-three new magistrates were elected, all of them publicly independent of Jake Sheridan and Elkin Garfinkle. Stripped now of his influence in the court as well as the sheriff's office, Jake had finally lost his political stinger.

Members of his old city council and county court coalitions began to shun him. Jake knew it was over when his longtime protégé Booty Draper came by to see him. Booty announced matter-of-factly that he no longer planned to attend Jake's strategy sessions. Draper's wife had tired of seeing her husband criticized in the *Tennessean* as a Sheridan lacky. She'd been on him about it.

"If it's all the same to you, Jake," Draper said politely, "I'd just as soon handle my own affairs at the council from now on. If you want something, well, you know I'd be glad to help you if I can. But I'd like to be in charge of my own business."

"Sure, Booty," Jake said. "I understand. That's fine."

No longer afraid of Jake's power, Ben West did as Tom Cummings had done and relented to Silliman Evans. He took the only course that would get both Jake and the newspaper off his back: he fired Sheridan as commissioner of public works. The best job Jake ever had in government would be his last.

Now, for the first time in over a quarter of a century, neither Jake nor Garner held an elective office. Only Garfinkle, still a county court magistrate from his city district, remained a public official. More important, for the first time Jake had no jobs to hand out in city government, no county law enforcement or court influence to trade on, no basis on which to levy tribute.

At its October meeting, the Davidson County Quarterly Court conducted its business without a script from the machine bosses. And for the first time since his election in 1950, the court allowed the county executive, Judge Briley, to appoint his own operating committees.

Except for seeking zoning changes on his own property, Jake Sheridan was never publicly seen taking part in politics again. He moved out of the city to the far north end of the county, near where the federal government was clearing and flooding a remote forest area with yet another TVA lake. There he built himself a profitable bait and fishing tackle store fitted with plumbing fixtures pointedly bought from one of Booty Draper's competitors in the hardware business. The big behind-the-scenes boss of Nashville politics, the wheeler-dealer of the Colemere Club, had become the victim of his own excesses. The personal relationships that had been his lifeblood had finally failed him. Silliman Evans had put him off in Treeville.

PART FIVE

Exile

The ups and downs of Sheriff Garner's political fortunes made bumps in all our lives. When Garner had to give up being sheriff in the early fifties, my granddaddy Dave once more gave up being a cop. Now instead of spending weekends with him on patrol, I spent them working as an errand boy at the motel and restaurant he managed a few blocks down the Murfreesboro Road from the Colemere Club.

It quickly became a hangout for cops and criminals— and the press. The first newspaperman I ever saw in the flesh was there one hot summer Saturday night. He was

stark naked except for cowboy boots and hat, a western
gun belt around his waist. He had a toy pistol pointed at
my granddaddy, who was about to die laughing.

"Stick 'em up," said the man cheerfully, to loud squeals
of female laughter from a lump under the covers of the bed
in his motel room. Even at age nine, I knew the gun was a
child's toy cap pistol and the squeal was probably the noise
the people in the adjoining room had been complaining
about. I had gone along lugging a jug of ice water, which
my granddaddy said might be needed to "douse the
ruckus."

"Looks like to me you've done enough stickups for one
day," said my granddaddy.

"Yes sir," said the naked cowboy. "I'm all stuck up." The
lump squirmed and let out another squeal.

"Hold it down in here, Red, willya?" said my
granddaddy. "Your neighbors are trying to sleep."

"Okay, Dave," the man said. He twirled the toy pistol
like a movie cowboy before replacing it in his holster so he
could take the ice water.

As I handed the pitcher through the door, the lump
jumped again and a foot with bright red toenails peeked
from beneath the covers.

"Did you know that man?" I asked my granddaddy as we
walked away.

He didn't answer, but when we got back to the motel
office, he handed me a folded newspaper. On the front
page was a picture of the man atop his daily gossip column
in the *Tennessean*. "It's one of old Sillyman's boys," my
granddaddy said. "I wish it had been old bald eagle
Hatcher or Sillyman himself."

From that day on my granddaddy and Garner referred to the columnist as "Old Stick 'Em Up." One night years later, after the writer had switched to the afternoon *Banner*, my granddaddy, once again back in the uniform of the county patrol, encountered him driving erratically. He tapped the siren on his patrol car and pulled him over. When the columnist rolled down his window, Dave pulled his police revolver from his holster. "Stick 'em up," he said. Both broke into laughter and the man's female companion, the less intoxicated of the two, was allowed to drive him home.

The columnist was still on the *Banner* front page and a celebrity in town when I became an adult. We worked in the same building and lived only a few blocks from each other. No matter how often I saw him, he was always naked except for his cowboy accoutrements. I had to bite my tongue to keep from saying "Stick 'em up."

Cootchie the Constable and Congress

Mayor West was reelected in 1955 running against a political machine that once again the *Tennessean* had only wished out of existence. When reporter John Seigenthaler wrote of opposition to West by the Sheridan-Robinson-Garfinkle crowd, Silliman Evans stormed out of his office brandishing a clipping of one of the newspaper's earlier proclamations that the machine had been crushed. Boss Crump had died in late 1954, two weeks after turning eighty. Jake Sheridan was in exile, and the old publisher's philosophy was clear: Once the *Tennessean* ran your obituary, you were dead, period.

Evans himself died later that year, only a few months after his
enemy Crump, and was succeeded by his oldest son, Silliman Jr., a
more accommodating man. But the old man's political prejudices
had a way of outliving him. A year later, it was no surprise that the
Tennessean neglected to acknowledge the pivotal role the machine
played in the epic political battle over who would replace Representative J. Percy Priest when he died in office in 1956.

The man with the most legitimate claim to succeed Priest was
J. Carlton Loser, who had first run for Congress twenty years before
as a reformer fighting Boss Crump's machine politics. He'd lost that
race but had served a record twenty-two years as county prosecutor,
banking significant political capital in the process. The *Tennessean*
had always opposed Loser, which of course assured him of support
by the *Banner*.

Only a month past his rafter-raising keynote speech at the Democratic National Convention, Governor Frank Clement figured he
was square on track to the White House, so he also had a keen interest in the future makeup of the state's delegation. He joined the
Banner in support of Loser.

Mayor West, meanwhile, was still mired in a three-way factional
struggle for local political supremacy. He didn't care if Loser became congressman but wanted City Attorney Raymond Leathers
appointed to Loser's prosecutor's spot. West also wanted control of
the local election machinery in 1958, when all the county offices
would be up for grabs. When neither Loser nor the governor went
for the deal, West put Leathers forward for the Priest vacancy, setting up another perfect situation for the East Nashville kingmakers.

The decision on who would fill Priest's spot until the next election belonged to a newly elected county Democratic party executive
committee, most of whose members owed their own elections not to
the mayor, the governor, or the newspapers, but to Garner Robinson, Elkin Garfinkle, or Jake Sheridan. This put the supposedly
crushed machine back where it had always been—with the deciding
votes in a crucial election. It also put a lot of people on the spot.

On the night before the committee vote, state Democratic party officials made a final attempt to dissuade the mayor from battling publicly with the *Banner* and the governor. At a meeting at the home of Buford Ellington, Governor Clement's campaign manager and political henchman, West refused to modify his demands. He boasted of fifty-five votes for Leathers and left a list of those pledged as proof. The minute he'd gone, the Loser people went to work to see how many minds on the mayor's list they could change. Among those targeted was a typewriter salesman who had just gotten a fifty-thousand-dollar service contract from the Clement administration. He got a call in the middle of the night saying if he voted for West, the typewriter deal was off.

Another was Mary Baker, an elevator operator who like many other committee members had been elected for no other reason than because she had friends and relatives among the machine politicians and could be controlled. Her son was a city fireman, and her only political ties were to her son's lawyer, Z. T. Osborn, Leathers' predecessor as city attorney and the man run off by Mayor West for carrying water for Jake. Early in the game Loser had called and asked for Baker's vote, which she had pledged. But then Mayor West himself had called and asked for her resignation from the committee, which she also signed. Her son, it seems, had been involved in a work-related legal dispute with the city but was still employed, and she didn't want to cause him any trouble by refusing the mayor's request. But Osborn, who had represented her son in the lawsuit against the city, obtained a signed statement from her saying she intended her resignation to be effective only after she voted for Loser. She gave Osborn her proxy.

And then there was the Constable, by his own admission caught "between the devil and the deep blue sea." A former county and state highway patrolman, he was a longtime personal friend of Leathers'. But he was also from east of the river and owed his political life to Jake and Garner, who'd given him his first job in law enforcement. So when Garner and Jake met at their Dickerson Road motel to count votes, they had counted the Constable for Loser—yet there was his name on Mayor West's list for Leathers.

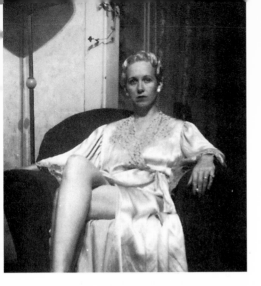

Above: Zoe Gillum of Yellow Creek, Tennessee, Dave White's second wife, in a 1944 portrait taken by a *Vanity Fair* photographer. Of her seven husbands she said she liked being married to Dave the best. *Right:* Dave White, Sallie, and their daughter Billye outside their Old Hickory home in 1930.

Above: Garner Robinson celebrates his first countywide election as sheriff in 1946. *Left:* The lovely "Skinny" Neiderhauser Robinson, who won Garner's heart and became his bride in 1929.

All photos courtesy of The Tennessean, *Maude Hopkins, and James Squires.*

Above left: Brilliant attorney Elkin Garfinkle (with cigar) was the "brains" of the Old Hickory machine for more than two decades. *Above right:* The "boss" Jake Sheridan called the political shots in Nashville from behind the scenes for twenty years until felled by Silliman Evans and his newspaper.

Above: Garner and Mayor Ben West at plant opening in Nashville with newly elected Senator Estes Kefauver *(left). Right:* Mayor West with Garner's twin daughters, Muriel and Maude, in the early 1950s.

Above: Sheriff Garner *(far right)* and his fledgling Davidson County Highway Patrol. *Right:* Dave on the highway patrol in 1944 with heavyweight boxing champion Max Baer *(left)* and "Big John" Cole *(right)*, who ran against Garner for sheriff in the infamous Hopewell Box election a year later.

Above: The Tennessee Highway Patrol, which was known statewide as "Boss Crump's Gestapo" in the late 1940s. *Left:* Crump's gestapo off-duty, heavily armed and hamming it up. J. J. Jackson in middle, Dave White on left.

Above: Black citizens of the "Minkslide" section of Columbia, Tennessee, under control of the Tennessee National Guard following the "riot" of 1946. *Right:* A contingent of highway patrolmen led by Captain Jackson and Sergeant White stormed a barbershop and tavern where armed blacks had holed up. Several were injured. *Below:* Confiscated whiskey was the favorite political booty of Crump's gestapo. Captain Jackson *(right)* and his sidekick Dave specialized in it.

Above: Sergeant Dave White *(center)* entertains a breakfast crowd attracted by Red Cross coffee and doughnuts during the sweep of "Minkslide." *At right:* Rival publishers Silliman Evans, Sr. *(top),* of *The Tennessean* and James G. Stahlman of the *Banner (bottom)* fought each other politically for twenty years in a newspaper war that knew neither bounds nor civility, despite remaining partners in a joint operating agreement that benefited both financially.

Left: Edward Hull (Boss) Crump *(left)* and Frank G. Clement, the last Tennessee governor elected by his powerful political machine. Branded the "gorgeous little stooge" by the newspapers, Clement keynoted the 1952 Democratic National Convention.

John Lewis, a young divinity student, leads one of the nation's first lunch counter sit-ins in downtown Nashville, which became the training ground for the civil rights movement. Lewis is now a distinguished congressman from Atlanta.

The firebombing of black leader Z. Alexander Looby's home on April 29, 1960, resulted in a long peaceful protest march that culminated in a street confrontation between civil rights activists and Nashville Mayor Ben West. . . . There on the steps of the Davidson County Courthouse, West became the first southern big-city mayor to publicly urge the end of segregation.

Left: Gene "Little Evil" Jacobs *(left)* and his mentor, Charlie Riley, represented the city's Second Ward, where the machine finally got caught stealing an election in 1962. Jacobs went to prison for it.

Right: Notorious Nashville gambler Jimmy Washer is buried in the family cemetery lot of the powerful sheriff who regulated his activities. Washer died a pauper, and another gambler wore his signature diamond ring and horseshoe stickpin to the funeral.

Above left: John J. Hooker, Jr., who brought the Kennedys' Camelot to Tennessee politics, helped get the *Baker v. Carr* case before the U.S. Supreme Court. *Above right:* Teamster boss James R. Hoffa, at podium, later hired Z. T. Osborn, Jr., at right in hat, mastermind of *Baker v. Carr*, to help him fight the Kennedy Justice Department in Tennessee courts. Both ultimately lost their lives.

Above left: Famed Nashville lawyer Jack Norman, Sr., defended Osborn on jury-tampering charges, faced off in court against his friend and rival, John J. Hooker, Sr. (*above right*), who acted as special prosecutor in the Hoffa case as well.

Above: Norman and Hooker together. *Left:* Garner's daughter Muriel is now one of Nashville's most popular and respected judges in charge of Domestic Relations Court.

Cootchie's voting plans might be a mystery, but his appetites and proclivities were not. Having been in the bait business of one kind or another for a long time, Jake knew exactly what it would take to catch Cootchie and keep him hooked. A shrewd and persuasive *Banner* political reporter named Neil Cunningham was assigned the task. Cootchie was reeled in to a lovely suite at the Hermitage Hotel, where Cunningham and friends worked furiously through the night eliciting and fulfilling his heart's desires. The next morning he was led, bloodshot and bleary-eyed, into the committee room, where in response to the sound of his own name he uttered a single word but the only one that mattered—"Loser."

When the committee secretary announced the results, it was forty-three to forty-two for Loser, with one member absent, an auctioneer working a sale in another county. But it had not been as easy as it looked. Twice during the day, the committee had voted, and both times the outcome had hinged on procedural decisions by the committee's nonvoting chairman, Sam Davis Bell, one of the first officers of the Colemere and a close friend of Garner's. Although the committee had a lawyer of its own present, on such occasions Bell took his cues on procedure from a former committee chairman and well-known expert on parliamentary matters, Elkin Garfinkle, who was prowling the county courtroom like an overseer.

At one point Mayor West had publicly challenged Garfinkle's right to speak to the committee chairman, but it was the mayor Bell ruled out of order, not Garfinkle. From this point Garfinkle relayed his advice through the committee's attorney, Elmer Davies, Jr.

Just as the final vote was announced, the mayor's brother, Wilson, rushed into the room with Mary Baker, a small, thin-faced woman dressed in black, wearing big round glasses, and carrying a shoulder bag. On the orders of the mayor she had been pulled away from her lunch and hustled to the committee room to vote in person. "Here is Mrs. Baker now," shouted the mayor above the confusion. "Let's see how she votes."

But Chairman Bell argued that her proxy vote had already been cast by Osborn and recorded.

"No," said Mayor West, of the woman whose resignation he had in his pocket, "this little lady wants to vote and has a right to cast her vote. She's here and she wants to vote . . ."

West insisted the vote had not been announced. Bell called in Davies for consultation. Both sides gathered around, banging on the chairman's desk and arguing over whether Mrs. Baker should be given the right to vote. Among them she stood tense, frightened, and silent, the mayor's arm around her shoulder. It came down to whether Bell ruled that the vote had been announced, thus recording the proxy vote. If it had, Davies told him, the proxy counted. If not, the process could be reopened, Mrs. Baker could vote, and the results would be reversed. Leathers would win.

"Is this your signature?" Bell asked, pointing to her proxy.

"Yes," Mrs. Baker said through trembling lips.

"I have consulted the county attorney," Bell told the gathering, "and he says the vote stands as announced. General Loser has been nominated."

Amidst the cheers and shouted complaints, reporters clamored after Bell, who was heading for an inner office to retrieve his hat and coat. One question remained unanswered. What about the election of a new chairman? Earlier in the session, by another one-vote margin, the Loser forces had won a battle to postpone the formal organization of the new committee until after the vote on the Priest vacancy. For an instant Bell considered calling the committee back to order for the chairman's election. What would happen if he did? Bell asked them. There was a good chance, the reporters pointed out, that if assembled again under a new chairman the committee might be whipsawed by the mayor into another vote on Loser and Leathers. "Give me my hat," Bell said.

That was it. A breakdown of the vote showed that among committee members from the city, thirty-eight had gone to Leathers and eighteen to Loser. In the county, however, the machine that didn't exist had delivered twenty-five of the twenty-nine votes— once more, just enough to win.

Thugs and Jackasses

Like all fallen governments, the Old Hickory political cabal saw exile as only the planning stage of its return to power. At fifty, Jake Sheridan had attained what he wanted from public service—financial independence. Now he had more interest in fishing bait and racehorses than politics. But Garner was as interested as ever in minding the public business. Not only was he planning his own comeback, he foresaw a political future for the next generation of Robinsons.

No matter what political office he held, Garner was always an undertaker first, and the base of his political operations had always been the funeral home. So giving up his badge and moving back there was not traumatic. He took his entourage with him, save the incorrigible jail prisoners he'd habitually favored in picking trusties. As sheriff, Garner had selected the con man Whim Wham to drive his children to school. As his own driver, he had chosen a killer and stickup man named Sonny Boy. "Daddy just loved a thug," recalled his daughter Muriel, who would follow him into politics. "We always had them around."

Just as he had at the courthouse, Garner wanted his children around him. For them and some other members of the younger generation of Robinson's political friends, the funeral home became a hangout, as Boss's store had been thirty years earlier. "You have nothing to fear from the dead," he told his twin daughters. "It's the live ones you have to watch out for." Preparing the dead and attending funerals became as routine as milking cows and feeding chickens were for farm kids. But the main attraction was the camaraderie of the colorful assortment of cops, saloon owners, gamblers, and political habitués who made Phillips-Robinson their headquarters.

• • •

One of Garner's two lifelong friends, the wallet retriever Dick Jones, who had been his shadow in the sheriff's office, performed the same function at the funeral home. But the other, Dave White, was not the mortician type. Careening through town in a speeding ambulance was okay, but Dave clearly lacked the sensitivity and decorum required of the professional funeral director.

For one thing, he found humor in death not often appreciated by the bereaved. For instance, he tended to see movements and hear noises from the dearly departed. And sometimes he posted the names of live Robinson family members or funeral home employees among the public listing of those in repose.

Because such irreverence was not in keeping with the Phillips-Robinson policy of quiet respect, Garner preferred to keep Dave planted somewhere in the world of lawmen and law violators as his set of political eyes and ears.

Keeping a man of Dave's temperament happily employed was never easy. Accustomed to rank and privilege not possible on the county patrol under Sheriff Cartwright, Dave went back into motel management, which he found equally boring and unfulfilling the second time around.

This made Dave adventuresome—and, now and then, drunk and dangerous. One Sunday afternoon he and Verna, accompanied by daughter Billye and her husband, Johnny, now a hawk-faced man of thirty-five, drove out to a roadhouse near Carthage for dinner. In the glove compartment of Dave's new red Pontiac was a pint of Jim Beam and a nickel-plated snub-nosed revolver. By the time they finished dinner, the pint was empty. As they emerged from the restaurant, Dave noticed a group of small donkeys in a roped pen nearby. "Come on, Johnny," he said, "let's ride a jackass."

When Dave stepped over the rope, a large and angry man—the owner of the donkeys—stepped from behind a truck. "What the goddamn hell do you think you're doing, you sonofabitch?"

Dave returned the hard look. "No use cussing us," he said. "Don't you see these ladies present here?"

The donkey man looked at Dave's wife and daughter like they'd crawled out from under a rock. "Well, goddamn your ladies. Get your goddamn ass outta that pen, you sonofabitch."

Dave punched the man in the stomach and doubled him over. Then he hit him in the ear and knocked him to the ground. The man got up, retrieved a sledgehammer from his truck, and raised it menacingly above his head. Dave stood his ground and watched as his son-in-law put his hand in his pocket and then moved quickly behind the man, who wheeled to face him. "Hang that knife in him, Johnny," Dave ordered, not knowing whether his son-in-law had a knife or not. "And he'll know you the rest of his life by the scar he carries."

Dave's bluff ended the confrontation. Police were called, but their response was to congratulate the donkey owner on his good fortune that Dave's pistol had been locked in the glove compartment of his car.

Garner soon learned of the incident and jumped all over Dave. "Well, you sonofabitch, the law up at Carthage told me they had a jackass fight up there Sunday," he said. "When they said one of the jackasses was drunk and driving a red Pontiac, I knew who they meant."

Soon Dave was again in quest of a policeman's job—at any rank. If Garner could get him rehired as a cop, he promised never to quit again. It didn't take Garner long. His successor as sheriff, Tom Y. Cartwright, rehired Dave, marking it down as a chit Garner owed him. But once again Dave had to start off at the bottom as a patrolman, a decade after he first attained the rank of sergeant on the state highway patrol. He was assigned to a car with a serious-faced, pipe-smoking partner named Walter Johnson. One day he and Walter crossed paths with Dave's saucy ex-wife, Zoe.

"Who's that sourpuss with you?" Zoe asked. "He looks like he washed outta his mama in a vinegar douche."

"Oh, Walter's all right," Dave replied, "but if that sonofabitch ever smiled, it would peel his pecker back to his navel."

Their bawdy revelry led to a rendezvous later on a rural road in neighboring Dickson County, the home county of the new governor, Frank Clement.

As the two sat in Dave's car sipping from a fifth of whiskey, they were accosted by a police officer, who arrested Dave for possession in a dry county. That he was a Davidson County sheriff's officer didn't matter, but that his name was Dave White did.

"You're Garner Robinson's buddy, aren't you?" the policeman said.

"That's right, but he's not the sheriff now," Dave replied.

"Doesn't matter whether he's sheriff or not, he's the best man I know. And the governor wouldn't want me arresting any friend of Garner Robinson's. You better get on back up there in your own county."

Garner's friendship might keep Dave White working and free of arrest, but it couldn't keep him married.

Like Sallie and Zoe, his third wife, Verna, had trouble coping, not only with Dave's meandering, but with his mother Ovie's meddling, which was epic. Once the old woman even confronted her daughter-in-law Verna with concern over the possibility she might transmit a venereal disease to her son. During a visit to their Madison home, Ovie said, she had come across Verna's douche bag and found that it had a break in the rubber. The story spread through the family like a virus, evoking a rare outburst of humor from Dave's son-in-law, Johnny—a formal offer to vulcanize Verna's douche bag in the interest of his father-in-law's health.

Frequent hilarity, however, was insufficient balm. Without even a good-bye note, Verna disappeared. A few weeks later she telephoned Dave from Chicago, where she said she had been visiting her sister. "I'm ready to come home," she said.

"Hell, you don't have a home," he told her. The divorce papers had already been filed.

As the truck carrying her belongings pulled away from their

rented house, Dave hung from the back of it a pair of ripped but colorful undershorts that he had been using as a cleaning cloth—and awarded himself yet another nickname.

"That'll give her something to remember her third husband by," he said. "Old Raggedy-ass Dave."

The shooting occurred in the middle of the day, quite unexpectedly. Men still stopped by Robinson's Store in Old Hickory to ogle the Boss's favorite daughter and Garner's favorite sister. Nearing fifty, Maude Muriel, now called "Maude Mammy" by Garner's children, was still lovely. She often suckered oglers like William V. Satterfield into a game of Far Away. The rules of Far Away were simple. Maude Mammy allowed a guest to get two Cokes from the cooler and the two would wager on whose Coke was bottled farthest from Nashville. If the guest won, the Cokes were free.

Being the one who had put the Cokes in the cooler in the first place, Maude usually won, as she did against Mr. Satterfield. But his response was unusual indeed. "I don't like to lose," he said, pulling a gun from his coat. He pointed it at Maude and began firing. She was hit and fell to the floor, and he kept firing, running her brother Dan out the back door and shooting the meat case to pieces in front of a fleeing female attendant known forever after as Leaping Lena. Just before getting into his car, Mr. Satterfield fired a final bullet in the air.

Why had he gone berserk?

"I don't know," Maude told the investigators sent out by her brother's successor, Sheriff Cartwright. "I was just talking to him, not dreaming of anything like that when he suddenly started shooting. He didn't seem mad."

But he was. Mr. Satterfield had lost more than a game of Far Away. He'd lost Maude Mammy, who'd once promised to make him her fourth husband. The Boss had told her, "You've been married enough for the whole family already. When he comes around here today, get rid of him for good."

Following her father's orders had nearly killed her. Mr. Satterfield's bullet had ripped through her dress just below the waist on her left side. There it struck a tube of lipstick in her pocket and ricocheted harmlessly into a desk, final confirmation to the women of Old Hickory that Maude Robinson's makeup was as bulletproof as it looked.

As for Mr. Satterfield, a whole passel of policemen loyal to the former sheriff and friendly to Phillips-Robinson arrested him on every charge possible, depriving him of his freedom for some time.

The banishment of Satterfield was among the Boss's last dictums as head of the Robinson clan. Not long afterward, at age eighty-one, he collapsed and died of a cerebral hemorrhage. He was ceremoniously laid out in his black serge undertaker's suit and buried by the politician son he once had worried might not amount to anything. The funeral was so large and grand it left no doubt that he had worried needlessly.

PART SIX

Resurrection

They went directly to the lunch counter, filled all the stools, and picked up menus. Nobody was at work in the drugstore but me, old Doc Bell the pharmacist, and the counter waitress, a bosomy Irish matron with red hair piled high on her head. She looked at them like they'd crawled from under a rock. "I ain't waitin' on y'all," she said. "Not me." She pulled off her apron and headed toward the kitchen. "I ain't waitin' on 'em, Doc," she yelled, and disappeared.

"Hellfire. Damnation," said old Doc Bell, staring at the black sea of faces around the horseshoe-shaped lunch area.

He began to walk in circles behind the prescription counter, wringing his hands and looking like a man trying to corkscrew himself into the floor. After a couple of turns, he grabbed his hat from the rack and pulled a plaid sport coat on over his white pharmacist smock. "I ain't gonna run no sodie fountain. No sir," he said to me. "Call 'em out there on Church Street and ask 'em what they want you to do. Tell 'em I'm out to lunch myself."

Me? What they want *me* to do? There I stood, Billye's boy, age eighteen, two months out of high school, wearing my one white short-sleeved shirt, my only necktie, and a look that said clearly that I didn't even have a telephone number for whomever it was on Church Street I was supposed to ask for help. And all around me at the Wilson Quick Drug Store at the corner of Eighth and Broadway was an organized black lunch counter sit-in, one of the first in the civil rights movement of the sixties.

My first inclination was to follow Doc Bell out the door. But the last employee to leave the drugstore full of black teenagers would surely be fired. I stayed.

The sit-in leader was a short, unsmiling, round-faced boy no older than myself, the color of chocolate with prominent lips and an intimidating stare. He took a step toward me. "You work here?" he asked.

"Yes."

"We would like some service," he said politely.

"Okay," I said, "but I don't work over here so I don't know much about the food. Whadday'all want?"

"Cokes," he said. "We want Cokes."

"Good," I said. "I can do Cokes."

I was still drawing and serving them up when a man

from company headquarters, which was only a few blocks away, showed up and took over. He walked with a pronounced limp and spoke that way, too—painfully, like a man half mad and half afraid.

"The fountain is closed," he said, shooing me from behind the counter. "There is nobody at work here."

"What about him?" the leader said, pointing to me. "And you?"

"We don't have health cards," the company man said. "You must have health cards for food service."

"Where's the woman who was here?"

"She quit."

The company man walked away from the fountain, leaving them there alone, and for the time stymied. After sitting around the counter for about an hour, they left as quietly and quickly as they had come.

Later that day my granddaddy came by and parked his sheriff's patrol car in front of the store. He was a lieutenant by then, with gold braid all over his sleeve. I went out to see him.

"Jigaboos came to see you, did they?"

"Yeah, they were here."

"I heard you had the big shot here—ya know, that John Lewis boy. He's the leader. Agitator from Alabama."

"I know which one. He's the one who ordered."

He grinned, showing the gold tooth. "Old Doc Bell left your ass, didn't he."

"Yeah, he took off."

"Sonofabitch. Well, you did the right thing. Serve 'em. Shit, why not? It's bettern' fighting 'em. That's what we're gonna have to do, you know. Fight 'em."

He shook his head at the prospect, but not so you could tell whether he relished it or not. I promptly changed the subject.

The day's events had reminded me that my granddaddy was trying to help me find more rewarding work.

"What about the other job?" I wanted to know. "You talk to anybody?"

"You mean down the road?" He nodded toward the Nashville *Tennessean* offices, four blocks down Broadway.

I nodded.

"Garner said he'd talk to Wayne."

It was the summer of 1961, thirty years after Boss Robinson gave my great-grandfather Will a Depression job, a quarter of a century after Garner Robinson got my grandfather a job as a cop. Now the Robinson clout had been enlisted for the benefit of a fourth generation—me.

Garner had recently returned to public life as a member of the Nashville delegation to the state legislature. And the Wayne of whom my granddaddy spoke was Wayne Whitt, the thumbless, whizbang city hall reporter for the *Tennessean* whom Garner had befriended in the forties. Garner was trying to use the chit to get me hired by the very newspaper that had opposed him so vehemently over the years. I figured it was impossible.

But Garner was now in a key position to help the *Tennessean* with one of its major political objectives— another change in the city charter providing for the consolidation of the city and county governments—and he had made a temporary peace with Silliman Evans, Jr., before Evans' unexpected and premature death that year. A few months later the *Tennessean* finally gave me a job as a clerk in the newspaper's morgue, perfect for a kid who'd spent so much time hanging around funeral homes.

The peace didn't last long. Soon, the newspaper, under Silliman's younger, more aggressive brother, Amon, was in another political war with the Robinsons, as rancorous as any between his old man and Jake Sheridan. But due to the timing of politics I had somehow leaped through a tiny window of opportunity that would shape my life with no less force than Boss's decision to take up undertaking had shaped Garner's.

My world was no longer obscured by being holster-high in a pack of gun toters or having to peer over dashboards through mud-spattered windshields. Before me was a nation's landscape in turmoil over the issue of race, another civil war of sorts pitting old against new, the country against the city, and white against black. My job as a reporter replaced the myopia of my youth with the vista of a front-row seat, a perspective distorted only by my own ignorance, and soon even that obstruction began slowly to diminish.

In 1963, I stood taking notes on a police line in a city street two blocks from my old drugstore, when the followers of John Robert Lewis, who later went on to become a distinguished and powerful member of the United States House of Representatives, were dragged from in front of Cross Keys Cafeteria and lifted into a police paddy wagon.

Naturally, my granddaddy was there in glistening brass and shiny leather with gold stripes up to his elbow. Nearly sixty now and still a superior officer who could have stood by giving orders, he was on the front line waving a lacquered billy club and growling at young men not even a third his age. "Son, if you don't back up on that sidewalk, they'll be taking you to Hubbard"—the city's only all-black hospital.

The following year, with his physical and political vigor now in more obvious decline, it was he who needed medical treatment after he fell or was pulled from a paddy wagon during a huge street demonstration. I found him sitting on a gurney in a hospital emergency room, his pants torn open at both knees, while a medic picked debris out of the bleeding gashes.

"What are you looking at?" he snapped. "You wanta put my knees in the paper?"

"What happened?" I asked him.

He pulled an answer from our past that instantly reversed our roles.

"I ran my bicycle into a telephone pole and fell in the gravel," he said, flashing the gold grin.

Later at the police station, I ran into Lester McKinnie, one of John Lewis's lieutenants and the leader of the demonstrators, who was there making bond for those who had been arrested. By now I had become a frequent interviewer of both Lewis and McKinnie and they knew me not as a kid who once served them in a drugstore but as a friendly white reporter on a newspaper totally supportive of them and their cause.

"How many people were hurt?" I asked.

"Fifteen or sixteen went to the hospital, I think," McKinnie said. Then he turned to one of the women with him, a fiercely aggressive student leader with a prominent Afro hairdo and a loud and ugly mouth. "Isn't that about right, fifteen or sixteen?" he asked her.

"Yeah," she said. "Sixteen of us. And two of them. One black police hit by the white police and that old white mothafuckin' police that fell off the paddy wagon and busted his ass."

They all laughed at the mental image of an old, failing enemy losing his footing and falling to his knees. And me, I smiled, too. Not at the humiliation of my grandfather, but at a Gordian knot of irony in which I was entangled. I was held fast by the rightness of their cause, doing a job I loved, which had been handed to me by the old policeman they hated and mocked as their enemy but to whom I was tied emotionally. He was at once both an accurate symbol of what they knew to be wrong with society—racism—and what I believed to be right about it—love of family. They could see him only as the oppressor of blacks and the enemy of civil rights, while I knew him as a man who was out there waving a stick only because that was his job.

It was a moment of true enlightenment. From my mother's father, who had taught me how to tie a fishing line, how to train a puppy, how to drive a car, how to get a job, how to really see what my eyes take in, I had finally learned something truly extraordinary. For the first time I realized that what you don't know is often the most important key to true understanding.

Because of my role as a *Tennessean* reporter and my friendly demeanor, Lester McKinnie and John Lewis knew and treated me as an ally committed to their cause. What they didn't know was that running through my veins was the blood of a man who had killed the blacks who rose up in 1946, and two decades later was still trying to put them down. If they had, they would never have given me a minute of their time, much less entrusted me with the details of their mobilization strategy.

By the same token, my family relationship would be meaningless if they knew as I did that my grandfather was on the police line not because he hated blacks but only because that was what was expected of him by the political system that bore him; that the only hatred he felt in his heart was for what he had learned from the day's experience—that he was getting too old to be a policeman; that in this new world he might not even know how to be one.

He had become a metaphor for what was happening to society as a whole—the crumbling of racial barriers in America.

Lessons from the Womb

Nashville was the perfect place for Martin Luther King to begin the civil rights movement because it was a pushover.

On its surface the city was tough and mean spirited enough to put up convincing resistance. Nashville whites could sneer, spit, and shout vulgar racial slurs with the best of American bigots. And they would come out in an eight-inch snow to do it, as John Lewis and his friends discovered when they launched their protest marches against downtown businesses in the winter of 1959. Nashvillians weren't adverse to violence either. Just before dawn on the morning of April 19, 1960, a firebomb flung from a passing car virtually destroyed the home of the town's most prominent black citizen, Z. Alexander Looby. But miraculously, as was the case in much of

Nashville's civil rights struggle, no real harm was done to anything but the city's reputation. In the final analysis, Nashville was too soft at heart to offer anything but foul-mouthed resistance that quickly collapsed to black pressure.

Politically, Nashville was set up perfectly if not purposefully to become the first major city in the South that would agree to desegregate in response to the nonviolent sit-ins and economic boycotts. That it did so was due in no small measure to the city's exiled political boss, Jake Sheridan, and the man who had sent him into exile, deceased *Tennessean* publisher Silliman Evans.

Sheridan's living legacy to the cause of civil rights was Nashville mayor Ben West, for whom he had stolen the 1951 election. Not only had the twenty-seven votes by which West prevailed come from a Black Bottom ballot box stuffed by Jake's black constituents, the election had been close enough to steal in the first place only because in order to have any chance at defeating the incumbent Tom Cummings, Jake had mobilized the city's black votes for the first time ever. Two black lawyers, Looby and attorney Robert Lillard, had ridden the same minority democratic uprising to become the first popularly elected black city councilmen in the South.

West had won his second and third terms with the support of the city's blacks. For years he had boasted of an affinity with blacks that stemmed from growing up alongside them in rural Tennessee poverty; in fact, he had actually made Lillard's and Looby's victories possible with his sponsorship of a single-member district law passed for the Nashville city council by the 1949 state legislature. Along with Evans' newspaper, the mayor would play the pivotal role in the defining moment of Nashville's place in the great racial drama of the sixties.

The *Tennessean*'s support for the desegregation of Nashville was the mere upholding of a long-standing institutional conviction, not a comfortable stance but one also assumed by newspapers in other cities such as Charlotte and Little Rock. But West's contribution was an act of pure personal and political courage rarely matched by public officials anywhere else in the South until much later and perhaps unequaled in its ultimate impact.

The city's moment of crisis occurred in the spring of 1960, two years after King had picked Nashville as the site of one of the first branches of his Southern Christian Leadership Conference. For months the Nashville chapter had been training protestors in the basement of the black First Baptist Church, which served a blighted area in the shadow of the state capitol. The group was led by the kind-faced, soft-spoken Kelly Miller Smith, who would become known as the "conscience of Nashville." But among its originators were three firebrand outsiders—John Lewis from Troy, Alabama, a student at the American Baptist Seminary; a Fisk University student named Diane Nash from Chicago; and their instructor, a thirty-two-year-old ministerial student at Vanderbilt University Divinity School, Dr. James Lawson, who was from Massillon, Ohio.

At a breakfast meeting of black ministers in March of 1960, Lawson electrified the Nashville establishment by announcing that the peaceful and relatively law-abiding street demonstrations were about to become exercises in civil disobedience. Marchers would be instructed to violate the law, he said, because the law was a "gimmick" to keep his race oppressed.

The *Tennessean* dutifully reported this news without emotion. But over at the *Banner*, it sent flag-waving publisher James G. Stahlman, who believed "separate but equal" was a God-given directive, into a rage. The following day, Stahlman labeled the Reverend Lawson a "flannel-mouthed agitator" and likened him to Ku Klux Klansman John Kasper, who had been trying to organize in Nashville. Both, Stahlman's editorial declared, were "paid agents of strife-breeding organizations" intent on disrupting the city. He called for Vanderbilt to expel Lawson from the divinity school. "The sooner both Nashville and Vanderbilt are rid of the presence and the baneful influence and tactics of Mr. Lawson, the better."

A major reason Nashville became the womb for the civil rights movement was its position as a center of black higher education, both public and private. It was home to Fisk University, Meharry Medical School, and Tennessee State University, a state-supported school then called Tennessee A & I. This bounty of black colleges had taken the pressure off wealthy, privately endowed Vanderbilt to enroll black students.

With a few token exceptions—Lawson among them—Vanderbilt had remained just like Stahlman's Belle Meade Country Club, a lily-white bastion of segregation. In 1955, a reactionary English professor, Donald Davidson, one of the original Fugitives and Agrarians, had helped organize a group of professors and local businessmen to mount a defense against federal intervention in southern race relations. The group remained moderate and civil, consistently rejecting the tactics and racism of the Klan. But in a gesture that spoke to the heart of the university, one of the group's attorneys, a graduate of Vanderbilt Law School, tore his diploma into small pieces and mailed it back to the university when it admitted the first black student.

Stahlman's demand for Lawson's ouster caused immense problems for both Vanderbilt and Mayor West, who earlier in the year had appointed the school's dean of students to chair a biracial committee to study integration. Not only was the publisher a stalwart on the school's powerful board of trust executive committee, his newspaper had been West's staunchest supporter for more than a decade.

Vanderbilt's student newspaper joined the *Banner* in calling for Lawson's dismissal. In short order, despite the presence of moderates on the faculty, the school caved in. When Lawson refused to withdraw voluntarily, he was kicked out of the divinity school for publicly advocating lawlessness. He became the leader of the Freedom Riders.

The *Tennessean*, meanwhile, viewed the civil rights demonstrations as another necessary step toward its beloved reform. Editorially, the paper was deliberate but somewhat cautious in support of desegregation. It saw peaceful protest as a legitimate right of free expression. But its news coverage of the civil rights struggle left no doubt as to its sentiments. Much of its reporting on the marches and sit-ins was being done by a young Jewish reporter from New York named David Halberstam, who had come to Nashville by way of Harvard and the Mississippi Delta brimming with conviction on the issue of segregation. Halberstam's sense of justice and outrage at the racial intolerance of the South, honed during a brief stint on a small Mississippi daily, was readily apparent in his journalism. A visionary even then, Halberstam could see what was in store for Nashville and the rest of the South, but the city's establishment did not like his previews. An aggressive and feared interviewer, he became for many local politicians the bearer of a message no one wanted to hear and a name on the newspaper whose policy they hated.

Among the police, who came to detest his presence at the street demonstrations, Halberstam was known as "that nigger-lovin' David Slobberstream from the nigger-lovin' *Tennessean*." The newspaper's political image had already been set in their minds by years of editorials against the poll tax and more recently by the activities of John Seigenthaler. Through his reporting of Teamster union violence, "Seig" had become acquainted with Robert Kennedy and took a leave from the *Tennessean* to work in John F. Kennedy's successful campaign for president. In the summer of 1961, while working as a special liaison between the Justice Department and the Freedom Riders who trained in Nashville before trying to integrate Birmingham and Charlotte, he was struck with a rock during a riot in Montgomery. Seig was from a large, well-liked Catholic family, but the sentiment in Nashville's political community was that he had gotten what he deserved.

Such hostility toward civil rights sympathizers was the rule rather than the exception in southern cities under siege. The exceptions were extraordinary acts of political leadership in times of crisis, such as those of Ben West. In the mid-fifties, when the Klan tried to build resistance to school desegregation by threatening school bombings, West's police put up protective barricades. Klan leaders were arrested and thrown in jail.

On April 29, 1960, after the bomb leveled the front of Looby's home, the mayor was among the first callers inquiring about his safety. That afternoon, a ten-block-long procession of demonstrators, three thousand walking three abreast, marched in total silence from Fisk University northwest of the city all the way downtown.

In his office, Mayor West listened as advisor after advisor, including emissaries from Stahlman's newspaper, told him the same thing: Not even the slightest violation of the law should be tolerated. If the crowd didn't disperse peacefully when ordered, the police should arrest the leaders and drive the rest back into their neighborhoods. Under no circumstances, they told West, should the mayor become personally involved in any confrontation with the crowd. If the blacks wanted to talk to the mayor, they should do so through Looby and Lillard.

Ignoring the advice, West met the demonstrators on the steps of the courthouse. He pleaded for interracial tolerance and publicly offered a ten-thousand-dollar reward for information leading to the arrest of the Looby bomber. He listened patiently as one of the march leaders, the Rev. C. T. Vivian, read a statement condemning him for not personally speaking out against segregation and for his biracial committee's recommendation for a "limited trial" integration. West, who relished eye-to-eye confrontations, defended his record eloquently. But the militant Diane Nash, who was also among the march leaders, pushed West to take a strong moral stand on desegregation.

"I appeal to all citizens to end discrimination," West replied.

"Then, Mayor, do you recommend that the lunch counters be desegregated?" Nash countered.

West hesitated. This was the moment of his reckoning. Either he responded positively, or he would be forced to stumble around for some lame excuse. Whatever he had accomplished by being there would have been undercut. He would end up having to send in the police.

"Yes," West said, resolutely.

The crowd applauded and went back to Fisk as peacefully as they had come. The next morning, as was its custom, the *Tennessean* exclaimed the victory in 120-point type: "INTEGRATE COUNTERS—MAYOR."

From that point on, the integration of Nashville and the rest of Tennessee, except for Memphis, was largely a matter of removing the obstructions embedded in the laws—a formidable undertaking nonetheless.

The Unholy Trinity

In the early sixties Tennessee's legislature was a marble monument to the status quo. For thirty years it had been run by the Great Triumvirate—a trio of elderly lawmakers from the rural rimland of Middle Tennessee who believed in one simple credo: collect the taxes where the money is—in the cities—and spend it where it is needed—in the country.

Even at the height of his power Boss Crump of Memphis had been unable to change things in the capitol, for the simple reason that the legislature had not reapportioned itself in fifty-five years.

Crump himself was demonic in his political battles, once writing in a newspaper ad opposing the reelection of one-time protégé Gordon Browning as governor that "in the art galleries of Paris there are twenty-seven pictures of Judas Iscariot—none look alike but all resemble Gordon Browning; that neither his head, heart nor hand can be trusted; that he would milk his neighbor's cow through a crack in the fence; that, of the two hundred and six bones in his body there isn't one that is genuine; that his heart has beaten over two billion times without a single sincere beat." But the tactics used by the triumvirate—Pete Haynes, Jim Cummings, and I. D. Beasley—were so villainous that even Crump had to admire them.

Crump had lost the key battle in 1933 when the unholy trio defeated his candidate for speaker and elected Haynes, a tough, brilliant criminal lawyer from rural Franklin County.

Believing the election of his candidate for speaker to be in the bag, the confident Crump had gone to Hot Springs, Arkansas, to bet on the horses, while his top Nashville lieutenant, Roxy Rice, went to the Rose Bowl in Pasadena. While they were out of town, Beasley, a roly-poly practical joker who had an extraordinary ear for voices and was an accomplished mimic, met in a Nashville hotel room with Cummings and Haynes with the goal of switching some votes.

I.D. was a classic backroom politician so adept at appropriating power he didn't have that he was known throughout his career as "Governor," even though he never held the office. His specialty was getting other people government jobs, which he worked at constantly. And his prowess was most clearly affirmed the day the real governor, Prentice Cooper, in a hurry and being chauffeured by a state highway patrolman, attempted to drive down a completed but still unopened highway near Beasley's hometown of Carthage. An old man who owed his state job to Beasley wouldn't let the governor's car pass, even though the trooper had explained they were late on official business. The quick-tempered Cooper jumped out of the car and joined the argument. "Don't you know who I am?" he demanded. "I'm Prentice Cooper, the governor of Tennessee."

"I don't give a goddamn if you're I. D. Beasley," the old state worker replied, "you're not going through here."

At five foot three, 230 pounds, I. D. Beasley in person was hard to mistake for someone else. But on the phone, he was a man of many voices, all of them impeccable impersonations. First, I.D. tried his mimic of Rice on a blind legislator, whose ear would prove an acid test. It worked. Satisfied, I.D. then called the backers of Crump's candidate one by one and in a voice they all took to be Rice's told them that Boss Crump believed Haynes had the job won and that they were free to vote for him. By the time I.D. was done calling, Haynes did indeed have the job and was accepting congratulations on the other phone.

A tobacco-chewing country lawyer who took ocean cruises, played bridge, and once rode a camel in Egypt, Haynes was an imposing man of quick wit and great theatrical skill, which he used to influence the legislative process the same way he swayed jurors in criminal trials. But none of his talents were more important than his skill at forgery. The triumvirate specialized in stealing the personal stationery and memo pads of legislators and governors, which Haynes used to facilitate their legislative goals the same way I. D. Beasley employed impersonation. During the ten years Haynes ruled the House, dozens of legislators lost their votes and their bills because they responded to a bogus call from Beasley or a phony note from the speaker.

All these tactics and skills were employed with one aim in mind—keeping rural control of the legislature. And it was from that speaker's podium in 1937 that Haynes beat back the first of many serious reform efforts aimed at diluting rural control of the legislature by abolishing the county unit rule, which had county delegations voting as a unit according to majority opinion. The fight was so intense that Haynes presided over the vote with a loaded pistol lying in plain view next to his gavel. The men of the triumvirate believed with all their hearts that urbanization represented a grave threat to the country. They knew that the rapid growth of cities would bring a demand for roads and schools that could only be met by sapping the lifeblood of rural America. And no weapon, scheme, or chicanery should be spared in the interest of preserving the values and priorities of agricultural life.

Men like them controlled state legislatures everywhere, producing identical urban crises as a result. The Pork Chop Gang of lawmakers from the Florida Panhandle, for example, split up the state's racetrack revenue at the rate of sixty dollars per person in rural Liberty County as opposed to twenty cents a person for the city of Miami.

A quarter of a century later in 1961, when Garner Robinson launched his political comeback by getting elected to the Tennessee General Assembly, the pistols had vanished, but the legislature was still unreformed. One-third of the state's population controlled two-thirds of the votes in the legislature, and the state spent one-third more on education for each child in the country than for each child in the cities, ignoring the rapidly developing urban crisis against which the new president of the United States, John F. Kennedy, had campaigned, calling it the "Shame of the Cities."

Garner came to the legislature as a replacement for his son Gale, who had been elected a member of the delegation in 1957 and had

been reelected two years later before deciding he preferred practicing law.

Getting a Robinson elected was easy because of the way the political system worked. There were no individual legislative districts,
so all candidates ran countywide, with the top six finishers elected—
a formula that assured that the six best-known white males got the
jobs. No name was better known in Nashville east of the Cumberland River than Robinson. And no family had more friends in high
places.

Boss Crump had gone to his reward but his "gorgeous little
stooge," Frank Clement, was in his second term as governor. The
state's most popular public official, Clement still harbored hopes of
being president, and he thought the world of the Robinsons. Surprisingly, Garner's personal friendship with Nashville mayor Ben
West had survived West's firing of Jake; with Jake gone, Garner had
found friends easier to keep. For example, Jack Norman, in a gesture
of kindness to his childhood sweetheart Skinny Robinson, had taken
the Robinsons' son, Gale, into his law firm, where the young man
had become close friends with Norman's sons. And it was not long
before one of the Robinson twins, Muriel, married the son of another Norman law associate, then joined the firm herself. This
didn't always make for good marriages, but it was the way to succeed
in law and politics, a form of intercourse by which a political organization reproduced itself.

New friends were added to the framework of the old. Many of
Jake's earliest ties were still in place and valuable. Nashville's congressman, J. Carlton Loser, owed his job to the proxy vote cast in the
party executive committee special election by Jake and Elkin's protégé and former Old Hickory lawyer Z. T. "Tommy" Osborn.

In choosing the local legislative delegation as the place for his
comeback, Garner drew on the earliest political lesson he had learned,
which remained the real secret of political power in America—that
those who count the votes can have more say about the outcome of
elections than those who cast them.

The local delegation still controlled the Davidson County Election

Commission, and controlling the election commission is how he, Jake, and Elkin had risen to power in the first place.

Although I. D. Beasley had died in 1955, Haynes and Cummings were still in legislative harness pulling the same load. Five years earlier Haynes had taken temporary leave from the assembly to become its lawyer, to battle the most serious and historic reform effort of them all—a lawsuit eventually known as *Baker v. Carr*, which raised the simple legal issue that if a man could not be denied equal treatment because of his race, how could he be denied the same because of his residence? If one was a federally protected right, why not the other?

Reapportionment was an easy issue for Garner because the driving force behind the effort to reapportion the Tennessee legislature, the man who had assembled the plaintiffs and spoke most eloquently for them in court, was Garfinkle's protégé Tommy Osborn. It was in Elkin's private law library that Osborn had come across the obscure 1946 Colegrove case from Illinois that had first raised the question about voting inequality being unconstitutional. Osborn and Mayor West had found the lawsuit common ground in which to bury their political differences. West had made the city of Nashville the main plaintiff in Osborn's lawsuit and was paying some of the legal fees. It had been at the knees of West and Garfinkle, during his brief stint as West's first city attorney, that Osborn had first formed his opinions on the plight of crowded, beleaguered, financially deprived urban residents.

Although little known outside scholarly legal circles, the reapportionment test case was one of the defining issues in Tennessee politics, dividing the reactionaries from the progressives, conservatives from liberals, Republicans from New Deal Democrats the same way the poll tax had done for so many years. After a long and bitter struggle, a federal appeals court had recently sided with Haynes and the legislature, but the reformers had succeeded in getting *Baker v. Carr* before the United States Supreme Court.

But just because the question of reapportionment was now a judicial one did not mean that the legislature was free of the problem. Financially strapped cities were trying to solve their revenue problems by annexing adjacent county property, which required legislative approval. In Nashville, old Joe Hatcher's front-page column now championed not only the one-man, one-vote principle at stake in *Baker v. Carr*, but the New Frontier of the Kennedy administration in Washington and—most fervently of all—an alternative to annexation, a proposed consolidation of the Nashville city and county local governments, wiping out the taxation and service inequities between them.

In all three instances, the newspaper couched its support under the old and familiar umbrella of better government. But with black protest marches occurring daily across the South, everyone understood that underpinning all reform was the question of how much power American blacks would wield at all levels of the democracy. While the core issue was simple as black and white, the implications were far more complex, separating old politics from new, rural interests from urban, and, in Nashville, separating the city's two newspapers and the old city and county political factions.

Although Nashville mayor West was one of the nation's leading proponents of urban empowerment and had supported a consolidated government proposal, he had also become an advocate of annexation. He and the Nashville City Council were now blocking the proposed consolidation by refusing to put it to public referendum a second time. And for good reason. West had the most to lose from the consolidation of city and county governments. The new charter was the brainchild of Davidson County judge Beverly Briley, a schoolmate with whom West had never gotten along. Backed by the *Tennessean* and aided inadvertently by Jake Sheridan's departure from the scene, Briley had emerged as West's main political rival.

A new consolidated Metro government would increase black representation on the council but would lower the black population percentage of a greater Nashville to less than a third. This would insure a white majority in the city for decades to come. And that meant that someone other than Ben West, who relied heavily on the big black vote, could get elected mayor—that someone else being Briley.

When Briley and the *Tennessean* had first tested their idea in public referendum in 1958, West and the city machine had been for it. But the Robinsons had mobilized the county voters and dealt it a crushing defeat at the polls. Now, as a freshman member of the Davidson County delegation, Garner came face to face with the issue again. Briley and the *Tennessean* now wanted a second referendum—one that would be held without the approval of Mayor West and the Nashville City Council.

Normally a freshman legislator wouldn't have much say on this, but Garner was hardly a typical first-termer. Old Jim Cummings himself, by then the seventy-one-year-old dean of Tennessee lawmakers and the legislature's single most potent member, had made it a point to stop by Garner's desk to offer congratulations and welcome him. "It's about time Nashville sent somebody up here who knows how to get things done," Old Jim declared.

A little man who wore smiles and bow ties like badges of good nature, Cummings was as courtly and cheery as Garner was polite and gregarious. The two were fast friends and quick to begin deal making. By the end of the 1961 session, Garner was clearly the Nashville delegation's most skilled and influential legislator. So when the law authorizing a second vote on the Metro issue got into trouble, the old ex-sheriff found himself holding the balance of power—exactly the kind of leverage Jake had always made the most of.

By killing the Metro government referendum bill, Garner could preserve many old friendships and loyalties. Because Governor Clement had to get along with Jim Cummings and his rural buddies in the legislature, he had been timid in his support of the Kennedy administration and had shied away from both the annexation and reapportionment issues, and anything else that threatened rural domination. *Banner* publisher Jimmy Stahlman had frequently reminded Garner of his desire that the Metro referendum measure never see the light of day. He and Ben West would have annexed all of Davidson County before they let Beverly Briley and the *Tennessean* run the city of Nashville.

Down behind the wall of resistance alongside the *Banner* and Jim Cummings would have been the natural spot for Garner to nestle in middle age. It was into this old-order politics that he and Jake had been spawned two decades earlier. And he was at heart an agrarian. After buying back the Robinson farm, which his more industrial-minded father, Boss, had sold to the manufacturers, Garner had put spotted walking horses and bird dogs on the land and tended them as religiously as he did the funeral business.

But backed up against the wall in the legislature helping old Jim Cummings block the path of progress was not where Garner wanted to be. For there, eventually, he would get his political ass knocked off for sure. Not Garner. Instead, he would do alone what he and Jake had done so many times together—walk to the other side of the tracks and catch a fast-moving express train in the opposite direction.

As time ran out in the legislative session, Garner used his friendship and influence with other members of the delegation to save the public referendum legislation wanted so desperately by his old political foes, Judge Briley and the *Tennessean*. How could he not? If there was one thing the Robinsons believed in, it was voting.

Almost instantly, the decision returned political dividends. A few weeks later, one of the most powerful and sought-after political jobs in the county, that of county trustee, was made available by the death of its occupant. Because the trustee collected and invested the taxes, both the city and county factions wanted control of the office. But neither Judge Briley nor Mayor West had firm political control of the group that controlled the appointment—the quarterly county court. Even after all these years, it was still a stronghold of the Sheridan-Robinson-Garfinkle faction. Taking another page from Jake Sheridan's book, Garner decided to seek the job himself. He didn't have enough votes to win without the support of either West or Briley, but even if he didn't get the job, he could probably decide who did and pick up another political chit.

Since he had just done the Briley and *Tennessean* forces a favor, Garner went first to the Briley camp, where he found himself face to face with the man who aspired to be the new Jake Sheridan—Briley's Svengali, H. E. Flippen, who represented the Nashville business community and had been handpicked for Briley by Silliman Evans, Jr., the *Tennessean* publisher. A classic chamber of commerce type, Flippen was better educated than Jake and moved in better circles. But he shared Jake's expertise in the machinery of politics and his understanding of what made it run—money.

Fifteen years earlier, Flippen had helped Garner campaign for sheriff in his first race for public office. It had been Flippen who had first recruited the hardware dealer W. Y. "Booty" Draper for the Sheridan-Robinson-Garfinkle machine.

A big bear of a man who sat like a Buddha behind the desk in his hardware distributorship, Flippen relished the behind-the-scenes king-making power that Jake had wielded so artfully. As the man who raised money for Briley, he had become the patronage chief who passed judgment on who got hired to county jobs, or whom Briley backed for this office or that. A drunk at the courthouse had dubbed him the "Honey Bee," as in "the big bee around which all the other little bees buzz." Garner called him "Flip," which is how he was known to his friends. But Flippen was none too friendly. "The group," as Briley's advisors called themselves, had reservations about supporting Garner for trustee.

"Garner," the Honey Bee said, "you have been known to switch sides. You don't always stay put."

Garner winced at this understatement. He looked around the room at the Briley supporters Flippen had gathered for the express purpose of watching Garner Robinson pay homage. He and Jake had not done it this way. They hadn't made deals by interviewing people as if they were job applicants. But this was a new day.

"Let me tell you-all this," he said. "I'll stick."

Which should have settled it, Garner thought. But it didn't.

"Let's hear that again," said the Honey Bee.

For some, the humility required would have been too much. Jake would have walked out. Elkin's temper would have flared. Though he would confide to Dave White later that "Flip wanted me to eat a little shit," Garner kept his cool. This was an important step in his political reincarnation. He could go along with these guys.

"Flip, I said I'll stick."

The deal was cut. Garner Robinson had become a reformer, of sorts—but not, he would soon discover, without high risk and serious consequence. For after he had left the room, the Honey Bee told the others what he had told Garner earlier in private—that Garner could hold the trustee's job only until the election the following year. "He'll never get reelected," Flippen declared. "The Robinsons are finished."

Old Dog—New Sandbox

The campaign for public approval of the new Metropolitan government charter for Nashville in the spring of 1962 had all the decorum of an alley brawl, and the issue of race shadowed it like an albatross.

With the Kennedys in Washington and a voting-rights revolution of some kind a certainty, the racial and political implications of a consolidated city and county government were thinly veiled and rich with irony.

The exodus of whites to the suburbs during the fifties had left the city nearly 40 percent black. Unless something was done, blacks would soon be in the majority, as in Atlanta, and would have all the city's political offices. But a majority-black urban area would be even more of a political orphan than the cities already were. The tax dollars and political power would stay in the white suburbs and the rural-dominated state legislatures.

In 1958, immediately after the first Metro charter was defeated by the county, Mayor West had annexed a large chunk of the all-white suburbs, accomplishing by legislative fiat what he had failed to do with public referendum. The city's percentage of black population dropped back to 25 percent. Yet blacks were still not represented in the government, except by the two black city councilmen, Looby and Lillard, who had been elected along with West in 1951. The political reality of a consolidated government was equally clear: by expanding its political boundaries, Nashville would remain a majority-white-controlled town. But under the charter provisions being pushed by Judge Briley and the *Tennessean*, the representation of blacks in both the city council and the legislature would be dramatically increased.

The irony did not stop there. The only hope for public approval rested in the annexed suburbs and farther out in the county. So once again the first real empowerment of blacks since West's election in 1951 rested with the same people who had elected West—the old Sheridan-Robinson-Garfinkle county machine. This time Judge Briley and Silliman Evans, Jr., took no chances. They picked a member of the Robinson family, Jim Roberson, son of Garner's older sister Leona, to run the campaign for approval of the Metro charter. At first many people thought he had broken with his family, which would surely line up again with Ben West in opposition. Nothing could have been further from the truth. Jim was like another son to Garner, every bit as close as Gale, and he never took a political step without Garner's approval. Rather than being a political gypsy for hire—even against his own family—Jim had taken the job at Garner's direction. After sending Gale out first to run for the legislature, he had dispatched Jimmy into the camp of the Metro advocates. He considered both of them second-generation advance men for the family's political comeback. So when Silliman Evans, Jr., needed help in the legislature in 1961, Jim Roberson deftly guided the publisher to his uncle Garner.

Silliman Evans, Jr., liked Jim Roberson personally, but he liked even better the idea of meshing the old Robinson political machine and the new county organization growing up around Judge Briley. Simply changing the minds of the Robinson followers who had opposed the idea of Metro in 1958 would assure its passage. And it was toward this end that Evans had convinced Briley and Flippen that Jim Roberson should be the campaign point man.

In his first assignment as heir to Jake Sheridan's role as election strategist, Jim proved to be a formidable grass-roots political organizer. A tall, striking man with prematurely silver hair, Jim combined Garner's folksy affability with Jake's high-energy work ethic. He lacked Jake's penchant for details and follow-through, but made up for it by recruiting an army of conscientious, hard-working women led by Guynell Sanders, a brassy buddy of Dave White's daughter, Billye, who had been Jimmy's childhood playmate.

Using money raised from the chamber of commerce crowd, Jimmy reorganized the elements of the two machines into a single impressive countywide network that was whipped into a fighting frenzy each day by a newly energized morning newspaper.

Following the unexpected death of Silliman Evans, Jr., from a heart attack at age thirty-six in 1961, the *Tennessean* had gotten a new publisher, Evans' younger brother, twenty-nine-year-old Amon Carter Evans. More liberal than Silliman Junior and more confrontational, Amon Evans was anxious to prove himself his father's son. Like Silliman Sr., Amon was a small man. But he disguised his stature with an exaggerated stride, an intimidating stare, and a giant sense of his own being. With his father's paper and his father's confidence, Amon automatically became a political force that demanded to be reckoned with. And the two men around him—Robert Kennedy's new Nashville pals John J. Hooker, Jr., and John Seigenthaler—soon made him an overwhelming one.

At thirty-one, Hooker was a tall, dark, lanky dandy with movie-star good looks, a rich and beautiful wife from a blue-blood Belle Meade family, and a famous attorney father who had been the number-one protégé of the great Seth Walker. Among his many good fortunes of birth, the junior Hooker had inherited a rare nimbleness of mind and mouth. A lot of people had better brains than Hooker and some more facile tongues, but seldom both. Hooker had yet to meet any perceived equals, so his confidence was unbounded.

When Silliman Evans, Jr., died, his mother, Lucille, had considered her younger son, Amon, too immature and liberal to succeed him as publisher, an assessment shared by the newspaper's lawyers and some members of its board of trustees. But Hooker, who had witnessed Jack Norman's rise to power as Silliman Sr.'s lawyer, could see a law practice of his own built around the *Tennessean*. So in the bold, carefree style that would become his trademark, he assumed on behalf of Amon an unlikely—and for most people impossible—role as the son's emissary to his mother.

Lucille Evans was a sinewy, rawboned Texan with a mean temper. Back when Jack Norman was her husband's attorney he had once delivered the old publisher home from an extended, alcohol-soaked trip to New York bearing a peace offering for his wife, a ten-thousand-dollar Tiffany diamond bracelet, which she promptly hurled out the window into the yard.

She proved a hard sell for Hooker, but he was persistent, haranguing her night after night in long kitchen-table conversations. Mrs. Evans was a chain-smoker; a four-packs-a-day man himself, Hooker matched her puff for puff. From it all finally came a strange, smoke-drenched agreement to install Amon as publisher, but only after a psychiatric examination by Hooker's own personal analyst showed that young Evans was indeed mature and stable enough to run the newspaper.

Doubt as to the accuracy of that doctor's conclusion was sufficient enough to cause the resignation of Mrs. Evans' most powerful board of trustees member, and ultimately also caused the departure of the gold-plated law firm of Bass, Berry and Sims, with which Mrs. Evans had earlier replaced Jack Norman. However, the new publisher did not have to look far for a new lawyer; young Hooker had already formed a new firm expressly for that purpose.

When he had maneuvered his way into a secure business relationship, Hooker instantly undertook a second mission, convincing Amon and his mother that Seigenthaler should be lured back from the Kennedy Justice Department to be the *Tennessean*'s new editor. Seigenthaler, who had been Mrs. Evans' late husband's protégé, was then thirty-six. Mrs. Evans considered him too young, too liberal, and—most important—too close to the Kennedys for the job. At one point, she told Hooker she feared both Seigenthaler and the Kennedys might be communists. But Hooker convinced Amon that if his mother prevailed in the selection of his first editor the full power of the publisher's job would never be his. Amon hired Seigenthaler.

Already streetwise and tough, Seigenthaler had been polished by a year as a Nieman Fellow at Harvard and steeled by the daily mental combat that came from constant association with the iron-willed Bobby Kennedy. He returned home, bearing not only the Kennedys' clout but their passion for politics, commitment to cause, and—as Tennesseans would soon learn—the same willingness to seize and exercise power in pursuit of both.

Under his hand the *Tennessean* would become the dominant power in Tennessee politics and Hooker its most flamboyant and charismatic player. For them, Metropolitan government was only the first battle in a decade-long newspaper and political war against the *Banner* and the remnants of the old Crump machine. The resulting fight would make previous struggles look like an Easter Sunday egg hunt at the Colemere Club.

Couched in principle, defined by the searing issue of race, and fought by some of the most prominent and colorful characters on the national scene, the war wrecked lives, ruined reputations, and left political carnage piled high in its wake. And never did the vanquished go down more stubbornly or count up more quickly than in 1962.

Jimmy Stahlman's *Banner* and the Nashville conservatives dug in against the idea of consolidated government as if preparing for Sherman's march to the sea. Metro was nothing more than a "political trick," the *Banner* assured their readers, "a false panacea" for urban ills. Joining them were the Ku Klux Klan and the John Birch Society, which saw Metro as a plot by desegregationists and foreign communists, whom they found indistinguishable.

The battle against integration, resistance to reapportionment, and the fight against Metro became a common political boundary separating city from county, black from white, communist from American, and the proven goodness of the past from the certain evil of the future.

In the trench with the past, in the most uncomfortable and incongruous political contortion of his life, was little bow-tied Ben West, the most progressive white politician in Nashville's history, who had done the most for its black citizens. But at this point, even a trench full of bigots provided the mayor with a badly needed refuge.

Desperate for revenue with which to finance urban services, West had pushed through the city council a ten-dollar wheel tax on any automobile using city streets. What's more, he had made the windshield tax sticker green, the color of money. It was a colossal political misstep, worse than annexation because it reached across all the suburbs. The *Tennessean* immediately seized on taxation without representation as the club with which to whip up voter sentiment for approval of the Metro charter. Relentlessly the newspaper flogged the mayor with acid editorial criticism and devastating political cartoons about the "Ten for Ben" green sticker, as if having decided to celebrate each day of its 150th anniversary year by extracting a new chunk of West's political hide.

West fought back the only way he knew how—with a small army of city ward heelers and precinct bosses, many of them disciples of Hilary Howse and Jake Sheridan whose election success had depended entirely on bribing or frightening voters and on outright vote fraud.

Ironically but predictably, opposition to consolidated government ended up concentrated in a few inner-city wards among the deprived, crowded, oppressed, and underrepresented poor black and white neighborhoods—the very Nashvillians whose plight was most likely to be improved by a new, more modern, and more powerful urban government.

The city's two elected black leaders took different roads. Courted by Jim Roberson and the *Tennessean*, Z. Alexander Looby broke with

Mayor West and went for Metro, taking many of the city's best-educated blacks and civil rights leaders with him. This gave the pro-Metro forces an important black voting base inside the city limits.

Robert Lillard, who was mainly a criminal lawyer, stayed with Mayor West, as did some of his more prominent clients. Black bootleggers and gambler Henry "Good Jelly" Jones remained West's political leaders in the black neighborhoods of North Nashville. And ten years after the *Tennessean* had photographed the "notorious ex-convict" hauling carloads of blacks to the courthouse to register to vote for Ben West's candidate to succeed Garner Robinson as sheriff, the newspaper photographed his car again, this time virtually covered with "No Metro" stickers and filled with anti-Metro voters.

The biggest anti-Metro vote came from the city's Second Ward, which stretched along the Cumberland River south of the courthouse and public square. Once the city's university area and long gone to seed, it had been for years the stronghold of a maverick city councilman named Charlie Riley. Tall, lean, and handsome in his youth, Riley had gained a reputation during Prohibition as the city's most prosperous and best-dressed bootlegger. When liquor again became legal, he pushed through a city ordinance giving councilmen the licensing approval to site liquor stores in their districts—a perk that kept him in chewing tobacco and whiskey for years to come.

By 1962 Riley himself had gone to seed. A bent, toothless, gallus-snapping old scalawag, he had retired to his rocking chair and had turned his ward over to a hand-picked successor, a grinning, moon-faced one-time sheriff's deputy from Chattanooga named Eugene Jacobs. Running in the council election to succeed Riley against an opponent of equal reputation and stature, Jacobs had managed to get a backhanded endorsement from the Briley organization, from the Hardware Store Honey Bee himself, that would brand Jacobs for life. When asked whom he was for in the council race, Briley's man H. E. Flippen said he figured Jacobs was "the lesser of two evils." And on the day Jacobs won the election, Riley, thumbs hooked in his suspenders, claimed he would still call the shots in his old ward.

"After the votes are in tonight, I'll go to the party and I'll say, 'Come sit on my knee, Little Evil,' and I'll tell him what to do."

From that day on, Jacobs, a tavern owner and junk furniture dealer, was known as "Little Evil," a nickname he spent a lot of his time trying to live up to. He sided with West on the Metro referendum, rivaling Stahlman and the *Banner* for the role of most vocal Metro opponent. Jacobs' South Side neighborhood was plastered with signs and placards that warned that "Russia Has One Government" and "Castro Has Metro."

Jones, Jacobs, and the other West bosses delivered a credible 55 percent of the city vote against the charter. But turnout was small, less than 35 percent. Roberson's combined county forces, meanwhile, turned out the vote in greater numbers, with a 72 percent landslide from the newly annexed suburbs.

The Metro election was a disastrous personal defeat for Ben West, whose term expired the following year. He would never win another election. The county machine had done him in. He'd lost the mayor's office the same way he'd gotten it eleven years before when Garner and the county machine turned on the incumbent Tom Cummings. By turning on West and abandoning their opposition to Metro, the Robinsons had handed the mayor's office to Beverly Briley. Through Cousin Jimmy, they had launched another generation, forged a new progressive black-white voting coalition, and joined the new urban era of Nashville politics.

Urban reformers maybe, but less than two months later the ghosts of the old Robinson allies, Boss Crump and Jake Sheridan, would again rise on the political landscape of Nashville in what would become known as the great vote fraud scandal of 1962.

A Little Evil

Nashville's famed Hermitage congressional district seat had been filled by the likes of Andrew Jackson and Sam Houston. So it was no wonder that both the city and state were embarrassed in 1939 when the incumbent representative Joe Byrns called the visiting King George VI and Queen Elizabeth "a couple of flat tires." The next year the voters tossed Byrns out of office and replaced him with the distinguished J. Percy Priest in what for years was regarded as the meanest, hardest-fought election in the history of the district. In 1962, they finally had a meaner one.

It was Priest's death that necessitated the special executive committee election in 1956 that put J. Carlton Loser in office. Six years later, nearing age seventy, Loser looked so unbeatable that the high-flying winners of the battle over Metro government didn't even bother to challenge him with a candidate they believed could win.

When Thomas H. Shriver, Jr., the son of a respected judge, wanted to test Loser in the Democratic party primary, he was told by the Briley faction to forget it. Their candidate would be a sacrificial lamb, State Senator Richard Fulton, who had already lost two bids for the seat and would surely be beaten a third time. About all he had going for him was the support of organized labor.

Loser had recorded enough antilabor votes to be included on the list of targets that Teamster president James R. Hoffa had said should be purged in the 1962 elections. But Loser picked the city's fastest-rising political and legal star, Z. T. "Tommy" Osborn, as his campaign manager. With Osborn's name atop his campaign, Loser ran harder against Teamster boss Hoffa than against Fulton, charging that the Teamsters and other unions were financing the challenge against him. But in truth Loser did not believe he'd have to run hard at all. He was on the same ballot with incumbent governor Frank Clement, who was a heavy favorite to win nomination for his third term. So Loser shook a few hands, made a few campaign speeches, and depended on his incumbency and the West city machine to get him nominated.

The *Tennessean* was supporting Fulton, as it had in 1960, but luke-warmly and as much out of dislike for Loser as anything else. The newspaper had opposed the congressman ever since 1947, when his brother Buck had been accused of misusing absentee ballots while trying to unseat Mayor Tom Cummings. To the newspaper's new young leaders, Loser, like Mayor West and Governor Clement, was simply another holdover from the days of Boss Crump and Jake Sheridan. Besides, all three had the support of Jimmy Stahlman and the *Banner*, which in itself was enough to disqualify them from public office. They were the old politics.

On election night, Clement won handily as expected, but Loser ran into trouble from the start, seesawing back and forth with Fulton, who showed surprising strength all over the district. When the voting machine count was completed, Fulton had an 80-vote lead. But there were 310 absentee ballots still uncounted, all from a single ward in the city—the one controlled by old Charlie Riley and Eugene "Little Evil" Jacobs.

This set off alarm bells in the city room of the *Tennessean*, where the institutional memory was engraved with the history of local election fraud. Every new reporter had heard how Ben West had won by twenty-seven votes and how Carlton Loser had won office on Tommy Osborn's single contested proxy vote. They knew also that Gene "Little Evil" Jacobs had been a member of that 1956 party executive committee and had cast a vote for Loser that day, too.

Gene was clearly a Loser man. That an unusual number of absentee ballots was being reported in his ward surprised no one. The *Tennessean* had figured as much and had been working on the story for more than a week.

In mid-July, a fierce young reporter named Bill Kovach, successor to the feared Halberstam who had just left for the *New York Times*, was patrolling a courthouse hallway outside the first-floor office of the county election commission when he saw a familiar sight—Little Evil.

As a city councilman and party committeeman, Jacobs had become a fixture in the lobby of the courthouse, hands in his pockets, bowling-ball beer belly lopping over his belt, his face a wad of raw red hamburger under a white straw Panama. The trademark hat, of which there were two—the larger one for special occasions—was always pushed far back on Jacobs' head, baring a large expanse of both nonchalance and sweaty bald head. Little Evil was nothing if not laid back. On this day, his thin summer sport coat bulged with what Kovach figured was most likely a bottle or a pistol, both of which Jacobs had brandished in the halls at one time or another.

Infectiously friendly, Jacobs knew Kovach and greeted him with a snaggletoothed grin.

"Whaddaya got in your coat, Gene?"

"Primary ballots," said Little Evil, patting his pockets.

"Ballots? Let me see."

Gene closed one bleary eye, grabbed his coat lapel, and flashed Kovach a peek at his inside breast pocket, which bulged with folded papers.

"Yeah, absentee ballots. For the primary, you know. For my people."

Gene patted the pocket closed. "Right here . . . is what's gonna beat your boy Dickie Fulton."

At the time Kovach did not figure the Loser-Fulton race to be close enough to be affected by a few absentee ballots. He thought that wily old Gene had just mentioned it as a diversionary tactic. Everyone knew that Jacobs was a big Clement man and that his daughter, Shirley, was running for a spot on the ward Democratic committee. Gene had bragged about "going whole hog" to get her enough votes to be vice-chairwoman.

What the councilman had in his pocket were actually applications for absentee ballots, which he planned to hand out in his ward. And there was nothing wrong with his having them. By law, the ballots themselves would be mailed to the applicants. Absentee voting was a regular feature of machine politics. Anyone could apply for a ballot. All they needed to say was that they planned to be out of town on Election Day, or were physically unable to go vote. As a result, councilmen and ward heelers always took the ballot applications to disabled voters and nursing home residents, anywhere they could get a sure vote for their candidates. The ballots were then notarized and returned to the election commission, where they were traditionally the last to be counted and seldom affected the election.

But when Kovach asked the election commission later in the day how many ballot applications Jacobs had requested, the answer was astounding. He had already gotten 218, compared with 194 for the rest of the entire county. Then Kovach checked the absentee ballot totals from the ward in previous elections. In each case, the numbers amounted to a third or a half of all absentees cast.

By election night, *Tennessean* reporters had already interviewed some of the Second Ward residents whose names had appeared on the list of those requesting ballots. At least two said they had not asked to vote absentee, but that Jacobs had come by with the ballots and personally marked and notarized them himself in their presence.

Little Evil's ballot perversion was centered in a once white and prosperous South Nashville neighborhood that was now a foul-smelling, firetrap shantytown for poor and mostly illiterate blacks. Frail, thin, well into her seventies, Hattie Morton, with her high school education, was an exception.

As her old chow dog thumped his tail rhythmically on the porch, Hattie kept time with her foot and shook her head ruefully as she served up the goods on Little Evil to the newspaper reporters.

"Their man came around to vote us for Mr. Jacobs' and Mr. Riley's side," she said. "We just signed our names . . . they did the marking for us."

Another woman told of watching Jacobs mark and notarize ballots in mass, most of them brought to him by black residents of his ward, many unable to read or write. One of them, Joe Henry Goodall, who didn't know any better, confessed that he had voted twice, once by absentee and once in person—both times for Loser, at Jacobs' request.

But not all the Second Ward residents whose names were on the ballot could be interviewed. By election night, the *Tennessean* knew that at least two neighbors of Hattie Morton's for whom Jacobs had requested absentee votes were dead. One had died a month before the election. The other had been dead for a year and a half.

It was the Hopewell box all over again. But this time, the *Tennessean* had some evidence. Twenty-four hours after the election, its reporters confirmed that the votes of the two dead men were among those still to be counted.

"2nd Ward Dead Men Vote," the newspaper announced. The scandal was on.

For once Garner Robinson and Dave White were in the clear. An election fraud had occurred that they'd had nothing to do with—a good fortune celebrated by their exchange of smug smiles in their ritualistic courthouse hallway meeting on the morning after.

The Friday after the vote found Dave with a huge silver flashlight in one hand and the other tucked in the pocket of his uniform, sauntering up to the trustee's office to enjoy the fruits of good judgment. It was nice to see the shoe heavy and tight on somebody else's foot for a change.

Garner and Dave were grandfathers now, with thinning hair and thickening middles. But in their minds they were still the lithe young lady-killers from the streets of Old Hickory. At age fifty-eight, Dave still sparkled and shined, now in the blue uniform of the sheriff's patrol, with a lieutenant's gold braid running up his sleeve. But his limp was more pronounced, gray sideburns glistened on his cheeks, and a slight paunch was finally beginning to show under his blue patrol jacket. Garner's uniform remained that of the impeccable funeral director—starched white shirt and keenly pressed suit. To these two old pals, the relentless advance of age was no more than a standing joke.

"Oh Dave, it's you," Garner said, in mock surprise. "I was wondering who that old man was hobbling down the hall."

To which Dave replied, "Well, you old sonofabitch, you're so goddamn fat I thought you were two people talking to each other."

Their talk quickly turned to politics. Whispering as if guarding some secret from a hallway with ears, Dave mentioned as to how he guessed "the shit has hit the fan now in the Second Ward."

Garner's face remained a funeral mask. "I don't understand people doing things like that, do you?"

Their burst of laughter echoed along the cavernous marble hallway like a volley of shots. Never in their wildest dreams could they fathom vote stealing.

Dave recovered to whisper again. According to his connections in the election commission, he said, the phony absentee balloting had been confined to the single city ward of Gene Jacobs. "Everybody else kept their nose clean."

Garner smiled his approval. He grabbed Dave at the elbow and ushered him down the hall, as if to move out of earshot, only to say something everyone already knew.

"Gene Jacobs has always been a stupid asshole. He did this to himself. He was showing his ballot applications to the *Tennessean* reporters and everybody else and braggin' about 'em. Remember fifty-six? Sorry sonofabitch sent me a telegram in fifty-six congratulating me on losing, remember?"

"When you lost to Tom B. Cartwright."

"Right. Only election I ever lost. And Gene sends me a goddamn telegram of congratulations. When I jumped him about it later, he said it was the worst thing he'd ever done. That he was sorrier about it than anything he'd ever done in politics."

"Until yesterday."

"They ought to put the sonofabitch in jail."

"They will. Sillyman's boys will see to it."

"Yeah. I ought to send him a goddamn telegram telling him 'bye."

As titular head of Loser's campaign, Tom Osborn was stunned and embarrassed by the accusations. What's worse, he was in a position to do something about them.

Just as the Hopewell box theft had seventeen years earlier, the disputed Loser-Fulton race fell into the lap of a machine-controlled election authority that included lawyer Earl McNabb, who was in the firm with Jack Norman and Garner's son, Gale; and Harris Gilbert, who had been Tommy Osborn's cocounsel in *Baker v. Carr*. For members of the old Robinson-Sheridan machine, keeping their noses clean suddenly seemed impossible.

The *Tennessean* went after Loser with teeth bared, its reporters confirming direct telephone communications between him and Jacobs only hours after the scandal broke. The *Banner* and the West crowd defended Loser, accusing the *Tennessean* of blowing the voting irregularities out of proportion in order to cloud Fulton's obvious defeat. Osborn, along with his impeccable reputation and his political aspirations, was caught in the middle, even though he'd had nothing to do with the controversy. As the heat from it rose, he vaporized, avoiding both Loser and his friends on the Democratic primary board. Neither ever heard from him. It was a wise decision.

Counting the absentee votes became a three-ring circus. Attorneys for Fulton pressed the primary board to throw them all out, while Loser's backers urged that they be counted. Organized labor sent crowds of Fulton supporters to demonstrate outside the city council chamber where the board was meeting. And Jacobs brought in carloads of Second Ward residents to counter them.

Under pressure from the *Tennessean*, both the local district attorney and the federal prosecutor announced investigations into the apparent vote fraud. Most of the witnesses had already given sworn statements to the newspaper's reporters and lawyers, and as they waited to be interviewed by official investigators they were openly lobbied and coached by Jacobs, who basked in the spotlight. "I'm Big Evil now," he boasted.

The primary board had no idea what to do. Secretly, McNabb took the problem to his law partner, Jack Norman, who was now head of the state Democratic party. Norman took the problem to the election lawyer—Elkin Garfinkle.

In 1946, Garfinkle had derailed the investigation of Lewis Hurt and Dave White's shenanigans with his insight into the election laws. Ten years later he had formulated the back-room strategy that legitimized Osborn's executive committee proxy vote. And now in 1962, still hidden from the eyes and ears of the inquiring *Tennessean*, Garfinkle assumed the role of judge and decided this case in typical fashion. The county primary board had no legal right to throw out the ballots, Garfinkle declared. In fact, the board should do nothing, which is exactly what its leaders wanted to do. Under Garfinkle's reading of the election laws, a challenge to any ballot had to be undertaken at the precinct level by the appointed precinct election officers. This, of course, was how Jake Sheridan had always wanted it.

The counting process moved back to the neighborhoods where the ballots had originated, into dingy school basements and cramped closet-size fire halls so tight that the sweat off the forehead of one combatant would fly into the face of another.

At one point, over a disputed ballot, Jacobs cocked his fist and threatened to bust Fulton's feisty lawyer, George Barrett, in the teeth, while Jacobs' mentor Charlie Riley could be overheard urging black residents of the Second Ward to "take a gun and shoot through the door at those newspaper people" who were harassing them. The dispute raged for eight days, at least one of them so long that a precinct official slept all night in the hallway, his ballot box cradled in his arms. Ultimately most of Jacobs' absentee ballots were counted—223 for Loser and only 17 for Fulton, wiping out the challenger's lead and giving Loser a 72-vote victory in the election.

But with McNabb and Gilbert on the primary board and Norman and Garfinkle calling the shots, there was no way to avoid the appearance of a coverup. Norman and Garfinkle were adamant in their contention that Loser had legitimately won the nomination, tainted or not. And the congressman was on the verge of accepting it when the rug was pulled out from under him.

In a front-page editorial, the *Banner*'s Jimmy Stahlman said no. A man of Loser's character and integrity didn't need a nomination under such a cloud, the *Banner* publisher wrote. He should decline it and meet Fulton in the general election on level ground.

Not even the *Tennessean* could disagree. The rematch was no contest. Fulton beat Loser handily and headed off to Congress for fourteen years. Little Evil headed off to the state penitentiary for a minimum of one.

"Just a little vacation," he said. "I'll be back."

Nashville hoped not, stated the *Tennessean*. "Nashville . . . wants no more of Mr. Jacobs. He is a political stereotype from the past. He is out of place in Nashville's contemporary political life. He has taken advantage of the poor people of his ward who need and deserve honest political leadership. The community has put up with Mr. Jacobs long enough. Now, for good reason, it wants done with him in the decent counsels of a progressive city."

Lost in the sound and fury of the Second Ward scandal was yet another sign that the old ways of Tennessee politics were yielding to the new. On the same night that machine man Little Evil had failed to steal an election in the second ward of the state's second-largest urban area, the leader of the rural forces in the legislature, the most powerful member of the Unholy Triumvirate, pistol-packing Pete Haynes of rural Lawrenceburg, was defeated in his bid for reelection.

Reform, it seemed, was on a roll.

PART SEVEN

Camelot

The *Webster's New World Dictionary* I bought while a part-time, nineteen-year-old college freshman in 1962 defined "Camelot" as "any time or place idealized as having excitement, purpose and a high level of culture . . . as in the town of Arthurian legend where the king had his court." Soon that definition would include the administration of President John F. Kennedy, with whom the country was having a breathless romance. To the bug-eyed, wet-behind-the-ears reporters who spent the Kennedy years at the Nashville *Tennessean*, nothing could have been more like Camelot than our own newsroom—except for the part about "the high level of culture."

The newsroom itself was a pigsty of scarred old metal desks strewn with paper and clusters of half-filled coffee cups floating cigarette butts and other indistinguishable lumps, sitting around on the desks like so many putrid little ponds. Here and there a big green trash can overflowed with snarls of old typewriter ribbon and wadded copy paper. One back corner had become a junkyard of maimed and invalid chairs; in another, the huge world map on the wall was so close to the back row of desks that its equator was clearly denoted by fist-sized black smudges from the hair grease of reporters who'd leaned against it.

The air in the place was so heavy it formed a low ceiling and so stale you could bleed from breathing. But the room's spirit was pristine and our vision crystal clear. The country was reaching for the moon then, and so was the newspaper's new editor, John Seigenthaler, home from Washington in his button-down Harvard shirts and pinstriped suits. He was our King Arthur, and we were his knights in polyester pants, five-dollar neckties, and a couple of J.C. Penney sport coats we shared. "I'm taking the coat" was an often-heard announcement indicating that one of us had an out-of-office assignment.

Of the reporters, only my granddaddy's friend and my benefactor, Wayne Whitt, who had been around since Jake Sheridan and was also a stringer for *Time* magazine, could afford more than one suit.

A few of the reporters were pedigreed Vanderbilt University students, but as a group we were—with the exception of the erudite Halberstam, who had just gone back east—a band of peasants, largely incapable of distinguishing a high level of culture even if one was encountered.

Excitement and purpose on the other hand were ours in abundance. My job was still brand-new when the Second Ward scandal broke. My first few days of work had been spent retrieving clippings from the newspaper's morgue, which I had ascribed to some morbid connection with having grown up around Phillips-Robinson. Then it got even more gruesome. Without warning, I was ordered to accompany a team of reporters into Little Evil's South Nashville neighborhood in search of bogus voters.

"You're the morgue man, right? Well, I have just the job for a man of your obvious qualifications, heh, heh," laughed Nathan Caldwell, a shaggy old tree of a man who was the newspaper's Pulitzer Prize–winning investigative reporter and the main writer on the story. "Unless of course you're afraid of the dead, heh, heh." He handed me a flashlight.

My stated mission was to check the gravestones in a shabby Second Ward cemetery for the names of the two dead men believed to have voted by absentee ballot in the congressional primary. But in truth, another husky youth named Jerry Thompson, the weekend police reporter, and I had been sent along for no other reason than to swell the ranks of the Vandy students with two big local kids who'd had a street fight or two.

It was a good idea. We hadn't been in South Nashville long when a car stopped beside us and disgorged four of the toughest-looking men any of us had ever seen.

Assuming the worst, a nervous photographer among us was going for his gun when I recognized the leader of our suspected assailants, a man with the size and demeanor of a refrigerator. It was Corky Ellis, friend and sometime bodyguard of a local Teamsters union tough guy named Don Vestal, who had been a source for Seigenthaler's *Tennessean* stories on labor violence. I had grown up with Vestal's sons and had once taken an ill-fated joyride in a purloined Cadillac with his youngest.

Seigenthaler, it turned out, did not believe in safety in numbers alone. Corky and his friends had been dispatched by the Teamster leader at Seigenthaler's request to protect the *Tennessean*'s boy reporters from Little Evil's gun-packing goons. Seigenthaler had realized what we had not—that we were searching for the evidence that would eventually put the ward heeler in prison. It was the first thing any of us had ever done important enough to warrant protection, especially on the orders of the man who was by all accounts best friends with the attorney general of the United States. Later that same year, as one of the newspaper's few researchers, I would be summoned to Seigenthaler's office, given a list of names, and told to check their backgrounds, using every technique possible short of directly contacting them or any member of their families. The list turned out to be the names of a panel of prospective federal court jurors in the Nashville trial of James R. Hoffa, then president of the International Brotherhood of Teamsters and the sworn enemy of Robert Kennedy.

The sense of purpose clings to the young from such high-minded pursuits, and I was covered forever with its residue, as Seigenthaler undoubtedly had been when Kennedy sent him to Alabama to protect the Freedom Riders. For him and the other white southerners it was the civil war of their time, a mission to free black Americans, the modern American city, and the political process itself from the imprisoning inertia of the last hundred years.

As a young man I would tag along with Seigenthaler as I had tagged after Dave White as a boy, learning the lessons of Kennedy politics the way I had learned those of the Robinsons—by being there, in both cases as a kind of appendage to someone they considered family. There I was, Billye's boy from East Nashville, lolling around the pool at Hickory Hill with Ethel and the children, sitting in Chicago convention strategy sessions with Kenny O'Donnell, Larry O'Brien, and Kennedy brother-in-law Steve Smith. When Seigenthaler was given William Manchester's controversial manuscript *The Death of a President* to review for the Kennedy family, he gave it to me to copy edit. When the eminent historian Arthur Schlesinger asked him for help in compiling his own recollections of the Kennedy White House, *A Thousand Days*, I got the editing job. When John J. Hooker, Jr., took on the task of raising money for the Kennedy Library in Boston, I was paid to compile and write the press releases.

So however ordinary and camouflaged the Kennedys' Camelot might appear to others in the cynical hindsight of history, it was indeed in those exciting, romantic days of 1962—from the perspective of the *Tennessean* newsroom— quite simply the quest for the Holy Grail.

Seigenthaler, his crusading publisher, the Evans family

lawyer Hooker, and their army of ragtag kid journalists were on a mission, a steamroll for right, justice, and a better America. Or so it seemed to us at the time—and undoubtedly to those who got in our way.

A Jockey for Gallahadion

If there was anyone in Nashville who looked liked he belonged in Camelot, it was attorney Tommy Osborn. He was a tall, grand-looking man with sandy hair, an easy, affable manner, a quick smile, and kind, laughing eyes. On Osborn, horn-rimmed glasses looked debonair, the way a mustache did on Clark Gable. He could have been a model for intelligence gracing the cover of *Fortune* magazine or the *Harvard Business Review*.

Yet he was completely unpretentious, the kind of man who would represent the son of his barber for free, or bring a class action suit on behalf of uninsured fire victims. Befriending an elevator operator in his office building or addressing a jury, Tommy Osborn radiated honesty and sincerity. Around the courthouse, they all said that Tommy Osborn could talk a vine out of climbing a wall. And they were beginning to speak of him in the same breath as the legendary Seth Walker.

But unlike Walker, who was a man of both wealth and social standing, Osborn had been a nobody, the son of a poor itinerant Kentucky preacher, a night-school lawyer who had worked his way through the lightly regarded Nashville YMCA Law School. Young lawyers knew Nashville as a "son-in-law town" where the best jobs in the best firms were reserved for the Vanderbilt graduates who married the daughters of senior partners or rich clients. Osborn's wife, Dottie, was charming, but she was from Oklahoma and without local connections. As a result his road to prominence had been full of potholes. After passing the bar at age twenty-one, Osborn had hung out his shingle in Old Hickory, where he did various jobs for the Robinsons and got divorces for Dave White's wives. After the war he joined a law firm that was friendly with U.S. Senator K. D. McKellar, an associate of Boss Crump. That had led to an appointment as an assistant U.S. attorney, a political debt he had repaid by working for McKellar in his losing 1948 campaign. Then the Old Hickory and Crump connections led him to Jake Sheridan and Elkin Garfinkle, who recruited him for Ben West.

After leaving West's administration to return to the courtroom, Osborn had caught the eye of Jack Norman, who had worshiped and emulated Seth Walker. Because Norman thought Osborn was made of the same stuff, he became Osborn's sponsor in the Democratic party. Meanwhile, through Garfinkle, Osborn had maintained his contacts with the Robinsons, and among those who shared his breakfast table everyday at Stumb's, a tiny eatery in the building where he and Garfinkle had law offices, were Garner's daughter Maude and her cousin Jim Roberson, who was rapidly assuming Jake's role as a strategist and spokesman for the family.

The law firms Osborn had passed through had been small and obscure. His income had been modest. But by the spring of 1962 none of that mattered. He had overcome every obstacle. With a combination of style and talent, he had become the city's most celebrated lawyer.

Osborn had doggedly pursued his beloved *Baker v. Carr* reapportionment case since 1955. Hardly a morning passed that he did not bounce his latest court strategy off his legal mentor Garfinkle. The old man with the bushy eyebrows and the photographic mind didn't particularly like the idea of reapportionment. He and Jake had never found the rural domination of the legislature much of an impediment to political success. But he was fascinated with the constitutional underpinnings of the case and wanted to see Tommy Osborn get it to the U.S. Supreme Court.

Finally, Osborn did. And on March 26, 1962, all his work paid off. The Court agreed with Osborn that federal courts had the right to intervene in state reapportionment cases. Further, the Court mandated that the test should be a one-man, one-vote principle, assuring urban residents their first equitable representation in state government.

In his maiden appearance before the high court in the spring of 1961 and at an unusual rehearing the following October, Osborn had made short but impressive arguments, but the end result was more a tribute to Osborn's political acumen than his legal talent. Like Seth Walker, Tommy Osborn had at every turn made a new and lasting political connection. In his pursuit of *Baker v. Carr*, he employed them all.

To get the case before the Supreme Court to begin with, Osborn had gotten Mayor West and the city of Nashville aboard as a plaintiff. West had helped him acquire as cocounsel a famous municipal lawyer named Charles Rhyne, who had been a law school classmate of Richard Nixon's and a friend of the Eisenhower administration.

But in the middle of his case, Nixon lost to John Kennedy, whose election created an entirely new political atmosphere for the high court. Fortunately for Osborn, it had also created a new group of political brokers in Tennessee, chief among them Nashvillians John Seigenthaler and John J. Hooker, Jr., and one of Hooker's law school classmates, E. William Henry, a Memphis native whose law firm had helped Osborn in *Baker v. Carr*.

All three had worked in Kennedy's campaign, and two of them had accepted jobs in the new administration, Seigenthaler as Bobby Kennedy's administrative assistant, and Henry as the new chairman of the Federal Communications Commission. These were the kind of personal friendships and cross-relationships that made the American system work. And they were what made law in *Baker v. Carr*.

As the administrations changed in Washington, Osborn brought his lawsuit to the attention of Hooker and Henry. A month after the new president's inauguration, Seigenthaler arranged for Osborn and cocounsel Harris Gilbert to meet with Attorney General Kennedy. They trooped through a heavy snow in Washington only to have U.N. ambassador Averell Harriman usurp their appointment at the last minute. They were shunted off to Kennedy's deputy, Byron

"Whizzer" White, who had only ten minutes and one question: "What does this case mean to the Negroes?" Osborn's answer was, "Everything." Without reapportionment, blacks would never realize their voting power. Their birthright to equality would be denied. White sent them to see the new solicitor general of the United States, Archibald Cox, alongside whom Hooker had worked in the 1960 Kennedy presidential campaign. The irrepressible Hooker had come along with them, in his pocket a copy of JFK's "Shame of the Cities" campaign speech, which eloquently made the case that urban residents were underrepresented. Hooker put his feet up on Cox's desk and waved the speech at him. "Archie, you've got to get in this case. This will put you in the history books." Cox already knew the case better than Hooker did—as well as its political implications.

Not long after that, at Seigenthaler's urging and ultimately Bobby Kennedy's direction, the Justice Department entered the *Baker v. Carr* case as a friend of the court, a third party with special interest in the reapportionment of state legislatures. Thus, when the case was finally heard, the weight of Osborn's argument was supported by two nationally known lawyers—conservative Republican Charles Rhyne, an expert on city law who had the respect of the Eisenhower Republicans on the court, and by the liberal Democrat Archibald Cox, representing the new president of the United States. Chief Justice Earl Warren later termed the one-man, one-vote case the most important to ever come before his court, more far-reaching than even the court's 1954 school desegregation decision.

Osborn's Supreme Court triumph sent his star shooting high in the sky over his hometown. At forty-two, he became the new darling of local politics, one of the few people in town welcome at both newspapers and in both political factions.

His renewed association with Ben West and his friendship with Jack Norman assured him of the good graces of the city machine and Jimmy Stahlman's afternoon *Banner*. But through his new relationship with Hooker and Seigenthaler and his image as a bona-fide reformer, Osborn now had friends at the *Tennessean* and in Washington as well.

As Garner Robinson had done with the issue of consolidated government, Tommy Osborn had ridden the reform issue of reapportionment out of the Boss Crump era of machine politics and into the New Frontier of the urban revolution. No one was better connected—or more sought after.

When Osborn agreed to manage the reelection campaign of the incumbent congressman J. Carlton Loser shortly after the Supreme Court decision had been handed down, it was taken as a sign that politics was as much of his future as the law. Loser was sixty-nine and had told friends that the 1962 election would be his last. Always attracted to public office, Osborn had announced his candidacy for the state senate in 1954 but had withdrawn before the primary. Now he was seen as the man most likely to inherit Loser's support from the *Banner*, Mayor West, the Robinsons, and Governor Frank Clement. And he stood a good chance as well of getting the support of Judge Briley and the *Tennessean*.

One warm, sticky morning in early July, Osborn came into Stumb's, cool and comfortable in a gleaming white shirt and a perfectly tailored suit of light tan linen. His breakfast buddies, among them a blonde who thought him as "cute as socks on a rooster" and an admiring politician who found him supremely confident, apparently capable of conquering even the city's terrible humidity, mentioned to Osborn that he was looking like the perfect man to run for office and perhaps unite the local Democratic party for the first time in decades. Not a chance, Osborn told them. At this point in his life he was not interested in public office. To the contrary: he had promised his new law partners at Denney and Leftwich that his future was in the courtroom, not in the political arena.

He wanted a lifetime of legal challenges like *Baker v. Carr*, he said, and compared his role in the case to that of a jockey named Bierman who won the 1940 Kentucky Derby on Gallahadion, a hundred-to-one shot. "That's what I want to be," he said. "The jockey on Gallahadion."

While the Loser campaign was sinking in the vote-fraud scandal, Osborn was out of town accepting enrollment in the American College of Trial Lawyers, one of the highest honors in American jurisprudence, with membership limited to 1 percent of the lawyers in any state. He had to be, Osborn repeatedly told his friends and family, "one of the luckiest men in the entire world." But they in turn insisted that Tommy Osborn was just one smart sonofabitch. Everybody turned out to be wrong on both counts.

An Enemy Within

If Tommy Osborn really wanted to ride a long shot like Gallahadion, he picked the right horse in James R. Hoffa.

The New Frontier was clearly not big enough for the arrogant, abrasive boss of the nation's Teamsters union, the man who had campaigned personally against John Kennedy and publicly upbraided Bobby as "a young, dimwitted, curly headed smart aleck." Hoffa's weight with union voters had been credited with tipping Ohio for a grateful Vice President Richard Nixon, who in turn had intervened with the Justice Department to delay a planned indictment of Hoffa in Florida until after the election.

Had Nixon won, Hoffa expected the case to be dropped. But from the minute Kennedy was sworn in, the volatile union leader became the Justice Department's number-one target.

The tangle of personal friendships and resulting political clout that had been employed on the issue of reapportionment was rooted in the issue of Teamster union violence in Tennessee, and the two soon became inextricable, tangled in both the political life of Nashville and the personal life of Tommy Osborn.

The reasons for going after Hoffa and the way best to do it had been the basis for Bobby Kennedy's best-selling book, *The Enemy Within*, documenting for the nation that both Hoffa and the Teamsters union were controlled by organized crime. Written in ten weeks at Kennedy's Virginia home during the summer of 1959 by Kennedy and his Teamster expert from Nashville, John Seigenthaler, the book's publication was timed to coincide with John Kennedy's campaign. Such timely meshing of moral crusade and personal agenda was one of the most potent and often-employed of the Kennedy political weapons and the one used regularly against Hoffa.

Much of the information in the book had been gathered during a Senate investigation of Teamster activities nationwide, which included the bribing of a Tennessee judge who was subsequently impeached. Seigenthaler had reported the story originally, and young John J. Hooker, Jr., had been involved as assistant to the special prosecutor in the impeachment case, Osborn's mentor Jack Norman.

Eventually, the judge's impeachment trial became an important source of information for some widely publicized congressional hearings for which Robert Kennedy was chief counsel. This led to Seigenthaler's friendship with Kennedy and to his being offered a job in the Justice Department.

Among the first acts of the new attorney general was recruitment of a group of young lawyers who became known as "the Hoffa unit." And among the cases the Hoffa unit were trying to build against the burly, hot-tempered union boss was one with a Nashville connection. During the fifties Hoffa and one of his union vice-presidents had collected more than $1 million from a trucking company, Test Fleet Corporation, that they had secretly set up in Nashville, which because of its geographic location had become the trucking center of the Southeast and one of the union's fastest-growing membership areas.

The Nashville case against Hoffa was not a strong one. The crime involved was only a misdemeanor, a violation of the Taft-Hartley Act, which prohibits union officials from receiving payments other than wages from their unions. Conviction carried a penalty of only one year in prison and a ten-thousand-dollar fine. The case was so weak in fact that John J. Hooker, Jr., whom Kennedy had invited to evaluate all potential legal actions against Hoffa, had recommended against bringing it. But Hooker didn't think much of the mail fraud case in Florida either, which had already been dismissed once, or a similar one that could be brought in Chicago. "You won't win any of them," Hooker told Kennedy, to his chagrin.

But Kennedy believed strongly in persistent prosecution of Hoffa on any charge, no matter how insignificant. Three times his slippery enemy had been tried by the federal government, and three times he had gotten off. Each time his main defense tactic had been jury-tampering, most recently and most obviously in his escape from a 1957 New York wiretap indictment. But eventually, Bobby Kennedy knew Hoffa could be caught trying to fix a jury.

Kennedy liked the Nashville case for several reasons. Not only had the evidence first surfaced during the McClellan Senate investigation of labor racketeering, for which he had been chief counsel, it was the kind of case that publicly discredited Hoffa among his peers. Truck drivers don't think much of union leaders who secretly own trucking companies.

This news would be particularly unsettling in Nashville, where the local Teamster leader, a maverick Texan named Don Vestal, had been such a strong Hoffa critic that he had been ousted as president of Local 327 and replaced with a Hoffa loyalist. A bitter factional rivalry had developed between the intelligent, smooth-talking, gangster-tough Vestal, who was trying to start a new local, and a bunch of slow-witted goons still loyal to Hoffa. It was a circumstance the Justice Department's Hoffa unit had already found conducive to gathering intelligence about Hoffa's activities elsewhere. Teamster union dissidents had become the Justice Department's best friends.

Dismissing Hooker's reservations, Kennedy ordered a federal grand jury investigation to proceed in Nashville. James F. Neal, a young Nashvillian and a law school classmate of Hooker's, was placed in charge.

Over all, Nashville looked like what Bobby Kennedy needed—a friendly venue in which to try Jimmy Hoffa. And when Seigenthaler returned in March of 1962 to be editor of the *Tennessean*, it became even more so. Two months later, Hoffa and the Detroit corporation he had used to set up the Nashville trucking concern were indicted in what would become known as the Test Fleet Conspiracy.

Tommy Osborn had a good reason for taking so little interest in the local elections of 1962. Being Carlton Loser's campaign manager was far less exciting than being Jimmy Hoffa's lawyer.

The opportunity to represent Hoffa had dropped into his lap unexpectedly, the natural result of his newly found prominence. Cecil Branstetter, a respected labor lawyer who had been the regular counsel for Teamster Local 327 during Don Vestal's presidency, had been representing Hoffa in pretrial motions. Branstetter was a shrewd cookie and a good politician who had helped County Judge Beverly Briley and the *Tennessean* break Jake Sheridan's hold on the county court in 1956 by managing a group of independent candidates to victory in the court election. But a few weeks after Hoffa's indictment, Branstetter filed a motion with the federal court asking to be allowed to withdraw from the case. Publicly he gave no reason, but privately he was concerned about the behavior and intentions of his client.

Hoffa wanted to replace Branstetter with "the best criminal defense lawyer in Tennessee." Two Nashvillians, both protégés of the great Seth Walker, stood head and shoulders above the rest. One, John J. Hooker, Sr., was out of the question for obvious reasons. The other was the talented, well-connected Jack Norman, who like the elder Hooker brought enormous experience and presence to the courtroom. Hoffa went to see him.

Every bit as tough and smart as Hoffa, Norman disliked the Teamster boss from the start and wanted nothing to do with the case. And he had the perfect excuse. He'd been special prosecutor in the impeachment of the Chattanooga criminal judge who had been bribed by one of Hoffa's union associates. The conviction of the man who had passed the bribe was then pending in federal court before U.S. district judge William E. Miller, who would most likely preside over the Test Fleet case. Claiming an ethical conflict of

interest, Norman declined the job. Hoffa asked if there was anyone
he might recommend.

As he considered the question Norman glanced out the window
of his office. There on Union Street below walked Tommy Osborn.

"Yes," said Norman. "The best young lawyer in Nashville is Z. T.
Osborn, Jr. He has represented the Teamsters in the past I believe."

Osborn was both flattered by Norman's confidence and sympathetic to Hoffa's insistence that he was the victim of Bobby
Kennedy's abuse of government power. Still, he was reluctant to
take the case and postponed a decision until after he'd called his
friend John Hooker, Jr.

"You know what's going on with Kennedy," Osborn said. "What
do you think about me representing Jimmy Hoffa?"

"Don't do it, Tommy," Hooker warned him. "Hoffa will try to fix
that jury and you'll get hurt. It's the wrong thing to do."

"You don't think I'd fix a jury, do you?" Osborn said indignantly.

"No, but he'll do it without you knowing it and you'll get caught
in the middle," Hooker replied.

"But this is such a tremendous professional opportunity," Osborn
argued. "It's the case of a lifetime."

"But it's not just a case," Hooker said. "It's a war."

Hooker heard nothing else from Osborn, but a few days later, as
he was emerging from his regular session with one of the city's most
prominent psychiatrists—the same one who had attested to Amon
Evans' maturity—Hooker saw the doctor's next appointment in the
waiting room. It was Tommy.

On September 5, Hooker read in the *Tennessean* that Osborn had
taken on Hoffa's defense and that as a result Nashville's congressman J. Carlton Loser was naming a new manager for his campaign
rematch with Richard Fulton in the November general election.
The real campaign issue, Loser said, was not the vote fraud scandal
during the primary but the support of Fulton by "Jimmy Hoffa and
others of his ilk."

But Loser went out of his way to praise his departing campaign
manager. His reaction to Osborn's decision was typical of the Nashville establishment. "Mr. Osborn's acceptance of employment by

Mr. Hoffa is in keeping with the highest tradition of the Nashville bar," Loser said, "which has never rejected a client's cause for the fact that it may be unpopular."

Not long afterward, Osborn assembled the Hoffa defense team at his office on Third Avenue. He asked Branstetter, who had been in charge of all pretrial motions, to attend. When Branstetter arrived he found a conference room filled with more than a dozen men. Osborn introduced them as Hoffa friends and associates from around the country who'd come to Nashville to help him with the jury selection process. Among them were some longshoremen from New York and some private detectives from West Virginia. One man Branstetter recognized was a slight, hunched-over former Nashville policeman and part-time Teamster named Robert Vick, whose face reflected long years of hard times. Branstetter knew that Vick had done investigative work for Osborn, that he was a man frequently between steady jobs and always in need of money for groceries and unpaid fuel bills.

When the discussion began, Branstetter was shocked by what he heard. Much of it centered on the names of prospective jurors in the case, with each Hoffa associate reporting on people he knew who knew jurors and how they were to be contacted.

A hatchet-faced man of unfailingly erect posture and unerring integrity, Branstetter was not one to bite his tongue. He called Osborn aside and admonished him on the spot. "I can't believe you-all are talking like this," Branstetter said. Pointing to a fireplace in the center of the room, he said, "Why, I'd lay you odds there is a bug in that fireplace right now. You people better be careful what you say."

The next day Branstetter ran into Osborn on the street and pulled him into a doorway. "What I heard yesterday goes way beyond what I consider appropriate in jury selection, Tommy," he complained. "Besides, the government is bound to bug you on a case like this. You're asking for trouble."

Osborn was defensive. "The government is violating every rule in the book in this case," he said. "They're going all out. Doing anything and everything. We're just fighting fire with fire, that's all."

Branstetter shook his head in dismay. "Well, think about that,

Tommy. Look at all the resources they have. There's no way you'll win that war. Their fire will be considerably bigger than yours."

But Osborn was still awash in the glory of the *Baker v. Carr* decision. No one was more amazed at his own success than Tommy Osborn. He had successfully defended worse people than Jimmy Hoffa, and had been stunned when juries actually returned the not-guilty verdicts for which he'd argued. The case against Hoffa looked to be exactly what his client said it was—a chicken-shit misdemeanor charge brought by a smart-ass rich kid from Massachusetts. Bobby Kennedy was only in his mid-thirties—a man far less experienced in the law than Osborn, yet one now able to swing the weight of the Justice Department simply because his brother happened to be president of the United States. Hoffa, on the other hand, had been a poor boy like himself, who by his own wits and muscle had become the most powerful labor leader in the country, the number-one spokesman in America for the working stiff.

Osborn saw Kennedy as both cunning and ruthless. On a tour of the South after taking office, the new attorney general had stopped in Nashville to pay a visit to Judge Miller, presumably only to get acquainted. But word was that during their chat Kennedy had raised the possibility of vacancies soon arising on the federal appeals court in Cincinnati. And earlier in the year, he had personally telephoned both of Nashville's newspaper publishers to talk about the importance of the Hoffa case and how crucial newspaper coverage was to the conduct of a fair trial. Jimmy Stahlman had thought so little of the gesture that he tape-recorded his conversation with Kennedy and ran the transcript on his front page.

Clearly Kennedy had sent a bunch of tough guys to do the job on Hoffa. Local policemen and FBI agents had told Osborn that Kennedy's taciturn chief investigator, Walter Sheridan, had made it clear that he would do anything to get Hoffa and that they should stay out of the way. And, deserved or not, Sheridan had gained a reputation during the McClellan hearings for intimidating and coaching witnesses and gathering evidence by any means necessary. The legal community was well aware that good old boy Kenneth Harwell, the regular U.S. attorney, had been roughly pushed aside in favor of the toughest and most ambitious of Kennedy's Hoffa unit lawyers, Jim Neal. Only thirty-one years old, Neal was a little powerhouse with a big mind, a permanently puffed chest, and a robust self-esteem to match. In addition, both of the city's newspapers were lined up against Hoffa, the *Banner* because it was supporting antilabor congressman Carlton Loser for reelection, and the *Tennessean* because it was clearly in bed with the Kennedys. Who knew better than Osborn how much clout Seigenthaler wielded in the Justice Department? Neal and Sheridan were Seigenthaler's pals. They were guests in his home. And although Osborn couldn't prove it, he believed Sheridan had bugged his home telephone and that the *Tennessean* offices were being used to interview prosecution witnesses. As far as he could see, the fix was in all over town.

Against such a vast army of resources, Hoffa, for all his power and popularity and despite all his boorish behavior and boasting, was still clearly the victim of a political vendetta. And most important to Osborn, Hoffa was the underdog, a Gallahadion whose slim chances of going home from Nashville a winner depended entirely on lucky Tommy Osborn.

Since his early days in law school, Tommy Osborn had had a recurring dream. In it he stood in front of a huge crowd, sometimes in front of a microphone attached to large speakers, and sometimes with a giant megaphone in his hand. He had something very important to say, but when he spoke into his amplified sound systems, nothing came out of the other end. No matter how hard he tried and how much he raised his voice, he could not be heard. Like Hoffa, Tommy Osborn still had something to prove. He had to make everyone hear. He thanked Branstetter for his good intentions and walked away.

While the Hoffa case proceeded, the men of Camelot were engaged on many other fronts. In late September, both the president and the attorney general were personally shepherding the attempt by

James Meredith to integrate the University of Mississippi. Breaking down the remaining racial barriers in the South remained a top priority on what was a carefully constructed but highly risky political agenda.

But they'd found that some events were well beyond their control and were threatening to overwhelm them. The White House had hardly recovered from the embarrassing debacle of the failed Cuban Bay of Pigs invasion when it discovered that Fidel Castro had turned the island into a launching site for Soviet missiles. On the eve of the opening of Hoffa's trial President Kennedy had to go on television to show the nation intelligence photos of the Cuban-based Soviet missiles aimed at the United States, the beginning of the Cuban Missile Crisis that would dominate the nation for the next week.

On that same Sunday afternoon Walter Sheridan watched at the Nashville airport as Jimmy Hoffa climbed down from a plush twin-engine Lodestar and marched jauntily off to a news conference, where he told newsmen that the attorney general "was starting out just like Hitler did." Hoffa then got into a red Thunderbird driven by Ewing King, a tall, blank-faced man with no chin who had been installed as Don Vestal's successor as president of Nashville Local 327. FBI agents fell in behind them and followed as King drove Hoffa to the Andrew Jackson Hotel, where an entire floor had been rented as defense team headquarters. Then Sheridan went back to his own hotel across the street, watched the president on television, and went to sleep wondering if both he and Hoffa would wake up dead together the following morning, victims of nuclear war.

But however preoccupied the Kennedys appeared to be with other things, nothing had been left to chance in Nashville. The trap for James R. Hoffa had been carefully laid.

Nine months earlier, on New Year's Day, another dissident Teamster, the head of a milk drivers' local in Cincinnati, had gotten a call from Edward Grady Partin, the chief of a Teamsters local in Baton Rouge. Although known as a close Hoffa associate, Partin complained that Hoffa had been pressuring him and had threatened his life if he ever told what he knew about the bribery of a National

Labor Relations Board official. The Cincinnati Teamster, already a Justice Department informant, passed the information to the Hoffa unit, which was at the time running a grand jury investigation of Teamster activities in Louisiana.

A month after Hoffa's indictment, Partin was indicted in an unrelated case for embezzling union funds. A month before Hoffa was to go on trial in Nashville, Partin was arrested in Louisiana and charged with kidnapping the children of one of his union members. It wasn't a kidnapping at all, only part of a domestic squabble involving one of his union associates, but Partin was held without bail. During his incarceration, he not only coughed up his earlier story about being afraid of Hoffa, but made a startling new disclosure: Hoffa had once talked seriously to him about assassinating Bobby Kennedy. The Hoffa unit asked Partin to take a lie detector test, which he passed. At that point the Justice Department struck a deal with the Louisiana Teamster that would ultimately be the undoing of both Jimmy Hoffa and Tommy Osborn.

From then on Partin began tape-recording his conversations with Hoffa. On the day the trial began, he flew to Nashville to meet Hoffa, now as an undercover government agent assigned to gather evidence of jury tampering. Partin had been in town less than twenty-four hours when he made his first report to Sheridan. He said that Alan Dorfman, a Chicago businessman later identified as a principle link between the Teamsters and the Chicago mob, was in town overseeing a massive effort to fix the Hoffa jury.

By now the town was crawling with FBI agents, private investigators, wire-tapping experts, and toughs of every description. For the next three months, nobody remotely connected with Hoffa or his defense moved or made a telephone call without Sheridan and his men knowing about it. Partin, using the code name "Andy Anderson," saw to that. Of the first three jurors tentatively seated in the case, one reported that a neighbor had already offered him ten thousand dollars in hundred-dollar bills to vote for Hoffa's acquittal. Several other prospective jurors reported to the judge that they had been telephoned by someone purporting to be a reporter for the

Banner who asked their feelings about Jimmy Hoffa. Miller ordered the jury sequestered. But despite warnings to Hoffa's lawyers, the attempts to influence the jury continued. A black business agent from Detroit made contact with the uncle of one of two black jurors in the case. And Partin reported to the government that the local union boss Ewing King was personally trying to get to a highway patrolman, the husband of one of the female jurors.

Early in December, the jury was temporarily removed from the courtroom for the argument of a motion when a young, itinerant restaurant worker wearing a raincoat walked into the courtroom and through the wooden gates that separate spectators from participants. He stopped short of the defense table, pulled a pistol from his pocket, and began shooting. The gun was an air-propelled pellet pistol, which did little damage. Hoffa leaped from his chair and struck his assailant on the jaw, knocking him to the floor. The man turned out to be a former mental patient, a bizarre intruder in the case apparently unconnected to anyone.

Regardless, the following morning the defense moved for a mistrial, which Judge Miller denied. The government then informed the court about attempts to influence the highway patrolman's wife. She was removed and replaced with the first alternate.

Meanwhile, Hoffa had picked Partin to guard his hotel suite, which meant that the informant now knew even more. One night Hoffa boasted to him that his black business agent from Detroit, Larry Campbell, had been successful and that he had one of the two black jurors "in his pocket." All the other attempts to get at the jury, he told Partin, were "just for insurance."

At Sheridan's insistence, Partin gave the government an affidavit attesting to what he had heard, which along with telephone records Sheridan obtained, built a strong case that the black juror, a man named Gratin Fields, had been compromised. After Jim Neal and Tommy Osborn gave their closing arguments, Neal showed the affidavit to Judge Miller, who resealed it and removed Fields from the jury, replacing him with a second alternate. On a Friday night late in December the jury retired to deliberate, but they could not reach a verdict. On Sunday morning, two days before Christmas, after seventeen hours of deliberation, the jurors reported—for the fourth time—that they were hopelessly deadlocked. Five of the twelve jurors had held out for acquittal. Judge Miller declared a mistrial.

A gush of relief washed over the defense table. Jimmy Hoffa had gotten off again. Four major government efforts to nail him had resulted in two acquittals and two mistrials. He and Tommy Osborn broke into wide grins and patted each other on the back. How lucky could Tommy Osborn be? He had ridden another hundred-to-one shot home to the winner's circle. A jubilant Hoffa wished the jury a Merry Christmas and jetted off to Detroit for the holidays.

The government had lost the battle but not the war. Early in January another grand jury was impaneled in Nashville to investigate three clear cases of jury tampering. In beating the misdemeanor charge, Hoffa had committed a felony. By April Kennedy was ready to indict Hoffa again, but this time he decided to add a Tennessee lawyer to the team as a special prosecutor. To convince a jury to put Jimmy Hoffa away he needed somebody outside the government, someone older, overpowering, and incorruptible. Again, there were only two possibilities—Jack Norman and John J. Hooker, Sr.

Kennedy asked the advice of Seigenthaler, who would not choose between them but instead told Kennedy an engaging story of how Hooker had just won acquittal for a woman who had slain her husband with a samurai sword. The tale fascinated Kennedy, who then called John Hooker, Jr. "If you really want to put Jimmy Hoffa away, you go get my daddy," the younger Hooker told him. "He can do it for you."

Because he had no special entrée to Norman and did not know him personally, Kennedy felt more comfortable calling Hooker. Either man would have served his purpose, which was to have his case against Jimmy Hoffa put before a Tennessee jury by a local lawyer as smart, as persuasive, and as believable as Tommy Osborn.

At sixty-three, John J. Hooker, Sr., was an imposing man, wide of girth with soft, intelligent eyes set in a ruddy face that betrayed both his good humor and his love of Jack Daniel's. He wore glistening shoes and expensive three-piece suits with a gold watch chain stretched across his vest and a colorful handkerchief usually over-flowing from his breast pocket. Hooker's chief attributes as a lawyer were his intelligence and supreme confidence, an actor's animation, and a distinctive voice that could boom, screech, or flow like warm honey depending on the desired effect. With few exceptions, every-one who listened to him for a few minutes wished he were their grandfather.

Like his friendly rival Norman, Hooker had two sons, Henry and John Jr., who had followed him into the practice of law. And like Norman's boys, Hooker's sons were smart, well-educated, and had made fine, successful attorneys. Hooker and Norman were proud of their children and often made them the subject of their conversa-tions. But when their talk turned to young lawyers who had their re-spect and admiration, they both agreed that one, Tommy Osborn, stood out above all the rest.

Hooker and Norman wouldn't ever want to be on opposite sides of a lawsuit with their own sons, and they felt the same way about Tommy Osborn, especially in a prosecution as ugly as this one was likely to be. How could there have been all that jury tampering going on under Osborn's nose and him not know it? For this reason, Hooker had reservations about becoming the special prosecutor. He didn't like what he might have to do to Tommy Osborn to get the job done. Before he agreed, it took several doses of Kennedy per-suasion, during which Hooker continually addressed the attorney general as "Mr. Kennedy," even though his son John Jr. called him "Bobby."

"Why do you continue calling him Mr. Kennedy when he's half your age?" John J. Jr. wanted to know. To which his father replied, "So he'll continue to call me Mr. Hooker."

In April, shortly before Hoffa, Dorfman, King, and the others were to be indicted on jury tampering, the elder Hooker reluctantly agreed to join Jim Neal on the prosecution team. Six months later, on November 7, 1963, as they prepared for trial, his worst fears were realized. One morning Walter Sheridan told them that Tommy Osborn had been caught trying to fix the jury.

Neither Mr. Hooker nor Jim Neal wanted to believe it. Not Osborn. He wouldn't. It was wrong. He was too smart, too good to do anything like that. But the "proof" was sitting right in front of them in the slinky form of Osborn's own private investigator, Robert Vick. Mr. Hooker found the man repulsive, but his story compelling.

For weeks Vick had been calling first FBI agents and then Sheridan, offering his services as an informant. Initially he'd hinted that he knew about more jury tampering in the Test Fleet case than the indictments alleged. Finally, he told Sheridan that he had arranged a meeting between Osborn and a Lebanon, Tennessee, attorney who knew the husband of one of the Test Fleet jurors. He said he didn't know the outcome of the meeting. The attorney, Harry Beard, admitted giving Osborn some background information on the juror but had denied any impropriety.

Now Vick had come forward again, this time volunteering the information that Osborn had only the day before instructed him to offer a prospective juror in the jury-tampering case five thousand dollars now and another five thousand dollars after the verdict to vote for an acquittal. He gave them an affidavit swearing to it and agreed to tape-record subsequent conversations with Osborn.

On the basis of the affidavit, Judge Miller authorized the FBI to tape a tiny recorder to the small of Vick's back, and he was sent to talk to Osborn in his office. When he returned, FBI agents removed the recorder and attempted to play the tape, but it jammed and then unraveled. There was nothing on it but Osborn's secretary welcoming Vick and offering him a seat. They put a new, smaller device on Vick and sent him back the following day, but Osborn never came to his office. Two days later, they tried again. And this time, Vick came back with a recording, which Sheridan played for Neal and Hooker. There was no mistaking Osborn's voice.

OSBORN: *Did you talk to him?*
VICK: *Yeah, I went down to Springfield Saturday morning.*

OSBORN: *Elliot?*

VICK: *Elliot.*

OSBORN: *(inaudible whisper)*

VICK: *Huh?*

OSBORN: *Is there any chance in the world that he would report you?*

VICK: *That he will report me to the FBI? Why, of course, there is always a chance, but I wouldn't have got into it if I thought it was very, very great.*

OSBORN: *(laughs)*

VICK: *. . . So he got to talking about the last Hoffa case being hung, you know, and some guy refusing ten thousand dollars to hang it, see? And he said the guy was crazy, he should've took it, you know, and so we talked about—and just discreetly, you know, and course I'm really playing this thing slow, that's the reason I asked you if you wanted a lawyer down there to handle it or you wanted me to handle it, 'cause I'm gonna play it easy.*

OSBORN: *The less people the better.*

VICK: *That's right. Well, I'm gonna play it slow and easy myself, and er, anyway, we talked about, er, something about five thousand now and five thousand later, see, so he did, he brought up five thousand, see, and talking about how they pay it off and things like that. I don't know whether he suspected why I was there or not, 'cause I don't just drop out of the blue to visit him socially, you know. We're friends, close, and kin, cousins, but I don't ordinarily just, we don't fraternize, you know, and er, so he seemed very receptive for, er, to hang the thing for five now and five later. Now, er, I thought I would report back to you and see what you say.*

OSBORN: *That's fine. The thing to do is set it up for a point later so you won't be running back and forth.*

VICK: *Yeah.*

OSBORN: *Then tell him it's a deal.*

VICK: *It's what?*

OSBORN: *That it's a deal. What we'll have to do when it gets down to the trial date, when we know the date—tomorrow, for example, if the Supreme Court rules against us, well, within the week we'll know when the trial comes. Then he has to be certain that when he gets on, he's got to know that he'll just be talking to you and nobody else . . . All right—so we'll leave it up to you. The only thing to do would be to tell him, in other words, your next contact with him would be to tell him if he wants the deal, he's got it.*

VICK: *Okay.*

OSBORN: *The only thing it depends upon is him being accepted by the jury. If the government challenges him, there will be no deal.*

VICK: *All right. If he is seated?*

OSBORN: *If he is seated.*

VICK: *He can expect five thousand then.*

OSBORN: *Immediately.*

VICK: *Immediately. And then five thousand when it's hung. Is that right?*

OSBORN: *All the way, now!*

VICK: *Oh, he's got to stay all the way?*

OSBORN: *All the way.*

VICK: *No swing. You don't want him to swing like we discussed once before. You want him.*

OSBORN: *Of course, he could be guided by his own—but that always leaves a question. The thing to do is just stick with the crowd. That way we'll look better and maybe not have to go to another trial if we get a pretty good count.*

VICK: *Oh. Now, I'm going to play it just like you told me previously, to reassure him and keep him from getting panicky. You know, I have reason to believe that he won't be alone, you know.*

OSBORN: *You assure him that, one hundred percent.*

VICK: *And to keep fears down that he might have—see?*

OSBORN: *Tell him there will be at least two others with him. . . . We'll keep it secret. The way to keep it safe is that nobody knows about it but you and me—where could they ever go?*

Hooker and Neal stared at each other in disbelief. Then Neal and Sheridan left for Washington to see Bobby Kennedy, and Mr. Hooker went home, where he visited with Jack Daniel's much of the evening.

The next day two Nashville FBI agents played the tape for Judge Miller. He just shook his head while he listened, saddened and speechless. Then he instructed his secretary to summon Tommy Osborn to his chambers.

When Osborn arrived, he found both Judge Miller and Judge Frank Gray, who was to preside over the jury-tampering case, waiting solemnly. Osborn maintained his cool confidence when the judges told him they had information of a substantial nature concerning efforts involving him in tampering with the jury. He denied everything, including ever discussing with anyone a prospective juror named Elliot.

The judges then served Osborn with an order for him to appear before them the following week to show cause why he should not be disbarred. Somber now and near a state of shock, Osborn was given a choice between a hearing in open court or in chambers. Grateful, he chose the latter and left.

Wild-eyed and afraid, Osborn returned to his office and tried to call Vick. While Osborn was en route to meet with the judges, Sheridan's men had moved Vick out of his home and into a room at a Holiday Inn. A deputy U.S. marshal was dispatched to stay with Vick's wife and children at his home, which Osborn telephoned frantically until after midnight.

The next morning Osborn sent John Polk, another of his jury investigators, to Vick's home to find him. But he found only the deputy marshal, who said Vick was no longer available. Osborn then obtained for himself the best attorney possible under the circumstances—a distraught and conscience-stricken Jack Norman, who blamed himself for getting Osborn involved. Ruefully Norman would say over and over again, "I never should have sent that man across the street to see that boy." Norman took Osborn's case for free. Together with Raymond Denney, Osborn's law partner, they went to see Judge Gray and asked for the information on which the show-cause order was based. The judge gave them all the evidence—the order authorizing the hidden tape recorder, Vick's affidavit, and a copy of the recording itself.

Tommy Osborn was devastated. Over the weekend he and Norman decided to do what all smart defense lawyers do in the face of overwhelming evidence of guilt—see what kind of deal they could get. Jack Norman went to see his old friend John Hooker, Sr., with one goal—to keep Tommy Osborn from going to jail and to save his future as an attorney. He reminded Hooker that if Vick was proved a government agent sent to entrap Osborn, the tape recording might not be allowed as evidence. Since Vick had made the whole thing up and no prospective juror had ever actually been offered anything, the case against Osborn might not be as good as it appeared. If Osborn admitted his guilt and agreed to testify against Hoffa, what would be the government's position?

Mr. Hooker wanted to help Tommy Osborn, too. What good could possibly be served by putting him in jail? He and Norman blamed Hoffa and Vick for Osborn's predicament. Hooker said there was no way to keep the federal judges from disbarring Osborn, but that if he went before them and confessed his guilt, the government would have no reason to bring a criminal prosecution against him. It was Hoffa they wanted, not Osborn.

On what authority could such a deal be offered? Jack Norman asked his friend. "Well, on this case I represent the full authority of the attorney general of the United States," Mr. Hooker replied.

Norman brought the offer back to Osborn, but cautioned him that their mutual friend Hooker might be overstepping his bounds. The deal might be something he wants to do but might not be able to deliver, Norman said.

If there were two people in the world in whom Tommy Osborn had faith, it was Jack Norman and John Hooker, Sr. Hooker, he knew, would not make Norman a promise he could not keep. Without a criminal conviction, there was always a chance that he could be reinstated to the bar.

Late Tuesday afternoon, November 20, Osborn appeared before the two federal judges and admitted having the conversations with Vick. He identified the voice on the tape recording as his own and forfeited his right to have Vick called as a witness. The next day, Judge Miller issued a memorandum detailing the chronology of events and disbarring Tommy Osborn from practicing in federal court. His "brazen" attempt to improperly bribe and influence a juror, the judge said, "is an indication of such a callous and shameful disregard of duty, such a lack of moral fitness and sense of professional ethics as to warrant no lesser punishment than the removal of his name from the roll of attorneys permitted to practice law in this court."

At the news a member of the board of directors of the Nashville Bar Association proclaimed the city's legal community in "a profound state of shock."

The rest of the nation soon followed. The next day, President Kennedy was shot in Dallas. Members of the Hoffa unit got the news flash in Judge Miller's jury room, which they had appropriated as an office while the court was not in session. Walter Sheridan tried to reach Bobby Kennedy in Washington, unsuccessfully. He then called John Seigenthaler, who was presiding over pandemonium in the newsroom of the *Tennessean*. Seigenthaler invited Sheridan to come down to the newspaper. By the time he arrived, live television coverage was under way in Dallas. It was not long before they learned that the president was dead.

The knights of Camelot were sick with grief.

Jack Norman proved himself a better lawyer than his client Tommy Osborn. As Norman had predicted, their friend John J. Hooker, Sr., was never able to deliver the deal Osborn thought they'd made. Robert Kennedy, Norman concluded, had nixed it himself, cutting the ground out from under Hooker.

The government didn't call Tommy Osborn as a witness against Jimmy Hoffa for the simple reason that doing so would have strengthened Hoffa's argument that his defense team had been deliberately infiltrated and undermined. Instead, in December, shortly before Hoffa's jury-tampering trial began, Osborn was indicted on three counts of jury-tampering himself. Despite Hooker's good intentions, the lives of Hoffa and Osborn and their treatment by the government had become hopelessly intertwined. If Osborn got off, so might Hoffa on the basis of an appeal that the government had subverted his lawyer-client relationship by entrapping his best lawyer.

The die cast, Osborn then showed up as a behind-the-scenes defense strategist in Hoffa's second trial, which began in January of 1964 in Chattanooga, where the trial had been moved on a change of venue request. Osborn supplied his old defense colleagues with an affidavit supporting their motion for a mistrial on grounds that the government had deliberately sabotaged the defense in the first trial. Disbarred now by the very Nashville Bar Association of which he'd expected to be president, Osborn was reduced to selling real estate for a living. He did, however, receive payment of more than $140,000 from the Teamsters union pension fund, which Hoffa was later convicted of looting.

The unflinching testimony of Grady Partin convicted Jimmy Hoffa and three of his codefendants of jury tampering. Early in March, Hoffa was sentenced to eight years in prison and fined ten thousand dollars. His attempts to overturn his conviction would last the rest of his life, as would his rancor for the Kennedys. On the day Hoffa was sentenced in Chattanooga, one of his followers in Puerto Rico wrote Attorney General Robert Kennedy the following letter:

Sir:

This is for your information.

The Undersigned is going to solicit from the membership of our union that each one donate whatever they can afford to maintain, clean, beautify and supply with flowers the grave of Lee Harvey Oswald.

You can rest assured contributions will be unanimous.

> *Sincerely,*
> *Frank Chavez*
> *Secretary-Treasurer*
> *Teamster Local 901*

Before Osborn's trial began in May 1964, Neal and Hooker went to Kennedy and told him that they did not want to prosecute Osborn.

If a prosecution had to be pursued, they asked that someone else be assigned the job.

Kennedy had decided to run for the Senate from New York and would soon leave the attorney general's office. He approved a plea bargain arrangement suggested by Hooker under which Osborn would plead guilty to a single count of obstruction of justice and be spared from going to prison. But he insisted that if Hooker and Neal could not get Osborn to plead guilty they would have to try the case.

Osborn refused to bargain again. A guilty plea to a felony would remove any chance of his ever reversing his disbarment, for his appeal rested on his entrapment claims. The odds against a jury finding him innocent were great. But given the chance to ride a long shot again, Tommy Osborn climbed up on Gallahadion one more time. Far guiltier men than he had gotten off, Osborn knew. He had gotten them off himself.

For John J. Hooker, Sr., and Jim Neal, prosecuting Osborn was a devil's deed. And for Jack Norman, the defense was a heart-wrenching mission of mercy. The trial took five days, the most important evidence, of course, being the tape recording of Osborn's voice authorizing Vick to "make the deal." Testifying on his own behalf, Osborn tried to convince the jury that he had been entrapped, that Vick had been a Trojan horse of the Justice Department.

Often in criminal cases, something or someone other than the defendant ends up being tried. In the spring of 1964 in the Nashville courtroom of Judge Marion S. Boyd, it was the system of justice itself, with the outcome hinging on a fierce and intimate struggle between two of the best courtroom performers ever to sway a jury.

Both men were big in stature and huge in presence. Norman resembled the actor Carroll O'Connor, who played Archie Bunker on television, except Norman was taller and thinner, robust and powerful looking. And he was always impeccably tailored in cashmere or linen. He had an impressive mane of white hair, which he was able to fling about with great precision and to great effect. In contrast, Hooker looked as if he had been born in his three-piece suits, thinning hair slicked back, his thumbs hooked in his vest pockets over his belly, and the wisdom of ages etched in his craggy face.

At the trial of their mutual friend, they were like two old herd bulls summoning up the courage and strength for one final charge, with their own immortality at stake.

On the day of summation, young Neal, who was good then and would in time gain enormous stature as a trial lawyer, was already wily enough to keep a low profile. His opening statement had been so simple and direct that Norman dismissed it forthwith, as if the jury needed an explanatory transition to the drama they were about to witness.

Shaking his head in dubious disdain, Norman began by saying that Neal had just committed Tommy Osborn to the penitentiary "with much formality . . . like a man reading from a dusty law book." A more accurate statement, he suggested, would have been the entrapment of Osborn by the government like "the capture of rabbits with a steel trap."

His voice exploding one minute, lowering to a whisper the next, Norman said he knew that "sometimes attorneys are tempted," and he confessed that "the lash of conscience has been on my mind" for sending Hoffa to see Osborn in the first place. But guilty conscience was not his alone, Norman said, because the entrapment of Tommy Osborn was "the scummiest, lousiest, most contemptible piece of trickery and fraud I have ever heard of" committed in the name of the government.

He said that Robert Kennedy could get a lot of his ideas through to the people of this country "through paid representatives" but that he should not be allowed to "cram this down the throat of a Tennessee jury."

Norman, who had conducted a devastating cross-examination of Robert Vick, flayed him some more. Pounding the lectern with his fist, perspiration beading on his face, he shouted, "We found out that Robert Vick had gone to the FBI not in November, as the government claimed, but in June. . . . What was the beginning of this thing? That's where you have to start. It has been testified here, and hasn't been denied, that Vick went to Walter Sheridan of the Justice Department and told Sheridan: 'We have to get rid of Tommy Osborn.' "

No matter how hard the government tried, he said, lowering his voice, the case against Osborn could not be divorced from the testimony of this paid informant. "Once you have poured ink in water, you can't get back the water from the ink."

As he neared the end, Norman's crisp shirt collar was curled and wet from perspiration. A few wisps of white hair were matted to his ruddy forehead.

"In all my experience, I have never seen a case rest upon the work of a person like Vick," he lamented. "Had he been Judas Iscariot he would have done the job for three instead of thirty pieces.

"It has been said that in the Louvre in Paris there are twelve different pictures of Judas Iscariot, painted by different artists, representing the concept of each individual artist of iniquity, indecency, loss from goodness, and there are no two of the twelve who look alike—but surely they all must look like Vick."

If the government could do what it did to Osborne—"take a man like Vick and strap a recorder on his back, and in order to get rid of a man, tell him to go get employed and gain his confidence, and make friends, and put his arms around and have him accept the generosity of a friend and find out what he is saying and doing . . . when my government gets to that point, I just think I will stay at home on Decoration Day."

John J. Hooker, Sr., realized instantly that he was about to follow the most effective closing jury presentation he had ever heard, by his most eloquent opponent in defense of a highly attractive defendant whom he himself didn't want to see go to prison. Mr. Hooker stood up and walked around, his hands resting proudly on his belly, his fingers slipping into his coat pockets, as if searching for an opening line.

"It is a proud position that you occupy, as one of twelve, like the twelve that followed the Master, that you have been chosen to pass upon the rights of the government and of the defendant, Mr. Osborn. . . . In all of the countries of the world where communism has taken over and infiltrated, the jury has vanished. There is only one country of the world, only one, not excluding even England, in which we have the free life, where we have trial by jury, by a jury of your peers. . . . And so I salute you as an important cog in a wheel of government."

He turned and faced them. "Ladies and gentlemen of the jury, like my friend Mr. Norman, I, too, have been standing at the bar in courthouses for forty years. This is the saddest day of my professional life. I would give anything on earth if I could run away and not be faced with the responsibility that faces me and faces you.

"I wish someone else had had this assignment. This is the saddest, darkest day of my professional career. But there was a sad, dark day before this, and that's the day Tom Osborn got mixed up with James R. Hoffa. Ever since he came into the courts of the Middle District of Tennessee, there has been a trail of jury fixing."

These instances were recited one by one, including those involving the defendant and Vick, whose character had been thrashed beyond redemption, a fact of which Mr. Hooker took subtle note. "You don't catch anybody trying to fix a jury with an elder or a deacon of a church," he lamented. "You don't catch them that way."

Hooker knew that Norman had been right, that he could not run away from Vick no matter how badly he wanted to. Norman's Judas Iscariot analogy had been devastating. The jurors had probably never heard it before. He needed some way to undercut it, to belittle it as an old story having nothing to do with the case. All the jurors were middle-aged, born during or soon after the era of Prohibition.

"I don't care how many witnesses they bring who swear they wouldn't believe Vick," Hooker continued. "I don't care how many portraits of Judas Iscariot he looks like."

He stopped and looked at Norman kindly, and then screeched in a loud voice, "If you knew where Jack really got that, that's what Jim Reeves said about Mr. Volstead . . . he said Volstead looked like all twelve pictures of Judas Iscariot." Hooker paused. The jury all looked at Norman, as if waiting for him to stand and respond, which of course Hooker had no intention of his doing. In fact the origin of Norman's story had not been the Prohibition debate, but Boss Crump's newspaper advertisement attacking Norman's gubernatorial candidate Gordon Browning in 1948. But Hooker was merely giving the jury time to digest the significance of his message: that the Judas Iscariot story was just old political rhetoric. Then, with a single line, he again leveled the playing field. "I don't care what he looks like," Hooker bellowed. "I am not asking you to convict on his [Vick's] testimony. I am asking you to convict him [he looked at Osborn] on his own voice."

Concluding, Hooker moved close to the jurors and lowered his voice to the point where they had to strain to hear. He wanted them to see a spent old man, out of breath and energy, about to clear his conscience. "I've rolled and tossed at night ever since this has been going on, wondering if there wasn't some way that I could be spared this."

Was the American justice system going to be "cast aside like, to use Mr. Norman's expression, an old hat, or an old cloak? What are you going to do about it?

"Of all the sorrow I have had about this, I hate to pass it on to you, but shortly I have got to take this garment off and hand it to you. Will you have the courage, will you have the fortitude, will you have the interest in justice to stand on the side of justice, to stand on the side of the courts, the judges?

"I hope you will not regard me as irreverent when I say—and I commend it to you—that I have gotten down on my knees at night like this," he said, dropping to his knees before the jury box, "and asked God that justice, and only justice, be done in this case.

"My only desire is . . . that you weigh the evidence justly and fairly, that you listen to the charge of His Honor, and do what you think your duty is. I am trying so hard to do mine."

He got up, composed himself, and finished by reading a transcript of the hearing in which Tommy Osborn had admitted having talked to Vick about fixing the jury. "And I didn't hear him say he was sorry in this trial . . . really."

Osborn's fate was in their hands, he told them. "There in the quietness of your deliberations, in the sight of your God, you will have to decide which side you are going to stand on. I have confidence in your honor and integrity."

When the jurors returned three hours later, Judge Boyd ordered Osborn to stand to receive their findings. Osborn thought he was about to be acquitted, as did most everyone else who had witnessed Norman's devastating assault on Vick and the government's case. Entrapment was the only possible explanation for Tommy Osborn's aberrant behavior.

Gasps were heard when the foreman announced that Z. T. Osborn, Jr., trial lawyer extraordinaire, was guilty of a single count of jury tampering on the basis of his conversation with Vick.

A month and a half later, Osborn stood before the bar of justice again and was sentenced to three and a half years in prison. He was there two years later in 1966 when John J. Hooker, Jr., son of the man who had put him behind bars and who had warned Osborn to stay off the Hoffa case, tried to parlay his Camelot credentials into a career in politics. Hooker, running for the Democratic nomination for governor, opened up his mail one day to find a letter from Osborn, then an inmate at the federal corrections facility at Montgomery, Alabama. Inside was a good-luck wish and campaign contribution of twenty-seven dollars, which Osborn said he had been able to save by working in the prison laundry.

PART EIGHT

Heroes
and Villains

F or a reporter still too young in 1962 to vote or buy beer legally, the easiest way to tell the heroes from the villains was to see how they were regarded by the exciting newspaper that paid my salary.

On the pages of the rambunctious *Tennessean* were good and bad Teamsters, good and bad cops, and of course good and bad politicians. By this measure, the Kennedys were veritable models of loyalty and patriotism. Jimmy Hoffa and his lawyers were puppets of organized crime, as was the likable and tragic Tommy Osborn, for whom everyone felt sorry.

Usually the core of distinction between good and evil was the simple and worthy cause of the equality of man. And what better end could there be for justification of any means necessary in its pursuit? For the young men of Camelot good and bad fell easily into categories of black and white, which was appropriate considering that racial division would mark the decade for history.

Good, of course, was black, as in Martin Luther King, John Lewis, and the others marching for the rights to be educated, to vote, and to have their vote count equally. Also good were all the elected white leaders who backed blacks' right to do so. These were the new breed of southern Democrats, mostly liberals, including Charles Weltner and Jimmy Carter in Georgia, Dale Bumpers in Arkansas, and in Tennessee, Albert Gore, John J. Hooker, Jr., and the new leader in the state legislature, Frank Gorrell. Tommy Osborn had been among them until Hoffa.

The bad, on the other hand, was white, more specifically white resistance to change—the old guard, including rural legislators, classic southern sheriffs like those who wielded the bullwhips at Selma, police who arrested demonstrators, Goldwater Republicans, and, always, the *Banner* editorial page.

So closely did the *Tennessean* become identified with the cause of black equality that thirty years after passage of the civil rights bill, old Jack Norman would still refer sarcastically to John Seigenthaler as "Nashville's most prominent black leader" and "a man who was never the same after he got hit with that rock in Alabama."

Still, somewhere in that black and white world of the

idealistic young journalist of the early sixties, room had to be found for gray. Not only is all politics local, it is all personal.

And in my own case, it was very personal. On the weekends, my reporting assignment was the police department where my granddaddy was still employed, but no longer able to survive politically. His fabled luck was gone now, having deserted him along with his youth.

In a strange and sudden reversal of roles, my job at the *Tennessean* gave me more politics than he could muster, and eventually he was reduced to coming to me for help.

As hard as it was to believe, the department brass had balked at taking him off the street. No longer with any political clout of his own, the man who only three years earlier had gotten me my job at the *Tennessean* stood before me in the police department press room completely frustrated, a lone patrolman's stripe on his uniform shirt.

"You know all the brass," he said. "See if you can get one of your friends to help me get assigned to the tow-in lot."

I took this request to a sympathetic young assistant chief, not much older than myself, who had married the sister of a lifelong friend. "We need a reason," he said.

"He says the reason is that he's old and sick and can't handle the drunks and street stuff anymore," I replied. The officer laughed in my face.

"Everybody in the place knows that's a lie," he said. "We'll have to do better than that."

Eventually, we did. But the department remained at the heart of the continuing struggle between good and evil, between the new politics and the old. And part of my job every day was to report "objectively" on the progress of the police department in the new consolidated government where the *Tennessean*'s hero was Mayor Beverly Briley, a paragon of progressive reform, and the villain was once more our old family friend Garner Robinson.

Lessons on Making Sergeant

The new mayor of the fledgling consolidated government of Metropolitan Nashville and Davidson County, Beverly Briley, was a tough, determined little man with a short temper and a long memory for political debts good and bad.

He didn't hesitate when the men of Camelot called and asked a favor for Robert Vick, the federal government's star witness against Tommy Osborn. The former deputy sheriff and policeman was in dire financial straits now that he was no longer in Osborn's employ and needed income to sustain him and his family while he waited to testify against Osborn for jury tampering in the Hoffa case. Osborn was after all a longtime friend and associate of Briley's arch political enemy Ben West, of whom he had not seen the last.

Briley readily obliged, ordering that Vick be hired by the Metro police department as a special patrolman third class and assigned full-time to the office of the U.S. marshal. For the next thirteen months, the federal government's debt to Vick was presumably borne unwittingly by the local taxpayers.

Mayor Briley figured that for his cooperation on a matter of such sensitivity, he could someday count on a handsome return from either the Justice Department officials in Washington or at least from their friends at the *Tennessean*. If there was one aspect of politics in which Briley took stock, it was the repayment of debts. And there was no better place for the settling of scores than the police department.

In an effort to keep the county sheriff's patrol from joining the city police department, in opposition to consolidated government, Briley had promised that no officers would be reduced in rank in the merged Metro department. Now the promise was coming back to haunt him.

Both of the old departments had been rife with corruption and had been cleaned out by a recent federal grand jury that nailed both the sheriff, a rising young political star named Leslie Jett, and most of the high-ranking officers of the city police department.

With most of them gone up the river on bribery and corruption charges, the only high-ranking officer left clean enough to be the new chief was a veteran administrative officer named Hubert Kemp, a kind, soft-spoken man with a reputation for being too dumb to steal. Except for him, most of the top rank in the merged department, including the deputy chief and his immediate subordinates, had come from the old sheriff's department. They were mainly grizzled veterans in their fifties, without civil service standing but with political connections reaching all the way back to Robinson and Sheridan. And there, in Briley's view, lay a problem.

Never could he forget that it was Garner, Jake, and Elkin Garfinkle who had stripped him of his power as county judge, turning him into an embarrassed and impotent eunuch for more than a year. Despite the good efforts of Garner's nephew Jimmy, who ran Briley's mayoral campaign as efficiently as he'd run the Metro referendum, Briley would never trust the Robinsons. To him Garner's pledge to "stick" was meaningless. So within days after becoming mayor, Briley repaid the debt he had owed Robinson for fifteen years. He stripped the trustee's office to which Robinson had been elected of all its traditional powers, including its patronage.

According to the mayor's interpretation of the new Metro charter, all two dozen of the office employees, save a single deputy, had to be placed under civil service, which meant that Garner no longer could hire and fire them. Also, the office would no longer function as county treasurer, Briley decreed, which reduced it to a funnel through which tax collections passed daily to a new office of Metro treasurer, which would now invest and dispense government funds.

Garner now understood why he'd had no opposition when he ran for reelection for trustee in the spring of 1962, and why Honey Bee Flippen had told him, "Garner, as far as I am concerned, you can have the office for the rest of your life." The office they let him have, Garner confided to his friend Dave White, "is not worth a shit."

When faced in the past with a problem of such magnitude and complexity, Garner had always turned to Elkin Garfinkle, and he did so again. A few days later, Garfinkle, who had been an advisor to the Metro Charter Commission and one of the charter's framers, filed a lawsuit claiming that the constitutional rights of the trustee's office had been violated. Briley was named as the defendant. To hell with reform.

But Garfinkle's magic had run out, and eventually the courts upheld Briley's interpretation of the new Metro charter. Now back on the outside looking in, Garner got a telephone call at the funeral home on the night after the final court ruling from an old friend who was out on the road in Maryland, driving a Buick with two racehorses in a trailer behind it. Jake Sheridan, Thoroughbred owner and trainer, had just telephoned to say "I told you so."

From then on Briley regarded Garner as certain to realign himself with Ben West, who was sure to rise from the political dead at the first full moon. The last thing Briley wanted was for them to have an escort by his own police department. All those years of fighting Jake Sheridan and the sheriff's patrol on Election Day had taught Briley the value of controlling patronage at the police department. Hiring the federal government's witness against Jimmy Hoffa on the police payroll didn't quite square with the mayor's promise to "take the politics out of the police department." But then having the department run by a bunch of county machine loyalists like old Dave White didn't either.

Old Dave still had his lieutenant's bars, but he didn't know for how long. Like Garner, he hadn't paid a lot of attention to the fine print.

The promise Briley made him and other members of the old sheriff's patrol about nobody losing their rank turned out to be subordinate to his other promise to "take the politics out of the department." To keep the police from ever being used against him, the mayor decreed that all officers except the chief and his immediate deputies be placed in civil service, which not only prohibited them from political activity but placed police promotions under a civilian review board. The board's first act had been to make all rank temporary and to determine that the rank of lieutenant in the old sheriff's patrol was equal to the rank of sergeant in the new department.

To be made a permanent sergeant in the new Metro Police Department, Dave would have to pass the civil service commission's written and oral examinations, which to him meant he needed political leverage with the commission. Naturally, he went to see Garner.

"They can stick that sergeant's examination up their ass," Dave said. "I'm sixty years old. I've been a sergeant for nearly forty years. I know how to be a goddamn sergeant."

"Go on and take the exam, Dave," Garner assured him. "They told us you'll be all right."

"I know what they told us, but what they say and what they do are not the same. I'm gonna need some help. Can't you talk to somebody? I need some politics."

"Hell, you don't have any politics anymore," said Garner, only half kidding. "Remember, you married a Republican. Or have you forgotten?"

Dave smiled. In the old days, the gold would have flashed. But he had a new bigger bridge that was all white enamel.

"How could I forget?" he said. And how could he? His fourth wife, Ann Richardson, whom he'd married a few years earlier, was a pert, pretty widow ten years his junior and the best thing that ever happened to him. She'd worked in the county election commission since the days when Jake Sheridan controlled it, and as the lone Republican appointee, was the only one on the staff not obligated to the machine.

"Why in the hell didn't you marry a Democrat, Dave?" Garner asked. "Hell, I know. You'd run out of Democrats. Married all them already."

Garner knew that Ann had been good for Dave. To Garner's knowledge she was the only woman he'd ever told the truth. "I have nothing," he told her. "No house, no furniture. No car without a bank note and no bank account."

"That's all right, Dave," she'd replied. "I have all those things. All I need is you."

For the first time since the twenties, Dave was solvent, happy, and—finally—as loyal to his wife as he had always been to Garner.

Dave knew his days as a policeman were numbered, but he didn't want to end up at sixty-five in the place where he'd started—at the bottom of the ladder.

"Shit, Garner," Dave told his friend the day he went for help. "All I'm trying to do is hold on to what I got. To Ann and these." He touched his lieutenant's braids. "And I need a little help keeping these."

"You'll be all right," Garner assured him again. "Now just take the goddamn sergeant's test."

From then on, Dave added two new items to the police paraphernalia he lugged to work every day. Along with his pistol, flashlight, handcuffs, and billy club, he now carried the new *Metro Police Department Operations Manual for Superior Officers* and a copy of the *Civil Service Board Rules and Regulations*.

The civil service examination was still a few weeks off. Before he could take it, though, he would have to pass yet another test—in the streets.

• • •

Dave was still Acting Lieutenant White in charge of a Saturday-night shift downtown when a call came across his radio that an officer was in trouble outside a normally quiet tavern in North Nashville called the Dew Drop Inn. There had been one killing inside the place already that night, so Dave checked the December sky for the full moon he held accountable for such unlikely occurrences. But he saw only a black December rain.

With responding sirens cracking through the night air, Dave was the first to reach the tavern. A police cruiser with both front doors open and its dome light flashing sat unoccupied in the street. Voices could be heard in the dark farther down the block—and then five or six loud reports. Pistol shots.

Dave pulled up on the sidewalk next to the vacant cruiser, reported his arrival to the dispatcher, and unholstered his revolver as he got out of the car.

No sooner had his feet hit the pavement than he detected the outline of a patrolman emerging from the darkness beyond the reach of the headlights of the abandoned cruiser. But something was wrong. The officer was backing up, his attention focused on something or someone still in the darkness. As he backed into the glow of the lights, the policeman fired, a streak of flame marking the direction, and then fired again. Dave could see the officer clearly now, a young black patrolman who quickly darted back toward his patrol car, the service revolver in his hand. Then into the beam of the headlights staggered a man in a white shirt waving a large butcher knife. Just off to his right, at the edge of the darkness, Dave saw another officer, the second man from the unit. He, too, was backing up, his pistol drawn. The man with the knife, a young black man crazy eyed and unhearing, was lunging at him wildly. The officer was dancing away from him, shooting futilely once or twice as he moved.

Trying to stay out of the line of fire, Dave stepped into the street. Crouching instinctively, looking down his arm over the sight of his pistol, he took dead aim at the stalker's midsection. He had been in this position before, nearly twenty years earlier, emptying his pistol at the young gunmen of Mink Slide.

Still retreating, almost to the car now, the patrolman leveled his revolver a final time and fired point blank, but the assailant, unhit or unfazed, kept coming. The officer's gun clicked again—on an empty chamber. Dave pulled back the hammer on his pistol. There was no more time.

Dave yelled a final warning, just as the blast from a shotgun filled the night. The gunfire came out of the darkness from the right side of the patrol car and was followed immediately by another blast and then a third, which lifted the man with the knife off the ground with its impact. He fell to the wet pavement in the wash of the headlights, a red hole in his chest. He had been shot by that first officer Dave had seen.

Never had Dave felt such relief at the sight of a dead man. It was the relief he always felt after escaping violence: relief that he was still alive, but also relief that the killing had been done by someone else. The young officers were now frantically trying to explain that the man had repeatedly ignored orders to surrender the knife and that they had almost emptied their weapons firing warning shots, deliberately trying first to miss him and then to wound him without taking his life.

Both patrolmen were temporarily suspended from duty. There would be an investigation and a grand jury just as there had been in 1946, and because the dead man was black, there would be a question about the possible violation of his civil rights. Good thing those patrolmen were black, too, Dave told Ann when he got home.

"If I'd had to kill him, they would have hung me up by my toenails. John Lewis and his boys would be marching in front of the house. I could forget about the sergeant's exam. I'd be up before the civil service commission just trying to keep my badge."

A few weeks later, with his dreaded civil service sergeant's examination only a few days off, Dave ran into Mayor Briley in the courthouse hallway. As usual the mayor was red eyed, in a hurry, and in the company of his secretary, with whom his relationship had become notorious. "Hello Dave," he said, throwing up his hand and scurrying along.

Briley had spent most of his adult life living in Garner and Dave's bailiwick of East Nashville. More than once when he was on the county patrol Dave had encountered Briley, then the county judge, hopelessly drunk and in need of assistance, which he had always rendered.

"Mr. Mayor, I need to see you a minute," said Dave, falling in step. The mayor was headed to his office. He stopped at the door, allowing the secretary, an officious and imperious woman, to enter without him.

"Yeah, Dave, what is it?" said the mayor, leaving no doubt as to his irritation.

"It's about this sergeant's examination. You know I've been a police superior officer an awful long time to have to take a test to be sergeant."

"Well, those are the rules, Dave. You know we've got to take the politics out of the police department. But you go on and take the test. I know you'll make a good score and be all right on that. You'll do fine."

"So all I got to do is pass the test, right? I mean, part of the test is an oral examination, which counts thirty or forty percent. That means you can promote who you want to, just like always."

"Well, we'll end up with a list of qualified candidates. And then as the promotions become available, we'll pick from the list. All you have to do is make that list, Dave, and stay on it. You'll do fine on that oral examination. You're a good policeman. Don't worry about a thing, now. You'll be all right."

Before the examination was administered Dave got a bootlegged copy of the written questions. He had never been a good student. His handwriting was like chicken scratching. His eyesight was failing. But he studied the sergeant's exam like a boy afraid he would fail the eighth grade and not make it to high school. He knew all the answers anyway, but he looked them up in the department's police procedure manual to make sure. When the test was finally given, he was ready. And of the sixty or so officers who took the test, Dave finished seventh.

But when the first promotions were announced, Dave was not among them. The handful of available permanent sergeant's jobs went to people who finished ahead of him—except for one. The civil service commission, noting the rising national concern for racial equality and the inadequate number of black superior officers in the police department, skipped down the list to number thirty-four, an impressive young black patrolman, twenty-seven or twenty-eight years old, the city's first beneficiary of something called "affirmative action." Dave knew and liked the young man and thought him a capable officer. In no time, the man was promoted to lieutenant, and then put in charge of police intelligence.

Meanwhile, Dave exchanged his acting lieutenant's bars for some acting sergeant's stripes and waited for a permanent promotion that never came.

The mayor had been right. Politics no longer had a place in the police department—at least not the kind of politics Dave knew. The new politics had to do with Washington and civil rights and the new guys at the newspapers whose names he didn't know. Dave was sure the new politics had some levers just like the old. But he didn't know where they were.

For a couple of years he held the rank of acting sergeant. Then he heard that they were going to abolish the list of qualified candidates. A new examination would be administered and a new list compiled. He wondered if they would put a sixty-two-year-old man on it.

Again he went to see Garner, who was preparing to run for reelection as trustee and to run his son, Gale, for attorney general, the one old county office that had been left intact by the Metro charter. Their daily meetings had become such a ritual that Garner was automatically waiting for him in the courthouse hallway, as if he could feel Dave en route.

"They're going to abolish the list and start over," Dave complained.

"I'll have to take another goddamn examination. What am I gonna do, Garner?"

For all the years they had known each other, Garner had always had an answer to questions like that. He had always had a button to push, or a chit to call in when Dave needed help. The sad truth was he didn't any longer.

"About all you can do is get yourself some new friends," Garner said soberly.

Dave's face took on that little sneer, which Garner knew meant he was either mad or afraid. "What the hell you talkin' about, Fat Pappy?"

"I'm talking about me. About us. You're not gonna get anything from Briley and Flip as long as they think you're my friend. You better cut loose from me."

"Hell," said Dave. He turned and walked off.

Garner yelled after him. "That's right. That's what you'll have to do."

Dave shook his head and turned around. "Well, if that's what I got to do to be a sergeant—well, I guess I ain't gonna be sergeant."

A few days later, Dave saw his friend from the *Tennessean*, Wayne Whitt, in the courthouse.

"Who do you have to know to get promoted at the police department, Wayne?"

"The man at the hardware store, I guess, Dave."

The Honey Bee. Dave knew that already. The *Banner* was full of stories complaining that all the patronage decisions in the Briley administration were being made by "the group"—or the "Seven Sachems of Metro" as Jimmy Stahlman called them in his editorials.

Dave was working the night shift, but he put on his police uniform early in the day, stopped at the barbershop and got his shoes shined, and went to the hardware store. Dave had known Ezell Flippen a long time, but not well enough to call him "Flip" like Garner did. He didn't have an appointment but he waited in a chair outside Mr. Flippen's office with his hat in his hands, turning it back and forth, slipping the shiny bill through his fingers. He caught himself staring down in his lap and jerked his face back up straight, so as to hide the growing bald spot on the back of his head from the woman who had greeted him. Dave had told Ann not to pay any attention to the bald spot, that the back of his head was older than the rest of him, which is how he felt.

Mr. Flippen greeted him like they knew each other better than they did. "And what can I do for you, Dave?" he asked in a courtly tone.

Dave explained that he would be retiring in a couple of years and that it would be nice if he could retire as a sergeant, which was the rank he had held nearly all the years he'd been a policeman. He told Mr. Flippen how he had finished seventh on the qualified-for-sergeant test and that now they were about to abolish the list. All things considered, Dave said, he thought he might deserve some help in getting promoted before the list was outdated. After all, he had worked for the passage of Metropolitan government, and for Briley's election. His daughter, Billye, had worked in both campaigns, he said, for Jim Roberson, and his grandson was writing politics for the *Tennessean*. "My politics are all right," Dave assured him.

"I'd like to help you, Dave," Mr. Flippen said. "But I don't know if I can."

Dave's eyes narrowed. Mr. Flippen was leaning back in his chair. The Honey Bee had swollen considerably since Dave had last seen him. His corpulence now tested his clothes. His hands were pudgy and soft.

"What do you mean you don't know, Mr. Flippen?" asked Dave, tight-lipped.

"Well now," said the Honey Bee, rearing back even farther in his chair. "It's like this. Putting those sergeant stripes on you would be just like putting them on Garner Robinson. And we just couldn't do that, now, could we? You know he's gonna be against us next time as well as I do."

That was not the answer Dave expected. But it was one he understood and he recognized it instantly as final. That was "the man" sitting there—the way Jake used to be the man. And there was nothing he could say or do, including renouncing his friendship with Garner, that would change things, and renouncing Garner was the last thing he would ever do.

Dave stood up, sucked in his stomach, and placed his patrol cap on his head, at a jaunty angle. "Well, thank you for your time, Flip," he said, with a familiarity he hadn't come in with. "If that's the way you feel about it, you can just take those sergeant's stripes and stick 'em up your ass, you old pustule-gutted sonofabitch, you."

Dave White stomped out of the hardware store without looking back, at either Flippen or the career he'd left behind. He never took the sergeant's exam again or pestered anyone for a promotion. Instead, he got that safe desk job Ann wanted him to have, as a clerk at the auto impoundment lot, where he worked until he was seventy-one years old. The minute he retired as a patrolman in 1975, hung up his uniform, and put away his gun, he began to die.

The Destruction of Chicken Man

"A big vote is necessary today to smash the old Robinson machine, drive its influence out of the courthouse and put important public offices in the hands of competent public spirited men," declared the *Tennessean.*

"The struggle . . . is between the powerful old county machine which has been on its last legs and, on the other hand, a group of able, dedicated candidates who want to bring a breath of fresh air into the courthouse."

It was primary election day 1966, but the words could have been taken verbatim from the newspaper's pages twenty years earlier. The old habits were ingrained. Despite its new leadership the *Tennessean* still felt most comfortable lumping whomever it opposed with its old nemesis the "machine," now personified by Garner and

Governor Frank Clement. After all those years, political machines—real or imagined—still made the best enemies.

Little Evil Jacobs, Big Evil Hoffa, and Tommy Osborn had all gone off to jail, and the Camelot men of Nashville were still out in pursuit of dragons. Two years earlier the newspaper had elected a liberal successor to Estes Kefauver and had come close to electing a blind man sheriff, only to have him lose at the last minute to the roly-poly Robert R. Poe, a former constable from Garner's side of town running as an independent.

With a veritable orgy of elections taking place in 1966, filling every office from constable to governor with enlightened, progressive young people aligned with the *Tennessean* was not only possible but, in the mind of the newspapers, imperative. This included the powerful county prosecutor's office being vacated by retirement and the now near-worthless offices of sheriff and of Metro trustee. The new political powers began anointing their candidates just as the old machine bosses always had.

Bright young Thomas H. Shriver, Jr., whom the Honey Bee had promised to support four years earlier, was a first-rate lawyer who would have been at home in any Kennedy administration. The *Tennessean* wanted him as prosecutor. But the people in the prosecutor's office liked someone else better—young Gale Robinson, who was already on staff as an assistant district attorney. Gale was hard on the bit to run, but he knew opposing the *Tennessean*'s candidate could complicate his father's reelection for trustee.

He went to see Daddy at the funeral home, where family matters were often taken up in one of the viewing rooms before only a single embalmed witness.

Expecting a request to postpone advancing his political career for a year or two, Gale diplomatically began by offering to do so. "I'm young," he said. "I have plenty of time. I can wait."

"No," the old sheriff told him without hesitation. "You're ready to run—and I'm not ready to quit. We'll both run and I'll help you any way I can."

Garner knew Ben West was planning a comeback against Beverly

Briley in the nonpartisan Metro election in May, a month before the June Democratic primary for county offices. He also knew that the *Tennessean*'s lawyer John J. Hooker, Jr., was planning on running for governor in the statewide party primary later in August. With elections almost every month during the spring and summer, it was going to be a political free-for-all all year long. There was no way he could escape opposition—if for no other reason than just to keep him preoccupied with his reelection.

Garner was right. A former city councilman named Glenn Ferguson, a close personal friend of the young publisher Amon Evans and anxious to claim the perks of the friendship, was ready to run for any office. He got the nod to run against Garner for trustee, and a local businessman, who had no experience with either jails or law enforcement, was recruited to run against Poe.

Garner made no secret of his support of West for mayor, and he made it known that he expected West's support in return. But shortly before the mayor's race in May, the *Tennessean* was tipped off that West was visiting the Robinson home in Old Hickory. A reporter-photographer team was sent out to document the fact that "a political machine" was still alive and meeting in the flesh.

Garner was surprised—and for once had trouble maintaining his traditional cordiality.

"Reporter? I didn't ask for any reporter myself," he told the young man at his door, "much less a reporter from you-all [the *Tennessean*]. . . . I don't think it is fair to send a reporter to a man's home."

The reporter was not admitted. "It's just a Sunday-afternoon gathering of friends," Garner told him. "But before you get through there will probably be some political implications from this. After all, I am in the political field . . . you know."

Cast back into the role of old machine boss, Garner made an easy target. And father-son machine duo—that was almost as good as the return of Jake Sheridan himself. The *Tennessean* could have its cake and eat it, too; it could act like the machine and run against one at the same time.

The turnout for May's mayor's race was huge, and Briley won reelection handily, which should have been a harbinger for the Robinsons. But even the bitter daily squabbling between the *Tennessean* and the *Banner* failed to generate much public interest in the county primary a month later.

In actuality, the Robinson machine the *Tennessean* continued to rail against daily now existed only in the imagination of editorial writers. The law enforcement agencies, the election commission, and all the patronage of the local and federal governments were in the hands of either Mayor Briley or the newspaper itself. Only the state government, which had plenty of jobs and state contracts to offer, was free of their control.

What was left of Garner's political power rested in his funeral home business and the thousands of loyal friends his family had made over the years. Garner and Gale had also both been popular leaders of the Al Menah Temple of the Shrine, an influential city-wide organization, and nephew Jimmy was a capable and experienced political organizer. The Robinsons put up a good fight, but their ability to win precincts was pretty much relegated to their East Nashville strongholds like Old Hickory, where old Dave White showed up in civilian clothes to work the polls. Warned by Garner that he was risking the loss of his police department job, Dave's response was, "To hell with it, I can get a security job in a parking lot anywhere."

Less than half the people who had voted in the mayor's race turned out for the primary, a circumstance the newspaper predicted would help the machine. Which was true. The *Tennessean*'s candidates won every race on the ballot, all by about the same margins of five thousand votes, except for Garner's, where Ferguson had won by less than three thousand votes. The most notable testament to the newspaper's power was the reelection of an incumbent judge who had died of pneumonia during the campaign. His wife, a little old lady with braided white hair who wore tennis shoes with socks rolled down around her ankles, carried on the campaign. On Election Day the *Tennessean* had declared, "The other candidate is totally unqualified" and urged voters to pull the lever for the deceased, which they did. It was an election coup of which even Boss Crump would have been proud.

Garner had never been one to wallow in defeat. He had always run as hard as he could, gotten his voters to the polls on Election Day, and then accepted the results. But this time he did not. He was mad at the *Tennessean*, which he thought had conducted a vendetta against him. What made it so hard to digest was that his nephew Jimmy Roberson was in Memphis working on behalf of John J. Hooker, Jr., the *Tennessean*'s lawyer who was now running for governor. The *Tennessean* had no greater political interest in 1966 than the election of Hooker, who was trying to end fourteen years of swapping the governor's office by Clement and his campaign manager, Buford Ellington, who was seeking his third term.

Garner knew that the August primary, held on the same ballot as the county general election, with the governor's office and both U.S. Senate seats at stake, would produce twice the voter turnout of the county primary he'd just lost. The Republicans, growing in numbers, would come out in droves to support their Senate nominee—a popular young East Tennessee congressman named Howard Baker. Jimmy Stahlman and the *Banner* would go all out to elect Baker and beat Hooker for governor. It was the perfect opportunity to try again. Garner told Gale he was not ready to quit. He decided to forsake the Democratic party and run against Ferguson in the general election—as an independent. The party line was about the only fence he had not already jumped over at least once.

Adopting the newspaper's own tactics, Garner ran against the "*Tennessean* machine" instead of Ferguson. The councilman, he told voters with a straight face, was "a machine candidate . . . a machine controlled by the morning newspaper."

Despite its preoccupation with the Hooker-Ellington primary, which was on the same ballot, the *Tennessean* found the time and space to fry Garner again. Glenn Ferguson's election was more important to Amon Evans than Garner had anticipated. The newspaper accused Garner of a "lack of grace" for deserting the party that had made him the most often elected man in Tennessee history. Even worse, the newspaper pointed out, Garner Robinson was being supported and was siding with—of all things—the Republicans.

The strategy worked. The voters had had enough of Garner Robinson over the years. He lost to Ferguson a second time, by more votes than before.

Dividing the monopoly proceeds from the city's newspaper business with his *Tennessean* partners had been a financially rewarding experience for Jimmy Stahlman and the *Banner*. At the same time, being able to spit editorial venom in the *Tennessean*'s socialist face each day was for the old flag-waving publisher a continuing spiritual invigoration.

He ducked no fights with his morning adversary and took his victories whenever and however he came by them. None was more enjoyable than the destruction of John J. Hooker, Jr.'s, political aspirations, which he carried out in the late sixties like he was driving stakes in the heart of a vampire who refused to die.

In 1966, from his position as the *Tennessean*'s lawyer, Hooker launched a race for governor, believing that he and his friend Seigenthaler could pull off in their home state what they had helped John Kennedy do nationally in 1960. Young, handsome, and charming, Hooker made a great Kennedy. Although not as wealthy, he was an even better speaker and had a beautiful and gracious wife and wonderful-looking children.

At the outset, it appeared that Hooker also had an asset most Democrats who ran for statewide office in Tennessee had never had—a substantial connection to and social standing within Belle Meade, the state's most important reservoir of money and power. John J. had married Tish Fort, the stunning and popular daughter of one of the city's wealthiest insurance magnates. One of his law partners, Gil Merritt, had married her sister, and John J.'s brother, Henry, had married an Ingram from the wealthy industrialist family of Nashville and Chicago. Henry's mother-in-law, Hortense, was among the rule setters at the Belle Meade Country Club and chaired a roundtable called "the committee" that passed on membership.

But despite his wealth and connections, Hooker was a refugee at heart. He had taken literally the Kennedys' philosophy "that a rising tide lifts all the boats." Running against an entrenched state administration, he made "Time for a Change" his campaign theme. But Hooker campaigned most effectively in the ghettos of Memphis, had his picture taken with black children crawling on his shoulders, and actively courted the burgeoning black political movement in Tennessee. When viewed in that context, his campaign theme made him undeniably the candidate of the poor and of organized labor— the tide whose boat needed the most lift.

Although his opponent, Buford Ellington, was more at home on a hog farm than in a country club, his conservative Boll Weevil Democratic politics were more welcome in Belle Meade than Hooker's classic liberalism. Belle Meade didn't raise its sons to wallow in the trough of politics anyway; it raised them to vote Republican in national elections and then to quietly give their money locally to conservative Democratic farm boys like Buford Ellington who would always hold them in awe and do their bidding when they got elected governor.

From the minute Hooker announced his candidacy, Belle Meade's voice, Jimmy Stahlman, condemned him as an unproven young squirt with a socialistic approach to government more welcome in Massachusetts where it had originated. Invariably the *Banner* political cartoons included a tiny bird somewhere bringing Hooker the same message from Washington: "Bobby says hello." The *Banner* news story reporting Hooker's endorsement by E. William Henry, the Kennedy-appointed chairman of the Federal Communications Commission, was accompanied by a picture of young Henry in a Batman costume. The photo had been taken at a masquerade ball, a fact the *Banner* didn't bother to mention.

In one of the great stump campaigns in American politics, Hooker and Ellington crisscrossed the state for weeks, each with a reporter from their sponsoring newspaper among their entourage and each stalked at every stop by a reporter from the opposition paper. Readers of both papers would never have suspected they were reporting on the same campaign.

Ellington, with a strong following within the Farm Bureau and the backing of both the incumbent governor and President Lyndon Johnson, defeated Hooker decisively statewide, losing only the black vote. Nowhere was his margin of victory greater than in Davidson County, where Hooker had been pummeled by Stahlman's *Banner*. Hooker lost his home county by twenty thousand votes, including a five-to-one humiliation in the Belle Meade precinct, a few blocks from his house.

The message was unmistakable. Voters had had enough direction from their morning newspaper for one decade. They had followed the knights of Camelot on civil rights, ending the segregation of their buses and lunch counters. They had supported reapportionment. They had made the *Tennessean*'s progressive dream of a consolidated city and county government a reality and had voted for its local candidates. But they would not give the state capitol to a rich liberal from Belle Meade, no matter whose lawyer he was.

Neither the *Tennessean* nor Hooker was discouraged by the defeat. They decided immediately that Hooker would run again four years later. Convinced that he had lost because he had no public record other than as a lawyer for mainly liberal causes, Hooker decided that in the interim he needed to become a successful businessman. Having played broker when his friend John Y. Brown purchased Kentucky Fried Chicken from Colonel Sanders, Hooker became infatuated with the franchise business. Brown, who had initially set up KFC in Nashville, envied Hooker's place in the social set, particularly his membership at the beautiful Belle Meade Country Club. But despite his family connections, Hooker could not help his kindred spirit Brown win over the Belle Meade membership mavens. They never gave him a second look. Peeved, Brown moved to Louisville, and John J., believing there was a greater appetite for chicken than the Colonel could satisfy, talked Grand Ole Opry star

Minnie Pearl into lending her name to a competing fried chicken company.

One of the world's great salesmen, Hooker had Minnie Pearl Chicken flying high. The franchise business concept was hot on Wall Street, and the initial stock offering soared, quickly splitting two for one. Soon Hooker was counting by the dozens the friends he'd made millionaires with the original issue.

But by the time the 1970 governor's race rolled around, the bloom was off the franchise rose—temporarily—and it was being picked apart by the financial press. Still, Hooker won the August Democratic primary easily, and there had not been a Republican governor in the state since early in the century. The unknown Memphis dentist the Republicans had nominated to oppose Hooker was given little chance.

But Stahlman was relentless. Unfortunately for Hooker, the Tennessee general election had attracted the attention of the Nixon administration. Senator Albert Gore, Sr., the leading Senate critic of Nixon's bombing policies in Vietnam, was being challenged by a wealthy young Republican congressman, Bill Brock of Chattanooga.

Stahlman convinced the Nixon crowd that the two races were inseparable. If Hooker could be stopped, Brock could unseat Gore and silence the president's loudest critic on the Senate Foreign Relations Committee. From that point on it was a simple matter for the Republicans to get the Securities and Exchange Commission to scrutinize a Kennedy follower's business at precisely the point he was asking voters to entrust him with theirs. The SEC came up with a few minor violations, which to the glee of Belle Meade Jimmy Stahlman quickly hyped into one of the great business scandals of all time. Before the newspaper was done, Hooker had the public image—quite unfairly—of a chicken flimflam man one step away from being roasted by the federal government.

He wasn't, of course, but he lost again, this time to a smiling Memphis dentist with no previous experience in politics. And from the bashing they took at the hands of Jimmy Stahlman, neither

Hooker's political career nor the Minnie Pearl Chicken business would ever recover.

Instead they became just more carnage strewn on the battlefield of the *Banner-Tennessean* wars. The political dead left by the wayside in Nashville during the glorious days of Camelot ran the gamut from little evil to big, from guilty to innocent. The victims included corrupt sheriffs and ignorant ward heelers; labor racketeers and their foolhardy lawyers; senatorial statesmen, brave city saviors, and idealistic pioneers of the New Frontier; and, of course, what was left of the old Garner Robinson political machine.

The Last Hurrah

Garner ran for public office one last time in 1975, the year Dave retired from the police department. The campaign gave them both something to do besides hanging around the funeral home. Garner was sixty-nine and Dave seventy-one. Together with Dick Jones, who was seventy-three and had been part of Garner's shadow as long as Dave, they resembled some kind of frosty-haired over-the-hill gang out to rob one more train.

The race was for a district seat in the forty-member Metro council. The district encompassed Old Hickory, which meant Garner had at least a chance of winning. But Mayor Briley was also retiring after thirteen years in office, and his handpicked successor, Representative Richard Fulton, who had been in office since the 1962 vote fraud scandal, was anxious to keep control of the council. Garner's history showed that there was no chance of controlling him.

The opposing candidate was a union man named Cotton Turner, a man half Garner's age who had learned his politics in labor-management wars where tire slitting and sugaring gas tanks were considered fair and manly tactics.

One of the twins, Maude, ran her father's campaign out of the Robinson store which had moved and modernized. She plastered the town with campaign signs and stickers, just like in the old days. But now the placards were torn down and destroyed as quickly as they were posted.

The family was shocked. Things like that didn't happen, not in Robinson country. Maude complained to the police, but nothing was done. Her cousin Jimmy Roberson, then a state senator, came in to help. Maude launched such a fierce counterattack against Turner that he publicly called her "a rattlesnake." His supporters responded by shooting out the lights in the Robinson store.

In the face of it all, Garner was nonchalant. He and his old pals went through all the usual motions, but times had changed. The Robinsons didn't own the Old Hickory voters anymore. Garner knew it, but by now he had figured out that while winning was better than losing, winning wasn't all it was cracked up to be either.

The real fun was in the running, the camaraderie with his old cronies, the scare he could still put into the political establishment that he had once personified.

For the old war horse, the tone of this campaign had been set the day he told Dave he was running. Dave came to the farm more frequently then, because it was one of the few places he had to go. It was closer to his home than the funeral home and he could be more certain of finding his way back. His memory had begun to slip. The old boys still met outside—always, no matter the weather. The privacy of Garner's driveway had replaced the courthouse hallway as the protector of their secrets.

Garner casually mentioned that he was thinking about going for the council seat, which Dave just as casually ignored. Maybe his mind was slipping faster than Garner had thought.

"What's that dog's name?" asked Dave, nodding toward an old speckled bird dog lying in the yard. Dave loved bird dogs and had never seen that one around Garner's.

"Oh hell, I don't know. He came here. I just call him Dog."

"I'll be goddamned," said Dave, shaking his head. "I'm gonna

THE SECRETS OF THE HOPEWELL BOX

take him home with me. Ain't nobody in Old Hickory gonna vote for a sonofabitch too sorry to name his dog."

"Well, by God, we'll just see," Garner replied. " 'Cause I'm running anyway."

"All right, I'll help you. But I'm taking this dog with me."

"Well, take him, goddamn it. I'll see you tomorrow."

The dog got a name—Blue—and a new wire kennel behind Dave's house beside his fishing boat, which he cleaned up a lot but seldom used.

The next time Dave showed up to campaign, Garner had left without him. Dave found an angry Skinny trying to break into a locked liquor cabinet. "Get in here right now, Dave White," she ordered, "and help me break into this thing. That sonofabitch Garner Robinson locked up my whiskey and took the key with him."

On the next campaign day, Dave loyally reported the incident to the candidate.

"And I guess to hell you helped her, too," Garner admonished. "You still can't stay away from whiskey."

"Hell no, you old sonofabitch, but I should've. It would've served you right for going off campaigning without me."

Garner did not win the council seat. Didn't come close. But he got the last laugh.

During the seventies, nephew Jim had become known as the "Senator" and wielded considerable power in the Tennessee General Assembly, including some influence over the appointment of the Davidson County Election Commission and the hiring of its staff.

Both Guynell Sanders, the executive director of the commission, and Dave's daughter, Billye, who was Guynell's best friend and worked for her, were Roberson loyalists. Dave's wife, Ann, still held her Republican staff appointment. The combination raised the specter that some chicanery might be possible in favor of Garner.

Incoming mayor Fulton had not yet consolidated his control, but he had supporters among the election commissioners, and they immediately showed up in Old Hickory and impounded the voting machines in the Twelfth District and hauled them off. As usual, the voting machine tallies were left with the precinct election officials.

When the Twelfth District reported its votes, Garner was well behind Cotton Turner, but one precinct summary was not included in the report. When Dave's daughter saw the district returns, she noticed that the missing precinct was the one encompassing the old Hopewell voting box, which she laughingly made a point of to her boss Guynell and her stepmother Ann. "Maybe Daddy and Lewis Hurt are riding it around in their car again," she said.

One of the election commissioners, a Fulton loyalist, heard the remark and raced to a telephone in the back office. Soon the place was crawling with commission members demanding the Twelfth District returns and a search for the missing precinct summary. The report turned out not to be missing at all, only misplaced. When it was found and tallied, Turner held fast to his winning margin.

Lewis Hurt was no longer the election officer in Old Hickory, and Dave White had long been home watching the returns on television, sitting in his undershirt on a sofa, with a mean-spirited little Chihuahua named Jingles on his lap. When his wife brought home the story about the commotion his thirty-year-old escapade had caused in the election commission, he had trouble understanding what she was talking about.

"I've been right here all night long with Jingles," he protested. The Hopewell box had long vanished from his mind. For the gang from Old Hickory, election stealing was not only no longer possible, it could no longer even be remembered.

Garner never brooded a minute over the loss. He was too busy over the next few years burying people he loved.

PART NINE

The Final Returns

W hen my brothers and I pulled up in his driveway that day in the summer of 1980, old Dave was sitting in a yard chair in a short-sleeved sport shirt talking to an empty dog kennel.

"Look at him, James," he said to me, his eyes fixed on the weeds where the dog had once lived. "Look at old Blue bare those teeth. He'd like to bite all of y'all in the ass. He would too, if I let him out." He laughed like a loon. "What're y'all doing here, anyway?"

Our granddaddy was mad as a hatter, the blood to his brain having long been slowed to a trickle through arteries clogged and hardened by years of smoking Home Runs, the strongest filterless cigarettes he could buy.

"To take you to the doctor," my brother said, only half lying. There would be a doctor there all right, preferably with several big, strong assistants to help us make sure old Dave stayed in the hospital for treatment, which he so far had refused to do.

My brothers and I had undertaken the task of delivering him there, only after his fourth and longest-suffering wife, Ann, living proof that it is never too late to do the right thing, had assured us she had located and secured all of his pistols. Even then we were afraid, not only that we might hurt him during the wrestling match we figured inevitable, but that he might still have some guns she didn't know about. At seventy-six, old Dave was still a helluva man to have to go after.

He had been well past sixty when he finally decided it was time to quit swinging billy clubs in street riots and voluntarily sought the tranquility of the police department vehicle impoundment lot. But the strong old man my brothers and I delivered to the hospital that day didn't stay strong very long. The next time we moved him we needed an ambulance. My mother asked Garner if he would do it, but warned him that his old friend no longer recognized anybody.

"I'll send somebody else to get him then," Garner said, painfully. "I'd just as soon remember the Dave I always knew."

Not long after her father was hospitalized, my mother got a telephone call from Zoe, wife number two now in her mid-seventies, from whom Dave had been divorced for thirty-five years. "If y'all have put Dave in some dirty old nursing home, I'm going up there and get him out," she threatened.

Dave died in a fit a few months later, and Garner sent a hearse to get him. His wake was a parade of old policemen, small-time politicians, and friends of the Robinsons. It was as if one of them had died. Dave's first wife, Sallie, my grandmother, came to sit alongside the widow. Zoe called in sick, and Verna, wife number three, telephoned her condolences.

Garner insisted on handling the funeral himself. All the boys from the old days wanted him to take care of things personally, Garner said, "especially Dave, who would be pissed off if I didn't."

I hadn't seen Garner for more than ten years, since the days when he was Metro trustee and I was a reporter for the newspaper that was lambasting him every day. No matter how often we had crossed paths, he never mentioned the *Tennessean* or acknowledged that I wrote about politics for it.

Whenever Garner, Gale, Cousin Jimmy, or any Robinson raised an election flag, my mother would report to the funeral home for duty, an expected and welcome member of the campaign brain trust that usually got set up on the upper floors of the funeral home. Despite my connection with the opposition newspaper, she remained as privy to their strategy and secrets as ever.

Remarkably, the newspaper never thought it a problem either, I guess because politics had always been such a personal thing with the *Tennessean*, too. Over the years it supported the people its owners and editors knew and liked, for whom they had done favors and expected favors in return.

No matter whom the *Tennessean* backed on its editorial pages, once inside the voting booth I pulled the lever for every Robinson on the ballot, always—a fact I would not have hesitated to confess in the publisher's office. That kind of "family" loyalty was what always made politics work in America. It was the foundation of the Irish Democratic tradition in Boston, the Kennedys' Camelot, and the Daley machine in Chicago. Questioned once about the awarding of city insurance contracts to members of his family, Mayor Daley indignantly demanded, "If you can't help your own family, who can you help?"

Working in the press carried no license to forget where you came from, nor an imperative to renounce your culture and citizenship. Neither did it mean you had to be mired forever in conflict. Although I worked at the paper for ten years, only once did the subject of my family ties arise. On that Sunday afternoon in 1966 when former mayor Ben West was rumored to be having a secret meeting with Garner at his home, a young city editor with no knowledge of my background asked me to accompany a photographer to the Robinson farm in Old Hickory and knock on the door.

"I can't do that," I said, refusing an assignment for the only time in my entire career. "I'd appreciate it if you would send someone else."

"Why?" he wanted to know.

"Because if I go out there and knock on that door Garner will let me in that meeting."

"Well, that's what we want," he said.

"No, it isn't. He'll let me in because I'm Dave White's grandson. Not because I'm a reporter. And if I go in that house under those circumstances, I can't tell you anything I hear."

Nothing else was ever said, and I was never asked to cover Garner again. But at my granddaddy's funeral I recalled the times I had spent as a child hanging around Garner's office, at eye level with the pistol barrels, peeking over the dashboards of his ambulances and police cars, and standing around on the Colemere Club lawn and in the driveway of his farm, watching chickens and dogs and spotted horses while he and my grandfather gossiped in some code I did not comprehend.

By then I had covered ten national political conventions, five presidents, and the Watergate scandal. I had interviewed President Reagan on national television and had been on "Meet the Press." In the world of East Nashville precinct politics, this bestowed some celebrity, which Garner acknowledged as having "been playing with the big boys." He was filled with questions about Washington and the Congress and what had happened to Jimmy Carter, as if I were some kind of expert on the country.

I knew full well by then that it was he who was the expert, that he and Jake and Elkin, their friends and their enemies had discovered the real secrets of democracy—at least for their time and place. They knew what had made America work all those years. And that thing was all around me at that very moment—an organization of friends.

Their old leader, standing next to me now, his arm

resting on my shoulder like I was four years old again, was thinner now, well below the 280 pounds he once carried. His suit and shirt collar were obviously from a fatter time, and the Stetson I remembered was missing, too, as were all but a few hairs on the top of his head. Instinctively, I looked for the bulge of a pistol under his coat that had always been there before. But it was not. I guessed that at seventy-two he decided it was time to keep it in a drawer with his newspaper clippings.

Otherwise, Garner was the same, always moving, always courtly, grasping elbows, shaking hands, patting backs, and moving people around, a politician working the crowd. As he prepared to bury his friend, Garner's face was—well, the face of a funeral director. He spoke to the family softly, as if giving us the professional solicitude that came with the price. But of course there was no price. It was, in the Robinson family parlance, "another big no-pay funeral." And when out of earshot of the widow and my mother, Garner's asides were hardly typical of your run-of-the-mill undertaker.

"Now, we have to do this right," he said, hustling my brothers and me out on the porch, "or Old Dave White will haunt us the rest of our lives. We can't have that."

To us that meant minimum ceremony and frugal mourning. And no one knew better than Garner what low regard Dave had for the dying and burying business. After a particularly tearful and soulful wake for one of Ann's relatives in Alabama, Dave sensitively observed during the drive home that, "If they loved him and missed him that much, they should've stuffed him and kept him in the living room."

There was a long list of honorary pallbearers, mostly cops, a couple of Ann's relatives, and Dick Jones from the funeral home. My three brothers and myself, our father, and Garner actually carried the box. Nothing was said among us until we had reached the driveway outside.

"Heavier than I thought," one of us commented, as we approached the hearse.

"It's top of the line," Garner whispered. "A lot better than Dave would have picked out himself."

We knew that was right. Our mother had once asked him if he'd thought about "arrangements" for his own passing. "Hell no, Bill," he snapped. "Just tell Garner to wait until I'm good and stiff and then sharpen my legs like stakes and drive me in the ground."

Garner had heard that. "He didn't even want a casket," Garner said. "Wanted to be driven in the ground. Dave would've picked the cheapest deal I had, so he could put the money in his pocket . . . to spend on a car or a boat— or a woman."

We tried to maintain our grief-stricken looks.

"There's a lot of extra stuff in there, too," Garner said.

I took the bait. "What's in there?"

"What he always had. Pistol, flashlight, carbine. Extra white shirts. Brass polish, stuff he wouldn't go anywhere without."

I tried to stiffen my lip, like I had a million times before as a kid at Holy Name School, trying not to laugh during daily mass. I knew my brothers were trying to do the same.

We got him into the hearse without breaking up and breathed a sigh of relief. But Garner resumed the commentary at Spring Hill, a cemetery where all the Robinsons and Whites and all the other dead we knew were interred. It was located on the Gallatin Road, the main route from Nashville to Old Hickory.

"I don't know how we got in here without Dave to stop the traffic for us," said Garner, gazing at the entrance where the man in the coffin had once been a gate fixture. "If he could've directed traffic at his own funeral he would have. Nobody else could do it to suit him."

I had figured out by now what was taking place. Garner was keeping a promise, that to help him and us he was having the same kind of conversation he and Dave always had. I, for one, was thankful. Going to the grave is always the hardest part.

"Reckon there'll be whiskey and women where he's going?" I asked. Might as well raise their favorite subjects. We were almost to the gravesite.

"Women for sure," Garner said without hesitation or smile. "Where *he's* going. And if not, he won't stay."

A pallbearer's solemnity soon became hard to maintain. I could see my own father's eyes laughing, even though his mouth remained taut.

"We almost never got this casket closed," Garner continued. Now, we hoped he was being serious. None of us wanted to laugh out loud while carrying our grandfather the last few steps to his hole in the ground. My mother would have understood but no one else would have.

"Why?" I asked sheepishly. Already I could see the shoulders of one of my brothers shaking under his coat. He knew what was coming.

"Hell, his pecker was standing straight up, hard-on a cat couldn't scratch. Must have been after the nurses when his heart quit."

One of us let his breath escape in a wail, which he tried to cover with a cough. Another laughed out loud—a single stifled grunt, but we couldn't look at one another to see who it was. Our eyes were fixed on the ground now, tears streaming down our faces—tears that no one could tell were not from our grief.

Garner meanwhile remained stoic, unshaken—and unrelenting. He was standing close to me now, still whispering.

"Isn't this a nice spot?" he said, as we set the casket on the apparatus that would lower it into the ground. "Hard to find a place in here next to somebody he hadn't made mad."

I finally looked at Garner and grinned, so he'd know that I knew and appreciated what he had been doing for us, but he remained poker-faced. "You know nobody liked the sonofabitch but you-all—and me."

After the dirt and the holy water had been sprinkled, Garner escorted us all back to the limousine and accompanied us on the ride back to the funeral home. Once there, he disappeared into the labyrinth of hallways and cubbyholes, and when time came to say good-bye, I couldn't find him. But as my brothers and I drove past the cemetery on our way home, we saw his Cadillac at the gravesite.

There he was, a lone figure under the tent, standing by the grave, hands in his pockets, presumably saying to Dave whatever it was they never wanted anyone else to hear.

Rewards of a Long Shot

From his prison cell in Alabama Tommy Osborn finally witnessed the legislative independence made possible by his triumphant *Baker v. Carr* lawsuit. By the time he went on trial for jury tampering in the spring of 1963, thirty-six of the fifty states were involved in reapportionment lawsuits. By the end of that year the number had grown to forty-two. Among the discriminatory practices stopped in its wake was Georgia's unique "unit rule" voting system, a kind of electoral college for congressional primary elections in which the popular votes counted only inside individual counties, so an urban county with three hundred thousand voters had no more say about who went to Congress from the district than a rural county with fifty thousand.

By 1966 the equal population rule had affected every legislative seat and congressional district in the nation, and within five years the political map of the country would be totally remade.

All over the South reapportionment increased urban representation immediately, including more blacks and more Republicans. For the first time urban delegations were able to contest what had previously been cut-and-dried decisions, such as the election of legislative leaders.

Nowhere, of course, did this happen more grudgingly or with more drama than in Tennessee. In the Tennessee General Assembly, the decline in power of the Unholy Triumvirate created a giant vacuum just perfect for the "gorgeous little stooge," Governor Frank Clement. Into it he promptly stepped in January of 1965, with the intention of naming Jared Maddux, a senator from rural Cookeville, as senate majority leader, or lieutenant governor, as the spot was then called.

But the *Tennessean*, which was active on every front, had been

instrumental in the formation of a caucus of independent Democrats, which selected its own candidate, a Nashville lawyer named
Frank Gorrell.

Gorrell was a new-breed politician. Attracted by the glamor and
ideals of Camelot, he had stepped into politics from an unlikely
stage—the social set of Belle Meade. Gorrell was literally the example frequently cited by the Vanderbilt law professor of the young
lawyer who gets hired into the good Nashville law firm because he
married the daughter of its best client. In Gorrell's case it was the
family who made Jamison Bedding.

A big, gregarious fellow with coal-black hair, swarthy skin, and a
barrel chest, Gorrell looked so much like an Italian mafioso that his
friends called him "Gorrelli" and accused him of wearing his large
horn-rimmed glasses so he would not be mistaken for a nightclub
bouncer. But the dashing young Gorrell was more than just a pretty
face who had married well. He was streetwise, too, and fun-loving,
with a deep, guttural laugh that was infectious with good humor.
Everybody liked him.

On the evening before the full Democratic caucus vote, Gorrell
threw a party at his fashionable home at which he signed up thirteen
of the twenty-five state senate Democrats on a petition. He had
enough votes to win, but included among them was another dapper
urban state senator, a Memphis bachelor named Charlie O'Brien,
who the next day failed to show up, leaving Gorrell and Maddux tied
at twelve votes each.

Overnight, O'Brien mysteriously disappeared, leaving only a
message that he had been taken ill and had gone back to Memphis,
where he had been admitted to a hospital and given sedatives for
what administering physicians said was a stressful situation. Stressful indeed. Charlie had his mind changed by Governor Frank Clement's most potent and charming political weapon, his lovely sister
Anna Belle, who not only kept O'Brien from voting for Gorrell, but
eventually got him appointed a judge and married him.

Although Gorrell followed O'Brien to Memphis, found him, and
got another pledge of support, O'Brien continued to abstain until

Governor Clement had cut a deal with the state senate's eight Republicans. They voted for Maddux and, more important, for the first time since Reconstruction had a say about who would lead the Tennessee legislature.

A year later, the indefatigable Gorrell won the post of Senate speaker through some deal making of his own. It was not long until urban independents claimed the speaker's office of the Tennessee house for the first time since 1919, and soon afterward a Republican, the first since Reconstruction, got the job.

More dramatic and more visible was the appearance of black lawmakers filling seats in legislative halls where only months before even the viewing galleries had been segregated. When the *Baker* revolution moved from the state to the national level, it changed the complexion of Congress, too, and made the black vote a potent factor in hundreds of legislative and congressional districts still represented by whites. All of this was for the most part the work of a forgotten convict still doing his time in an Alabama federal prison.

In 1968 Tommy Osborn almost got his conviction overturned. While in prison he found out that Robert Vick, a man who could never keep his mouth shut, had told his neighbor Harry Childress that for testifying against Osborn, Kennedy's man Walter Sheridan had promised him thirty-five dollars a day during the trial, a job, money, and education for his children. At the trial, Vick had testified that he had been promised nothing.

Up to this point Osborn's appeal had been based on an allegation of entrapment. Now, he could seek a new trial on the grounds that he had been convicted on perjured testimony bought and paid for by the prosecution. He got his old law partner Maclin P. Davis, Jr., to file a new motion to vacate his sentence. A Belle Meade blue blood, Davis was a rarity among them in that he had always had an abiding interest in politics. More important, he was Tommy Osborn's closest friend and a good lawyer himself.

Davis was able to prove that ever since Vick testified, he had been benefiting financially from his role as a government witness. First, he had been put on the Metro police payroll for thirteen months and placed on special assignment with the U.S. marshal's office. And then, even though he had no experience in the insurance business, Vick was given a lucrative insurance contract by Teamster Local 327, where Hoffa enemy Don Vestal had regained the presidency. And in between the two jobs, Walter Sheridan had requested and subsequently passed along to Vick three thousand dollars in cash from Robert Kennedy's brother-in-law, Stephen Smith. But Sheridan had second thoughts about the transaction a few days later, took the money back, and later replaced it with Vestal's arrangement for insurance commissions. By this time Sheridan was an investigative reporter for NBC News. But along with Neal, who'd served briefly as U.S. attorney in Nashville and then gone into private practice, he was still involved in trying to make sure that Vick and their other star witness in the Hoffa trial, Edward Grady Partin, did not recant their testimony. From prison Hoffa had let it be known that either man could get a million dollars for changing his story.

Based on the new information, the Sixth Circuit Court of Appeals ordered the trial judge to hold an evidentiary hearing on the question of Vick's perjury, which produced the most bizarre irony yet.

The government's lawyer was Neal's successor, a brilliant young Nashvillian named Gilbert S. Merritt, who had been an assistant city attorney when Mayor Briley's administration had put Vick on its police payroll. Merritt, John J. Hooker, Jr.'s, brother-in-law, a former member of his law firm, and one of John Seigenthaler's closest friends, argued that Vick's statements to his neighbor Childress about the promises from Sheridan were not believable because Vick was a notorious liar who often made up stories to convince people he was an important man—except, of course, when he was under oath.

In denying Osborn a new trial, Judge Boyd issued a finding of fact in which he said the court did not believe what Vick told Childress because "Vick has apparently made wild and untrue statements when not under oath on a number of occasions." In other words, Vick was a terribly unreliable liar except on the day he testified for the government against Osborn. Eventually, the Sixth Circuit Court of Appeals agreed. However unbelievable Vick might be, Osborn's voice on the tape directing him to tamper with a juror remained the overwhelming piece of evidence. That this evidence was obtained under dubious circumstances seemed to matter little, even in an era when criminal convictions were being thrown out right and left because evidence had been obtained without warrants or because defendants had not been properly informed of their rights. When all was said and done, Osborn could not overcome the evidence of his own voice or recover his own treasured credibility and power of persuasion.

After his release from prison in 1969, Osborn fought the whole case over again in an effort to stall his permanent disbarment. But in September of that year, the Tennessee bar expelled Osborn for life. His last hope was that the Supreme Court would overrule the Sixth Circuit and grant him a new trial. But on January 14, 1970, the Supreme Court refused to hear his appeal.

Two weeks later, on February 2, Osborn's wife, Dottie, left their comfortable home in fashionable West Nashville to do some shopping. Her husband, who had been selling real estate since his release from prison, was home alone. When she returned about 4:30 P.M., she could not find him, although his automobile was still in the driveway. Alarmed, she called Maclin Davis and the police. Davis arrived just in time to see a young ashen-faced policeman step out of the garage. Tommy Osborn had put a .38-caliber police revolver beneath his chin and fired. He was fifty years old.

The note Tommy Osborn left Dottie assured her that he was not taking his own life in a moment of haste or without deliberation. Convinced now that he could never "undo the wrongdoings against me," he did not want to face life as a disbarred lawyer. For his many triumphs, Osborn had credited luck, never fully buying into those frequent tributes to his superior legal mind. But for his one great failure in life, Osborn blamed not luck but himself. He could untangle the complexities of law, read the minds of jurors, and win the respect of friends and foes alike. But for the life of him he could not understand how he had been so stupid as to be taken in by Robert Vick. Osborn's confidence in himself, his essence, had been destroyed.

A short distance from Osborn's house, John J. Hooker, Jr., who had lost his race for governor in 1966 and was preparing to run for the United States Senate, was winding up his day hitting golf balls at the Belle Meade Country Club driving range. Someone came from the clubhouse with the message that he had an emergency telephone call from his father. Having never gotten such a call from his father in his life, the younger Hooker raced to answer it. His father was distraught and disoriented.

"John J., a terrible thing has happened. You must come and talk to me. Please come over right now."

"What is it, Daddy?" John J. asked. "What's happened?"

"Tommy Osborn killed himself this afternoon, John J., and I believe I may be the cause of it. I'm afraid I'm to blame for it. Please come and talk to me."

John J. spent the early evening consoling his father, trying to convince him that Tommy Osborn had been duly warned and had to bear the responsibility of his own misfortune. John J. could not understand why his father had assumed so heavy a burden. Later, John J. left the task of consolation and companionship to one of his father's protégés and admirers, a young lawyer named Hal Hardin, who would go on to be the U.S. attorney in Nashville himself.

In the wee hours, as Hardin and the old man stared into a rapidly disappearing bottle of Jack Daniel's, a ringing telephone shattered the silence of their private wake. When Hooker answered, a voice he claimed not to recognize said simply, "Well, I hope to hell you're satisfied now, you sonofabitch."

Mr. Hooker died the following December in his sleep.

Burying the Machine—For Real

Tommy Osborn, the youngest of the Old Hickory crowd, was the first to go. His funeral was a huge gathering of lawyers lamenting injustice and a wasted life.

Skinny Neiderhauser Robinson died in 1977, after forty-seven years as Garner's wife, much of it plagued by alcoholism. Her services were planned by her twin daughters, who had inherited her good taste. It was a solemn but not sad occasion. The Robinsons did not plan and carry out sad funerals for themselves.

A few years later Garner married a younger woman, a union his children never regarded as anything more than a gesture of friendship on the part of their father. She never became "family" in the full sense of the word, but the marriage was notable for its ceremony.

Ruth Oakes and Garner were married by his son, Gale, who had become a criminal judge. In keeping with his casual manner on the bench, Judge Robinson administered the vows by asking, "Daddy, do you take Ruth to be your lawful wedded wife?" And when she replied in the affirmative, he said, "Ruth, do you take Daddy to be your lawful wedded husband?"

Garner had always been close to his daughters, whom he and Skinny had raised to be independent, ambitious, adventuresome, and unbounded by limitations of gender. After Skinny died, he grew even closer to them. Muriel would eventually follow him into politics. But Maude became his partner in farming and raising spotted walking horses on the 132-acre family farm and replaced her aunt and namesake Maude Mammy as the overseer of the funeral home. There, she assisted her father in what had always been his labor of love—burying the dead.

Jake died of a heart attack in April of 1981 at age eighty, after returning from the Laurel Race Course in Maryland, where he had been racing his horses. His passing resurrected on the pages of Nashville's newspapers some of his most memorable exploits, including his consumption of the poll tax receipts in 1942.

Garner was in charge of the services, which attracted an unusual number of black Nashvillians, who were treated like family by Jake's widow and his son Jake Jr. Jake was a colorful and wealthy man who could afford the best send-off. But his funeral that year was not the most memorable one held at Phillips-Robinson.

That honor went to the king of Nashville gamblers, James T. "Jimmy" Washer, who had paid for more John Doe funerals at Phillips-Robinson than everybody but the Robinsons themselves.

In one of those strange twists of fate, his sister called one day to report that Jimmy had died penniless—presumably after giving his last shoebox full of cash to Jack Norman's wife in a final act of gratitude. Jimmy was in danger of having a John Doe funeral himself.

Garner sent the hearse after him, and Maude rolled out top-of-the-line treatment for the man she'd always known as Uncle Jimmy. He went on to the big game in the sky clad in a new black-and-white pinstripe suit, laid out in a stainless steel casket inlaid with black onyx under a stunning pall of white roses and black orchids.

The only thing amiss was that Jimmy was not wearing his signature horseshoe-shaped, diamond-studded stickpin and his five-carat solitaire diamond ring. But to the dismay of Maude and the rest of Jimmy's friends and admirers, they showed up that day on the lapel and finger of a gambler known as Pee Wee, to whom Washer had apparently hocked them before dying. Everyone there who knew Jimmy thought Pee Wee was disgusting. Jimmy was buried in the Robinson family plot.

To his disappointment Garner did not handle the services for Elkin Garfinkle, who died two years later at age eighty-nine. The lawyer's funeral was planned by his old-maid sisters, who then fought a legal battle over his $250,000 estate, giving the newspapers yet another opportunity to recall the Sheridan-Robinson-Garfinkle machine.

Mayor Beverly Briley and Ezell "Honey Bee" Flippen died about the same time, but neither chose to entrust their remains to Phillips-Robinson—and not surprisingly. There was always the possibility that with Garner in charge, they might have ended up too close to Jake Sheridan or Ben West, which would not have made for a tranquil eternity.

When he died in 1976, crusty old Jimmy Stahlman did not avail himself of Garner's undertaking services either, despite the men's close political association. This might have had something to do with the fact that Phillips-Robinson emergency service attendants, called to the scene of an automobile accident in the early seventies, had inadvertently dropped Stahlman's wife, Gladys, one of the victims, while attempting to place her in an ambulance. It was an unfortunate and uncharacteristic departure from tradition for which the Stahlmans promptly sued the funeral home. The suit was settled by the Norman law firm.

In 1989, in what everyone agreed was his most painful duty, Garner buried his nephew Jimmy, who had died of a heart attack aboard a plane on his way to Mexico for a vacation. In the seventies, Jim Roberson had become a major power in the Tennessee legislature, where he was known as "Mr. Democrat." Remarkably, he didn't have a single newspaper clipping in his scrapbook linking him to any political machine run by his uncle.

Garner himself lived a vigorous and active life into his eighties. At seventy-eight, he was still able to run down a wounded, chicken-thieving fox on foot, kill it, and have it mounted as a trophy for Maude's farm office. Even in advanced age, it was not unusual for him to climb aboard a rank young horse that was giving Maude trouble and "ride the buck" out of it for her.

But the year Jim Roberson died, Garner's health failed noticeably, the result of chronic heart problems. He spent some time in the hospital, where, despite the contraband strawberry pie and chicken and dumplings smuggled in by Maude and Muriel, his weight dropped to 120 pounds. But he recovered enough to go back to work at the funeral home and on the morning of December 29, 1989, he ate a hearty breakfast of eggs, bacon, biscuits, orange juice, milk, and coffee. He had just settled back on a sofa at the funeral home to watch a morning talk show when he had a heart attack and died.

His funeral, not unexpectedly, was the biggest, best-attended "no pay" funeral in the history of Phillips-Robinson. Flowers covered the place, and cars lined the side streets around the mortuary for blocks. His children made the arrangements and his friend Dick Jones, by then nearing ninety, handled the services. As a send-off, a recording was played of Frank Sinatra singing "My Way."

The *Tennessean* ran a long, flattering front-page obituary that did not mention the Sheridan-Robinson-Garfinkle machine until the forty-fourth paragraph, and then only matter-of-factly. The next day it ran a nice eight-paragraph editorial summing up Garner Robinson not as a political boss but as "a gentleman of resolve and forcefulness" whose success in life should gratify and comfort his mourners.

Epilogue

The Robinson family political legacy did not fall to the expected heir, Garner's son, Gale, who ran often but finally gave up after losing his bid to become Nashville's mayor in 1987. It fell instead to Gale's sister Muriel, twelve years younger, a domestic relations court judge and now one of Nashville's most popular politicians.

Both Muriel and Gale had inherited their mother's patrician good looks and outgoing personality. But while Gale got his father's appetite for life and interest in people, he failed to get his superb sense of political timing. Like Muriel, Gale became a judge, which in Tennessee during his father's era was defined as "a lawyer who knows the governor." In Gale's case, his judgeship came not through his father's connections but through the lawyer that knew every governor—Jack Norman, who arranged for his appointment. But even

that episode reflects a kind of missed beat that thwarted Gale's natural inheritance.

From the beginning, Gale's problem was that his political style
was that of his father's generation. As a boy, he had ridden around
in the ambulance with guys like Dave and his uncle Dayton who
taught him to cuss, smoke, drink whiskey, and ogle girls. The only
political currency he ever knew was based on personal friendship
and favor swapping. Unfortunately, his political ambitions blossomed
at precisely the moment in the late fifties and early sixties when the
nature of politics began to change, when the combination of image
and the most valuable tool for its construction—money—began to
take over the election process.

Wily Jake Sheridan, as steeped as he was in the old ways, had been
among the first to see the potential value of television in an election.
As early as 1952, when he was desperately trying to install the young
patrol captain Oscar Capps as Garner's successor as sheriff, Jake
had bought live paid political announcements on the fledgling
Nashville television station in which Capps stiffly introduced himself as "the only FBI-trained candidate for sheriff." But for the most
part the Robinsons relied on their friends, not their advertising, to
do their image building. Gale always made his home on the east side
of the Cumberland, and none of the Robinsons ever passed themselves off as anything other than what they were—a family of undertakers from Old Hickory good for at least thirty thousand votes
in almost any election. But once beyond geographic and demo-
graphic boundaries, the power of personal friendships and favor
swapping is limited.

Without Jake's election-fixing skills neither Garner, Gale, nor
cousin Jimmy proved to be much of a vote-getter once they got
south or west of the Cumberland River or up into the voting ranks
of the rich and well-to-do. By the late sixties and early seventies the
urban population boom had made good old boys like them and their
personal political styles as obsolete as horse and buggy drivers.

After Gale lost his race for county district attorney in 1966,
Norman asked the new governor, Buford Ellington, to appoint the

younger Robinson to a vacancy in General Sessions Court. Norman was so politically stout that Ellington agreed. But the governor backed off when he discovered that Gale was out campaigning against his state senate floor leader, handing out soft drinks at the polls for his cousin Jimmy, the floor leader's opponent.

"How can I get you appointed judge when you are out there handing out Coca-Colas against Ellington's man?" Norman demanded. "Why were you doing that?"

" 'Cause my family told me to," Gale replied. "If Jimmy loses, they'll all be looking at me the rest of my life like I am responsible because I didn't work for him. If it's a choice between being a judge and having my family mad at me, I'll have to not be a judge."

Fortunately for Gale, his cousin's campaign was successful. Jimmy Roberson beat Ellington's man, which meant the governor had lost an important power broker in the senate and now needed to do a favor for the new one. Gale got the appointment, and Jack Norman personally escorted him up to the governor's office to receive it officially.

"Which branch of the court is this judgeship in?" Ellington asked his new appointee. Gale had to apologize. In truth he did not know the precise court vacancy for which Norman had put him forward.

"Damn," said Ellington, laughing. "I believe you might be the dumbest judge I ever appointed."

Consequently, Gale got his only substantial political job the old-fashioned way. To extend the Robinsons into a fourth decade of political prominence and to a new generation of voters, it took a different kind of candidate with special credentials and wider appeal to modern voters—a woman.

The *Tennessean* didn't support Garner's daughter Muriel the first time she ran for public office, the only female candidate among four seeking the powerful domestic relations court judgeship. But it didn't matter. She ran countywide, spent only eleven thousand dollars, and beat her closest competitor by fifteen thousand votes. Like her brother, Gale, Muriel was a lawyer in the Norman firm. Had she been male, chances are she would have been regarded as just another good ole Robinson boy. But as a smart and stunningly attractive woman, she had a valuable and trendy political credential of the eighties and nineties. She had built a successful career in the legal community—still a man's world—while mothering a daughter of her own and a whole brood of stepchildren acquired in a second marriage.

Her public image was fixed by her résumé and what voters came to know about her from a twice-monthly television talk show where she dispensed advice on domestic-relations law. Even if the Nashville newspapers had still been in the business of attacking political candidates in their news columns, which they no longer were, Muriel was both too young to be tarred by machine association and too fashionable to be criticized. She had an image that was beyond assailing.

While Muriel escaped her father's political liabilities, she profited from his assets. In one of her first public appearances in the black wards of North Nashville, she proudly announced that the old gentleman standing close by was in fact the first black deputy sheriff in the history of Davidson County, appointed by her father in 1946. "And not only that," the old man interjected, "he let me carry a gun."

While Garner Robinson was without question a man of his times, he was in at least one respect a second-generation pioneer. Boss had raised his daughters to be strong, independent women quick to seize and shoulder responsibility. Garner raised his twins the same way, to eagerly enter a man's world—or to take charge of it. As a result, Muriel had the brass to reject even her father's advice when it conflicted with her own convictions or political instincts.

He fretted when she became the first family member to move to the West Side. "You need to stay on this side of the river where the people have been good to you." And when Muriel enrolled her own teenage daughter in Harpeth Hall during the eighties, Garner wanted to know what was wrong with the public school. She told him in detail and refused to move back. "Well, maybe when Cathy Gale gets out of school," he said, "you can move back on our side."

Garner knew well the secrets of his own political success but he did not understand immediately the secrets of Muriel's. But he soon realized that she understood more clearly what was going on socially and politically in American society than he did.

Early in her tenure on the bench both Garner and Muriel's legal mentor Jack Norman, her mother's old boyfriend, fretted that she was spending too much time on television and had become too media conscious. But Muriel had the same feel for the families of her generation that her father had for his. She knew how to do her job and make them feel good about what she was doing.

Her father frequently visited her courtroom to watch her dispense justice, which she did with aplomb and sometimes with harsh words for irresponsible fathers and chauvinistic male attorneys. Once, after witnessing a particularly scathing upbraiding from the bench, Garner called her aside and reminded her that she was a Robinson. "Sister, we didn't use to do it that way. We kind of took care of our friends."

But the more time Garner spent hanging around her courtroom, the more he realized just how politically in touch she was. After overhearing a woman tell her friend in the hallway that "Judge Muriel Robinson is the best thing that ever happened to this county," Garner went back to his daughter and retracted his earlier advice.

"Sister, I've been thinking it over," he said. "Maybe you just better keep on doing whatever it is you're doing."

Muriel Robinson has held but one public office. As a judge she has been able to win reelection on the basis of an image projected largely through the goodwill of clients and lawyers who come before her bench. But among successful vote-getters in Tennessee, she is an exception, and should she seek higher office, she, too, will have to mount an expensive television campaign.

The mayor of Nashville in the nineties, Phil Bredesen, did not grow up or go to school in Tennessee. He did not have to build a political base of personal friendship to get the job. A wealthy health care entrepreneur from upstate New York, he in effect bought himself an image of trust and competence—not necessarily undeserved—with two lavish television advertising campaigns financed largely with his own money, the first one in a losing effort. In 1994, he tried to advance in politics by extending that image statewide, spending $6 million of his fortune in an unsuccessful campaign for governor. He won the primary but when he got to the general election he ran into opponents with the same kind of money and image-making capability. They looked a lot like him except they were Republicans.

As political systems go, Tennessee's is now as truly diverse and free of prejudice as any in the country. The state has had black congressmen, black judges, and black mayors. The ethnic and racial diversity of its cities is reflected in the makeup of its legislative delegations and city councils. Women are prominent on its courts and a Jewish woman, Jane Eskind, is chairwoman of the state Democratic party. Garner's old job of sheriff was held during the early nineties by a former FBI agent, Hank Hillin, who spied on both John Lewis and Jimmy Hoffa during the sixties. Hillin is a card-carrying Republican, though definitely not the purebred, highbrow kind. He once sent out five hundred invitations to a punch and cookie office-warming party that neglected to include either the time or the place.

The television money politics of the eighties and nineties has had a leveling effect on candidates for public office, not all that unlike the one *Baker v. Carr* had on the voters. Now, one well-heeled candidate has as good a chance to be elected as the next, whether he comes from Black Bottom or Belle Meade. And this constitutes a dramatic change for the people in both neighborhoods.

The late Tommy Osborn's best friend and lawyer, Maclin P. Davis, Jr., has one of those thoroughbred-sounding names found in old yellow Nashville newspaper clippings that tell about goings-on at the Belle Meade Country Club. "Among those attending were . . ." That's appropriate because his family name was always there, listed alongside those of Brownlee Curry, Mrs. Will T. Cheek, or Guilford Dudley, Jr., people who as a group over the years generally could only wonder how the other half lives.

One time the wife of the renowned lawyer Jack Norman, who had risen from more modest circumstances, was visiting the beautiful Belle Meade golf course as a guest. Because of her husband's love of the city and desire to be close to the courthouse, they had resided for much of their married life in a luxurious penthouse apartment on the edge of Nashville's notorious nightclub strip, Printer's Alley. Due partly to her husband's prominence and partly to her attire, which included a floral skirt and decidedly unmatching checkered blouse, Carrie Norman found herself the object of considerable curiosity.

"Tell me, Carrie," said one of the Belle Meade matrons, "what are the whores in the Alley like?"

"Oh, they're just like the ones around here," replied the delightful and well-traveled Mrs. Norman. "I can't tell the difference."

Davis, who grew up around the Belle Meade Country Club, remembers when the curiosity there extended not only to prostitutes but to Republicans. Back in the days when Walter Stokes, Jr., was out trying to form his citizens' group to police honest elections, the club had only one member of the Grand Old Party: the town's premier investment banker.

"When he walked by, somebody always said, 'That's J. C. Bradford,' " Davis recalled. "Then they would quickly put their hand up and whisper behind it so you would have to read their lips, 'HE'S . . . A . . . R-E-P-U-B-L-I-C-A-N.' I was twenty-five years old before I knew there were more Republicans than two—Wendell Willkie and J. C. Bradford."

Davis was among the few sons of Belle Meade interested and courageous enough to try his hand at politics. He was in the Tennessee legislature in 1945, introducing reapportionment legislation, which of course went nowhere. And he was in the courthouse that night in 1951 when the fracas broke out over custody of the voting returns in the mayoral race.

Such behavior was frowned upon. Frank Gorrell, son of the state senator by the same name who was the first independent to break through the rural dominance of the Tennessee legislature, says his father's political trailblazing did not sit well with the proper West End society in which he grew up. Now head of the bedding company started by his mother's well-regarded old Nashville family, young Gorrell remembers feeling a bit smudged by his father's front-page prominence in such distasteful affairs.

Davis became a Republican himself in 1970, after his years of battling the Democrats in Washington on the Osborn matter. Not only more comfortable for him politically, the GOP had finally also become fashionable. That year Nashville helped traditionally Republican East Tennessee elect the state's first Republican governor in modern times—and another United States senator, giving the GOP both seats. The governor's office has swapped back and forth evenly since.

Now that you can be in politics without actually having to touch it, Belle Meade likes it better. In 1994 it sent out handsome Bill Frist, a well-bred young heart surgeon who had never even registered to vote before 1988, to run for the U.S. Senate. And see how easy it was. He won, displacing incumbent senator Jim Sasser, a man who had been in politics all his life and in line so long he was the top-ranking Democrat in the Senate. Dr. Frist spent $2 million of his own money and at least that much more raised by the Republican Senate Campaign Committee on television advertising to convince voters that Sasser was a flunky for President Clinton who did not deserve another term in Washington.

In the 1994 elections, the Republicans took control of both U.S. Senate spots again, and a Republican congressman from Memphis defeated the Democratic mayor of Nashville to reclaim the governor's office for the third time in twenty years.

Such noticeable Republican swings by southern voters have happened frequently since Barry Goldwater made the first inroads into the "Solid South" in the 1964 presidential race. They are almost always attributed to a continuing regional ideological movement toward conservatism. To the extent that southern voters are like those in the rest of the nation, this is true. The homogenization of American politics is undeniable.

But everything that has been going on in southern politics in the last twenty years, including these outbursts of Republicanism, could not have happened without the leveling of the playing field that began in Nashville in the sixties. The cumulative result of both Tommy Osborn's rebellion in the courts and John Lewis's rebellion in the streets was the equalization of voting power among all citizens. This meant that rural blacks in Montgomery, Alabama, and suburban Republicans in Nashville's Belle Meade could stake their claim in American democracy with the same hammer—the one-man, one-vote equality of the ballot box. For black and white alike, the right to vote was the spoil of a political revolution. And among the first shots fired were the Nashville *Tennessean*'s long campaign against the poll tax, Ben West's sponsorship of single-member districts in the Tennessee legislature in the forties—and eventually the West administration's capitulation to Martin Luther King's boycotts of the late fifties and early sixties.

That most of these skirmishes involved the same cast of Depression-era blue-collar characters from the Nashville suburbs is remarkable indeed. Who in the great cities of the Northeast and Midwest, where political power was enhanced considerably, knows that the "Baker" in *Baker v. Carr* was not the distinguished Republican senator from Tennessee, but merely a neighbor with whose name lawyer Tommy Osborn began his class action suit. The nation now recognizes John Lewis, who represents the city of Atlanta, as one of the leaders of Congress, but the contributions of his old adversary Ben West to the quality of city life in America are all but lost to history.

Ben, Elkin, and Jake, Silliman Evans, Straight-from-the-Shoulder Stahlman, and the rest of their friends and enemies in the Nashville political wars were not men of like mind, as the men of Constitution Hall were not. And it was from the settling of their differences in an often personal and disorganized manner that liberty has benefited.

Were the motivations behind the *Tennessean*'s assault on the poll tax entirely altruistic? Or Jake Sheridan's meticulous courting and organizing of the black vote in the forties free of selfish and manipulative intentions? Probably not. As Carrie Norman suggested to the ladies of Belle Meade about another old profession, it is hard to look at politicians of any era and distinguish the whores among them. Back then they at least knew one another and rose to power on the basis of personal relationships not carelessly cultivated. Their constituents knew them by sight and name and were usually as close as the neighborhood mortuary or fire hall. But that system could not survive the onslaught of modern urban life and mass communication.

Before Little Evil's mentor, grizzled old Nashville ward heeler Charlie Riley, died in 1977, he identified the most important casualty of the change in the way people elect their leaders. "A man can get on television today and talk to a hundred and fifty thousand people and no one can ask him a question. I like the old kind of personal politics better, where you can look a man in the eye and see if he's lying."

The 1994 Tennessee elections were a far cry from the knockdown, drag-out front-page hell-raising of the past, no doubt irking both Jimmy Stahlman and Silliman Evans, wherever they are. The boys of Camelot have aged and moved on. Amon Evans is a farmer now, not a publisher, and the controversial John J. Hooker, Jr.—now truly the political refugee he always wanted to be—is unable to draw a crowd. Despite his talents, he lacks the right image. John Seigenthaler has retired from active newspapering to a prominent academic post at Vanderbilt University, where he is viewed as an elder statesman of both politics and journalism. His fabled, fighting *Tennessean* still pursues reform, but now in the more restrained, respectable style demanded by its absentee corporate ownership. Newspapers and their publishers can't behave the way they used to. It's bad for the image of their business.

Nashville's neighborhoods have become more image conscious, too. In 1994, only 30 years after the passage of the Civil Rights Act and 130 years after the Civil War, the Belle Meade Country Club admitted its first black member—a rich guy from Atlanta, who is rumored to own McDonald's franchises. And as far as is known, no old members resigned as a result. And finally, Belle Meade has acknowledged the existence of Nashville's music industry.

For all its success, the Nashville music industry has not been integrated into old Nashville society, although Tennessee Republicans have in the past called on such big-name entertainers as Roy Acuff and Tex Ritter to sacrifice their popularity in losing statewide races against entrenched Democratic incumbents.

This has not, of course, kept the wealthy music crowd from moving into the neighborhood. The legendary Minnie Pearl long resided near the governor's mansion on lovely Curtiswood Lane without a single raised eyebrow. But there was much angst and lawsuits galore when aging Grand Ole Opry star Webb Pierce began luring tourist buses to his residence in the same area by personally handing out miniature guitar-shaped bottles of water from his swimming pool of the same configuration.

Today, the country music crowd is no longer ignored. Dr. Bill Frist even took a struggling Nashville musician along on his anti-Democrat campaign.

Nonetheless, no matter how striking and significant the political and social change, some barriers remain too subtle and strong even to challenge, much less overcome.

By the time the senior Frank Gorrell choked to death during dinner in a restaurant in 1994, he was no longer married to Betty Jamison, the bedding company heiress. She had died four years earlier. But he was still firmly entrenched in society's premier institutions, including the West End Methodist Church, the preferred place of worship for the city's elite. Young businessmen on the make were often advised that the two certain ingredients for success in Nashville were to be seen with the *Wall Street Journal* every work day—and at West End Methodist on Sunday.

Naturally, Gorrell's second wife, Candy, planned his memorial service there. But in keeping with her husband's eclectic tastes, she wanted the music to include a soulful version of the hymn "Amazing Grace" by a Tennessee gospel group known as the Wilburns, who are from Vice-President Albert Gore's hometown of Carthage. Her husband had been listening to the Wilburns on a cassette in his automobile tape deck the very day of his unexpected death. But having the group sing live at the funeral would have required that the church relax its rules against the use of amplified sound systems at services. This it refused to do. The pastor informed the widow that only music provided and chosen by the church would be possible.

At the last minute Mrs. Gorrell had to shift the service to a large and modern Pentecostal church farther west of the city. The public explanation was that West End Methodist was too small to accommodate the large political crowd anticipated. And indeed it was, in more ways than one.

No matter how strong the political winds or how swift the change in public attitudes, some chasm always remains—is indeed demanded—between the southern aristocracy and the rest of us. The precise nature of it was perhaps best illustrated at the recent wedding of one of Belle Meade's adopted sons, the Honorable Gilbert Merritt, now a sitting member of the U.S. Sixth Circuit Court of Appeals.

Merritt grew up in the working-class neighborhood of Hermitage, which abuts Old Hickory to the east. But like Frank Gorrell, he had acquired through marriage an elevated social standing that he maintained long after the early and tragic death of his wife, who was also John J. Hooker, Jr.'s, sister-in-law. The judge remained single for nearly two decades, raising the couple's children with the help of his mother, and he attained such judicial prominence that he remains on the Clinton White House short list for appointment to the Supreme Court.

Merritt was enjoying the publicity attendant to such consideration when he wed for the second time shortly after Clinton took office. A sizable collection of anxious friends on both sides of the Cumberland River received invitations to an evening ceremony at the old and dignified Wightman Chapel on the downtown campus of Scarritt College. To his Belle Meade friends, the evening wedding automatically meant black tie required. But to those in Hermitage and elsewhere, it meant only that ol' Gil was getting married at night. When the crowd assembled, half the men were in tuxedos, the other half were not. No zip codes were necessary to determine where each fit in the chronology of the judge's life.

Although in Old Hickory "black ties" are still more likely to be associated with railroad track construction than with parties, it, too, is a much improved community. No one who lives there is ashamed to claim it as their home, as was often the case when "the village" was drawing comparisons with mining towns of the California Gold Rush.

The Du Pont Company still operates the textile plant there and provides jobs. The plant is cleaner though, no longer requiring smokestacks and coal trains. The sour smell of garbage no longer wafts across with the breeze, and there is no "burning ground" to separate the residences of black and white. The population is older, quieter, and less in need of recreation.

As a breeding ground for politicians, Old Hickory has lost both its appeal and its prominence, its once feared political clout gone forever along with the up-close and personal family politicking style of the Robinson-Sheridan-Garfinkle machine. And as far as social prominence is concerned, it—well, it still has a ways to go.

At the local high school, they have student enrichment programs, including a career day at which prominent Nashville leaders are invited to appear as role models. Judge Muriel Robinson, a celebrated graduate and frequent invitee, was on a women's panel there a few years back, along with Annette Eskind, Nashville socialite, philanthropist, and sister-in-law of the state Democratic party chairwoman.

A few days before the event was to occur, Judge Robinson got a telephone call from Mrs. Eskind, who of course resides in the town's West End. She wondered if the two of them might drive out together because "I don't even know how to get to Old Hickory."

Postscript

My mother Billye, Dave White's only child, died of cancer in March of 1995. She got a predictably nice, below-cost funeral from Phillips-Robinson, including a grand wake that could have passed for a Democratic party precinct meeting. The attending crowd reflected the modest sum of her life's accomplishments, mainly the five children she'd raised and scads of political acquaintances—including both friends who'd come to mourn and enemies there for proof that she had indeed worked in her last election.

Among the mourners were all the Robinsons themselves, including Garner's first-born son, Gale, who'd raised his own family two blocks away from the house where I grew up. After paying his respects, Gale, who had inherited his mother's alcoholism but had been on the wagon for several months, went out and got drunk. On his way home a few hours later, he lost control of the car he always drove like a bat out of hell, wrecked it, and was killed.

My mother was seventy years old and Gale was sixty-three. Although Gale had been a frequent candidate for public office, neither his nor my mother's life was marked by extraordinary accomplishment, nor had they been as interesting, eventful, or public as those of their fathers. That their deaths closed another generational chapter in the history of the Robinson-White family relationship and might be notable for the coincidence of their timing was significant only to those of us close enough to know. Yet their passing received unusual media attention. The newspapers gave each a long obituary and their names and pictures were on television repeatedly for one simple reason that in itself made them exceptional today.

Billye and Gale were dedicated, full-time participants in the process of democracy. For them politics was a family obligation, a duty. My mother's death was one of those long excruciating bouts with lung cancer that had spread to the brain. Refusing to give in, she struggled for days, in and out of a dope stupor during which her children vainly tried to maintain communication. At one point to test her coherence, one of my brothers mentioned the name of Jim Roberson, her long-deceased best friend and fellow election warrior, in connection with the prospect of an approaching spring primary. The sound of "the Senator's" name and the word "election" brought this bird-like, decrepit, and hairless figure straight up in her bed. "Well, tell him to get me the voter list so we can get started," she declared, with new life in her eyes. "Tell me when we get the list."

Had Jim Roberson been alive to summon her into political battle, no doubt my mother would have tried to get up and get dressed. Love and appreciation of politics had been passed on to her and to Gale by their parents as surely as had my mother's temper and Gale's inability to cope with alcohol. And they in turn passed it on to their children. But with all due respect to the apocryphal suggestion that politics is somehow in the blood of the Scotch-Irish, this is not an inherited trait. It is learned behavior, a family value.

Of all the things my mother expected of me, few were higher on her priority list than involvement. And of all the things she taught me, none was more often stressed than the three-way relationship of freedom, independence, and the election process.

"In this country whoever gets the most votes gets to decide things," she told me when I was a child barely old enough to understand. "Even if you don't get the most votes and lose, you can still have a say and influence how things turn out. And there is always another election just around the corner. But if you don't participate and speak up, you won't even have the right to complain."

If money was needed to be involved in twentieth-century democracy, or if it required exceptional intelligence or television celebrity, the Whites and the Robinsons would never have been participants. But in those days it did not. And fortunately we were rich in what for the time and place was the most valuable currency of politics, that precious and vanishing gold that has been correctly termed the most democratic of all virtues—fraternity.

Acknowledgments

This book would have been impossible without the support of Maude Robinson Hopkins, my childhood friend, who believed in its worth; the resourcefulness of Ashley Woods, whose research enriched it greatly; the splendid recollections of three people who died during its writing: my mother, Billye White Squires, her friend Gale W. Robinson, and renowned Nashville attorney Jack Norman, Sr.; the talents of my editors, Ruth Fecych and Paul Golob; and the patient assistance of the staffs at the Nashville newspapers, the *Tennessean* and the *Banner*, and the Archives of the State of Tennessee.

Sources

INTERVIEWS

Interviews on which this book is based include Rudy Abramson, Bob Battle, Dick Battle, Cecil Branstetter, Pamela J. Brown, Robert Cross, Larry Daughtrey, Maclin P. Davis, W. Y. Draper, Verna Eakes, T. G. Fite, Ethel Garfinkle, Frank Gibson, Harris Gilbert, Zoe Gillem, Candy Gorrell, Frank Gorrell, Frank Gorrell, Jr., C. D. Graves, Mr. and Mrs. Oscar Grey, Jack Gunter, David Hall, Hal Hardin, Mr. and Mrs. Les Hart, John J. Hooker, Jr., Jack Hurst, Eddie Jones, Bill Kovach, Harry Lester, Dwight Lewis, Joe C. Loser, James F. Neal, Jack Norman, Sr., James H. Roberson, Dan Robinson, Gale W. Robinson, Judge Muriel Robinson, Robb Robinson, John Seigenthaler, Mr. and Mrs. Jake Sheridan, Jr., Billye White Squires, Joseph Torrence, Ann White, Weldon White, Jr., Wayne Whitt, Eleanor Willis, Judge Thomas Wiseman, Frank Woods, Jayne Ann Woods, Ralph Worthy, and Eugene Wyatt.

BIBLIOGRAPHY

Ashmore, Harry. *Hearts and Minds.* New York: McGraw-Hill Books, 1982.

Bowles, Billy, and Reemer Tyson. *They Love a Man in the Country.* Atlanta: Peachtree Publishers, 1989.

Carter, Jimmy. *Turning Point.* New York: Times Books, 1992.

Doyle, Don H. *Nashville Since the 1920s.* Knoxville: The University of Tennessee Press, 1985.

Graham, Gene. *One Man One Vote.* Boston: Little, Brown and Company, 1972.

Norman, Jack Sr. *The Nashville I Knew.* Nashville: Rutledge Hill Press, 1984.

Sheridan, Walter. *The Fall and Rise of Jimmy Hoffa.* New York: Saturday Review Press, 1972.

Tidwell, Mary Louise Lea. *Luke Lea of Tennessee.* Bowling Green, Ohio: Bowling Green State University Popular Press, 1993.

Index

About the Author

JAMES D. SQUIRES began his newspaper career at the Nashville *Tennessean* in 1962, and later served as Washington bureau chief for the *Chicago Tribune* and as editor of the *Orlando Sentinel*. During his eight and a half years as editor of the *Tribune*, the paper's staff won numerous awards, including seven Pulitzer Prizes. Since 1990 he has lectured at Harvard University on the press and democracy and at Middle Tennessee State University on the First Amendment. In 1992 he served as media adviser for Ross Perot's presidential campaign. He and his wife live in Versailles, Kentucky. His critique of the American press, *Read All About It: The Corporate Takeover of America's Newspapers*, was published by Times Books.